In My Hands

Stories of the Land and Animals I Love but Can't See

Reyna Bradford

Flint Hills Publishing

D1118331

**In My Hands: Stories of the Land and Animals I Love
but Can't See © Reyna Bradford 2019**

All rights reserved.

Cover and Interior photos by Ann Palmer
annpalmerphotography.com

Cover Design by Amy Albright

stonypointgraphics.weebly.com

⫯Flint Hills Publishing
Topeka, Kansas

www.flinthillspublishing.com

Printed in the U.S.A.

ISBN-13: 978-1-7332035-0-0
ISBN-10: 1-7332035-0-8

This book is dedicated to the memory of Glacier,
my faithful guardian.

.

INTRODUCTION

THROUGH MY EYES

When I was fifteen months old, I had a brain tumor.

To be more accurate, that's when the doctors diagnosed it and performed the surgery. It had been there my entire short life, growing, expanding, and destroying. By the time it had reached the size of a malevolent apricot, it had stretched and damaged the optic nerve. My horizons were darkening. My world was going gray.

By the day of the surgery, my vision was almost completely gone. And although the tumor was successfully removed, the destruction in its wake could never be repaired.

Blind, my parents were told. *Nothing anyone could do. No facial recognition. No color perception. No depth perception. If you're extremely lucky, maybe some light perception. But maybe not. Maybe nothing at all.*

Only time would tell.

Thirty-plus years later, I homestead my own hobby farm, called Goldengreene, in northeast Kansas. I raise Nubian dairy goats. That means bottle feeding the babies, milking the moms, and making cheese, soap, and yogurt. I live with ten dogs, and I

1

train and show more than half of them in several competition sports. I walk miles with them every day. I love life. Physically speaking, the doctors were deadly accurate. My visual world is a muddle of light and dark, shadows and contrasts. Color is only a concept. Faces mean nothing to me. And that's just in my left eye. The right eye is totally dark.

But there's a lot more to life than being able to see. Love, joy, courage, and endurance are not things you can see. Even beauty is not something you truly see. It's something you feel.

That's why I've written this book. It's not meant to be a book about myself. It's a book about dogs, goats, and life on the land. It's about the sun and the wind and the seasons. It's about Kansas. If the stories inspire you, then I have done my work well. At the end of the day, remember the stories. Remember the challenge and the hope and the beauty that can be *felt*.

As we journey through the next chapters together, come and catch the vision with me. Step out onto the windy Kansas prairie, love my dogs, meet my goats. Savor the struggle and the sweetness and the goodness of life. Because, to quote a line from the movie *The Polar Express*: "Seeing isn't believing. Believing is seeing."

PART ONE

AUTUMN

Long before the first frost chills the nights into crisp silver and melts the days into warm gold, there's a change in the air.

It begins in August. On those scorching, wavering afternoons, when the world is so hot that all the grasses smell like baking bread, there will sometimes be a stealthy breeze from the northwest. I expect it now. But still, the first time it comes, I stop short, turn to the northwest, raise my head and feel it. Breathe it in and smell it. The sun burning into my back, sweat soaking my T-shirt, the cicadas rasping in the trees like miniature power tools. But that wind has an edge to it.

And suddenly I'm four months in the future. Steely clouds overhead—fine, powdery snow underfoot—the northwest wind slicing like a knife, dark falling early, and the sun rising in the morning late, stiff and cold, like an old cat reluctant to meet the frigid day. I think about frozen water tubs and wind-washed roads, and about my cozy house and the snug barn, full of sleepy goats and the fragrance of brome hay. I might even shiver slightly, wondering, worrying.

And then the wind falls, and more sweat trickles into my

eyes, and I remember that it's only August. Summer still ruling supreme, and hot, sticky work still to be done. But that wind. Autumn is coming, and hard on its heels—breathing out malice and loneliness—winter.

The birds usually quiet by August. The chattering, charming dickcissels—tiny birds of the tall-grass prairie which nest by my mailbox every May—suddenly go silent. I don't think they're gone yet, but they are considering going, not raising babies anymore but storing up strength for the long migration down to the pampas grasslands of Argentina. The meadowlarks and blackbirds have been quiet for weeks. The doves and killdeer, the whistling bobwhite quail and the burbling barn swallows, have gone silent. Even early mornings, any bird's favorite time of day, are sober and quiet. Usually only the stalwart cardinals have much of anything to say, but cardinals talk all year round.

The cicadas and locusts, on the other hand, get louder and louder as the weather turns. Both of them are a torment to me from mid-June through most of October, so loud that they can actually be disorienting. One blessing of the frosts as they begin to cloak the fields and touch the trees is that they irreversibly start to kill off the bugs. And slowly the racket subsides. By the end of October, I can train dogs outdoors with more confidence. Less background noise means it's much easier for me to hear the dogs responding to hand signals, picking up an object I've asked them to retrieve, or coming over the correct jump.

On our walks I can hear vehicles approaching much sooner than I could when those stupid cicadas were sawing away. Even going out to the chicken coop after dark is easier, since the oak trees that shelter it and the weeds that grow along the outside of the fence have gotten rid of their six-legged summer citizens. What a relief. Life just got a whole lot better.

Jeans and sweatshirts become routine. Gradually, I remember what it's like to do chores and walk dogs without dripping sweat.

Acorns begin to patter down from the chinkapin oaks that shelter the house. They shake loose in any kind of breeze, bouncing and tapping onto the roof and patios like woody hail.

The wind sharpens. Its sound even changes. It doesn't frolic and laugh anymore, or rush through the trees in loud, standing ovations of applause. It sighs and gusts, restless and eager after the relative calm of summer. Sometimes it sweeps down from the north in gales, carrying with it the allure of far places and changing times. Roaring at forty miles an hour through the disintegrating trees, it arrives in my little valley to clatter the wind chimes and claw at the vents on the house roof until they whirr and squeak. It snatches first fistfuls of leaves, teasing and swirling them, but there is still the noise of green in the crackle of sound. As the days pass and shorten, the wind takes the leaves in great armfuls, all gentleness forgotten, shredding and ripping them from the trees, scudding them along the ground in dry drifts and whirlpools of sound. It blows cold now, almost always from the northwest. Now the nights are truly cold. Mornings bring thin, timid sun and ice half an inch thick on the water tubs. The goats and the miniature donkey are putting on their winter coats. The house is beginning to feel cozy.

The migratory birds are long gone, and I'm back in the habit of filling feeders for the year-round residents. The afternoons are still often warm and golden. The cottonwood leaves smell spicy in the sun, and I can take off my sweatshirt for a few hours to work dogs or clean the barn.

But nothing stays for long in the fall. Cold fronts come in fast, pummeling the farm with piercing wind and stinging sheets of rain. Then, by next morning, the wind can switch back to the south, settle in to blow at thirty-five miles an hour all day, and by afternoon, temperatures will brush seventy degrees. And I'll wonder why the crickets have moved into the barn and laundry room to get away from the cold.

This is autumn on the Great Plains. The world is changing.

It's beautiful, stirring, and unpredictable. Its magic tumbles in on me with excitement and restlessness, hope and despair. I dread the winter that is to come. I rejoice in the glory of what is now.

CHAPTER 1

BREEDING: THE SEASON OF LOVE, GOAT STYLE

Goats are seasonal breeders. This means that during spring, summer, and most of winter, they aren't interested in romance at all. It's autumn that gets them feeling frisky. So as the days shorten and the weather cools in the fall, the love life out in the pasture is just beginning to heat up. And spoiler alert: it does get pretty hot and steamy by the time things are all taken care of.

The mature males (technically called bucks) come into rut every autumn. Interestingly, bucks will come into rut whether there is a female present or not. It's just the way of the goat world. The triggers seem to be the shortening days and the cooling temperatures, rather than the flirtation of a female. But of course, she is the key player in the whole drama.

The females (technically called does) go through a heat cycle every three weeks in the fall and early winter, usually between September and January. In the long run, this is a good method to determine whether or not a doe is pregnant. If she is, she won't go through a heat cycle again. If she isn't, her body will produce another heat cycle, and we'll have to go through the dirty flirting all over again and hope that he "gets her settled" this time around.

But let's not get ahead of ourselves. The first thing you notice about goat romance is the smell. The boys are old-fashioned in their unshakable belief that the ladies are always impressed by a good, heavy dose of cologne. By mid to late July, my two Nubian bucks are starting to apply it.

There's no delicate way to say this, so I'll just come right out with it. They spray themselves with urine. And they do it generously. They can pee to reach places you would never imagine possible, let alone socially acceptable. Heads, chests, front legs, and faces are the favorite target sites. They spritz, sprinkle, and outright spray until by October their front halves are pretty much untenable.

Because the urine doesn't just soil and stain. It stinks. The smell hangs on them like a palpable, poisonous haze. It reminds an innocent bystander of raw sewage, accented with heavy undertones of serious BO and filthy socks and a liberal mixer of angry skunk to complete the ensemble. It's quite overpowering, even alarming, especially to someone who has never before witnessed this bizarre ritual. The more bucks you have, the stronger the smell. I only have two of them, yet by October or November, when the rites of autumn are in full swing, you can smell the billy goats from halfway up my driveway. Especially when the wind blows from the south, the musky stench wafts in and clings to everything in the front and back yards, chicken yard, even encroaching as far as my enclosed front porch. It is, quite frankly, disgusting.

And the lady goats love it.

At about the same time that Epic and Petra start spraying themselves and stinking, they also start checking out the available women. By which, of course, I mean the female goats in the area. Actually, the guys check out the girls even if the girls aren't available. Because, I guess, a fella never knows. She may not act interested, she may not smell interested, but she may also just be playing hard to get. Anything's possible.

On my farm we do not believe in free love. Both Epic and Petra are separated from the does all year, each in his own secure and reinforced corral. Each has his own shelter hut strategically situated in the middle of the corral. And each hut is located far enough away from the fence to prevent wild capers. Because it does occasionally happen that desperate, love-crazed Romeos will figure out that they can bound onto the roof of a hut situated too close to the corral fence and leap into the pasture to join the girls. I've never seen it, but I'm not taking any chances.

Still, confined as they are, my two guys never pass up an opportunity. If she's within reach she's a potential bride. At the beginning of the season they are somewhat polite about it. At least for billy goats. They mostly just sniff. They wedge their crusty faces doggedly through the squares of the corral fencing and crank their necks to get a good angle. The girls move away. You can almost hear them muttering to each other. "Honestly, did you see the way he was looking at me? What a creep! Disgusting!"

By mid-October, though, everyone is feeling far less prudish. The girls are definitely changing their tune and finally noticing just how handsome these two blokes really are. Fence line trysts become longer and more fervent. The does linger, lulling their heads through the boys' gates, pushing each other out of the way, and, as a true mark of caprine love, wagging their short tails. Talk about something that will turn the fellas on.

This is when the sound effects begin.

Nubians are a vocal breed. The does who are in the mood bleat and whine, and every so often they scream. It can go on for hours, especially if the one in heat is locked in the barn for the night, or if she's the only one interested in the boys and all the other ladies in the herd have drifted away to better pursuits. The poor doe left behind stands along Epic or Petra's fence, bleating hideously, telling her friends exactly what they're missing and her chosen gentleman exactly what she wishes he could do to her, furiously wagging her tail to prove the point.

Nothing, however, compares to the noises the bucks make.

Moaning. Wails of despair. Growling bellows of unrequited desire. Wild bursts of up-and-down blubbering, crescendoing into a blood-curdling alto range, wavering and often cracking with emotion. And deep, rumbling belches that ought to win any woman's heart. Fifty percent of this horrifying rendition is directed at whichever hussy they happen to be ogling, and the other fifty percent is performed for each other. One can only imagine the epithets, murderous threats, and vulgar slurs that one buck hurls at the other, lobbed over his shoulder between frenzied head-rubbing and bursts of urine. I probably better not include them in print.

Accompanying these comments is a good round of tongue flickering. The bucks stand with mouths agape, eyes glazed, sticking their slimy tongues out and flicking them back in with such amazing rapidity that you just have to pause and marvel for a minute. And let's not even discuss what they're doing at the other end of their anatomy. Suffice it to say that these guys have no inhibitions.

The bucks work very hard during breeding season. At least, they're ready to work hard. They pace and paw and constantly patrol the fence line closest to wherever the ladies might be hanging out. They rear up on the fences and gates, ever hoping to force a way through. They eat less hay during this time, and they drop weight.

And they fight. They definitely become more belligerent and aggressive with each other and will square off any chance they get, literally butting heads and wrestling through the fence. One autumn the two bucks I had at the time ripped off about a ten-foot section of the cattle panel fencing separating their corrals. They were up on their back legs, their front legs supported by the fence, head butting and chest slamming each other so violently that the poor fence finally just gave up. Until my dad fixed the fence, they had a grand time, jostling and sparring to their hearts' content for about a day. Later on, they actually broke several bars in the same section of the panel fencing. They are impervious to pain when it comes to sparring, and they will crash their heads together with startling force if allowed to.

The reason for all this violence is that age-old culprit—testosterone. It makes the bucks act like deranged maniacs until sometime in January. By then, all the does have either been bred or else their bodies have just quit cycling as the days grow slowly longer. In the wild, the buck that dominates the herd wins the hearts of and the rights to the most ladies, and he does that by slamming and intimidating the younger, weaker bucks into submission. So even in their separate corrals, Epic and Petra still contend for dominance over the group.

Thus far I've been fortunate to have bucks that are fairly laidback and easy to handle when it comes to human interaction. Some can be very aggressive with people during the breeding season, and they're big enough to make it matter. Nubian bucks usually weigh between two hundred-fifty and three hundred pounds, and their heads come up to my chest. They're pretty big boys, and when they're in rut, they basically lose their minds for three months or so. Most of the time, though, they remember that I'm the one in charge. The two I currently have are pretty easy-going. Epic is still young, just a goofy jock, still essentially a teenager. He oozes punk and machismo when there's a beautiful girl around and when Petra is safely on the other side of the fence, but he really doesn't have it all together yet. He's a little awkward and pretty wimpy—he hasn't yet tried to challenge my authority. Petra is big but not very bad. He knows he's easily the top buck between the two of them, and he knows he gets most of the girls. He also knows I'm the one who brings them to him. The farthest Petra has pushed me is to body block my progress across his corral, or if he's feeling really ambitious, to shove me. I give him a shove right back, and so far, that settles it.

My first Nubian buck, however, did try a little more. His name was Rock. I had just brought him home a week or two before, and because it was not yet breeding season and because we hadn't gotten the bucks' corrals set up yet, he was in with the does for a few weeks. It wasn't quite breeding season, but it was pretty close, about the middle of July. One of the girls I had back then, a Nubian-alpine cross called Daisy, was notorious for coming in heat early. I would learn that, for her, even late July was a good time, and mid-August was running tardy. I would learn what Rock had already figured out. She wasn't available yet, but she was thinking about it, and, as you've probably already guessed after reading the last several pages, so was he.

I turned my back on him for two seconds to open a gate, and the next thing I knew he had thumped his grungy chest onto my back and was in the process of twining his filthy front legs around my neck. Without giving it a second thought, I wheeled around and decked him. That boy never knew what hit him. I flipped him onto his back and straddled him and was seriously considering doing some rearranging to his face and a few other bodily regions, when common sense began to prevail. I did read him the riot act, though, and informed him in no uncertain terms that there are just some things I will not tolerate from so-called gentlemen. We came to an understanding. He never tried that trick again, although there were still a few times that I felt safer carrying my riding crop when it was time to do his chores. Sometimes their brains are just so missing in action, and that doe just beyond the fence is just so flaming hot, the bucks simply need a little reminder not to, *ahem*, substitute.

I think I speak for most of us dairy breeders when I say that we love our boys. I mean, they can't help it that they're revolting. And they can't help it that their brains are between their back legs for three months out of every year. They do pretty well, considering. No, seriously, we appreciate our boys. Not only do we need and rely on them for obvious reasons, but they really aren't as tough as they'd like us to think. For whatever reason, the bucks are the ones most susceptible to ailments like parasites, colic, and pneumonia. They put up a good front, but those of us who deal with them every day know the truth. They're really big cream puffs who need to be loved, understood, and just a little bit pampered. They just also happen to have a Napoleon complex.

It has been scientifically proven that the earlier in her cycle a doe is bred, the greater the likelihood will be of getting doe kids. And because these are dairy goats, used for milk production, everyone wants doe kids. So as soon as we hit October (which means kids will be born in March, my target time) and I catch a doe acting silly, I drop everything and hustle for the wedding. I have planned months in advance which doe will be bred to which buck. Lots of factors go into this decision, including genetics, milking ability (which you hope will be passed on to the kids), temperament, and who is related to whom.

I bring the doe to him, which is much easier since he already has a separate pen, get her through the gate, yank it shut behind me and hang onto her collar.

As passionate and sordid as the flirting might have been, the act itself takes only seconds. It's kind of anticlimactic, really. He certainly spends enough time ogling her, rubbing on her, offering her cologne samples, and doing other unspeakable things just to sweeten her up. But the consummation of the marriage, as it were, is rather low-key after all that hoopla. It only takes ten or twenty seconds. A quick jump and hump and he's done.

The older and more experienced does don't usually need much persuasion. They know the routine and will generally just stand still and take it. Oftentimes, though, the "maidens" (dairy goat-speak for girls who have never been bred before) will get cold feet and try to cut and run at the last second. You can just see them start to put the pieces together. It's like, "Wait a minute. . . I didn't realize. . .but he was on THAT side of the fence. . .I was just having some fun. . .I didn't really think he was gonna. . ." Yeah well, honey, that was then and this is now. I just clamp a death grip on her collar, get a knee into her chest, and let him do his thing.

What keeps me motivated through this whole crass, crude, and creepy process is the excitement and hope for the kids. All innocence and sweetness, all legs and ears and pleading eyes, nudging my knees and sucking my fingers. Totally, totally cute. This one should turn out to be a superb milker. That one should have excellent conformation. And this set of triplets should sell for a really decent price. Excitement and hope and all the anticipation that a crop of new babies can bring. They arrive in five months.

CHAPTER 2

GEM: A DIAMOND IN THE ROUGH
GOLDENGREENE SOJOURNER

I have loved border collies ever since meeting my first one up in South Dakota the summer I was fourteen. He was a working stock dog on a big cattle ranch, and he had all the presence, athleticism, and whip-smart intelligence that draw so many diehard dog people to the breed. I had never met a dog like him before and I fell in love. Someday, I promised myself, I would have a dog like that. Not for a while yet, because even back then I knew how demanding a breed like this would be. But someday I would have my own border collie.

Decades later when I first met Gem, I was open to the possibility of another dog joining the household, but I wasn't yet sold on its needing to be a border collie. By then I already had Meg. Still, on a whim I contacted Pam, a breeder who I'd gotten to know thanks to a few herding lessons with a couple of my other dogs. I liked Pam and the feeling was mutual. Plus, I knew that she had feelers throughout the border collie world. She placed dogs all over the country, fostered dogs for BC rescue, and didn't think twice about skipping across the pond to bring home breeding stock from Wales and Scotland. A serious BC person.

So, I dropped her an email: *Do you happen to know of any border collies currently looking for homes? My preference would be for a rough-coat male, but I'm open to anything that needs me.*

She wrote back that yes, actually she knew of a dog exactly like that, and would I like to come and meet Happy?

A few days later we were in the car headed out to her farm. I wasn't getting my hopes high, but Happy did sound worth investigating. Roughly a year and a half old, he was a failed herding prospect who had been turned over to Pam in order to find him a good, pet home. Apparently, he had been bought for high dollar by some famous baseball player (she never did give me his name) and had been touted as coming from excellent working lines. "He should have lots of drive and potential," the seller had said.

"I don't think I've ever met a border collie that had less potential," Pam told me as we stood in a loose circle, the dogs skittering between us. "But he certainly lives up to his name."

She grabbed the lolloping, grinning dog by the collar and hauled him to her knees. "Happy, honey, come on. She is NOT INTERESTED!" She shook her head and reached to corral the other dog, the one supposedly not interested in Happy's boisterous advances. The little, tricolor female gave her a look, hovered just out of reach, then ducked away and rushed over to me. She was a smooth-coat, very small and quick, with intense, searching eyes and hard, bunched muscle under her sleek coat.

"That's Gem," Pam said. "She's one of my puppies, a return from somebody who didn't want to put the work and time into her."

Happy, sensing distraction, abruptly darted away from Pam and came straight for Gem, and the little dog at my feet gave him one fleeting glance as he burrowed his nose between the ground and her bottom. Then they took off running, dashing and feinting as only border collies can do.

As we stood there and I tried to learn more about Happy, gradually bits and pieces of Gem's story also wove themselves together. It would take me a year or so to work out most of the details, but I knew enough then to be both intrigued and drawn.

Gem was the product of a whoopsy-breeding. Her mom, Shot, was a decent working dog on sheep, very people-oriented but with a pronounced shy streak. Her dad, a hard-as-nails dog named Butch, didn't care about anyone except Pam and could work cattle. Not a breeding she would have chosen, Pam told me, but she shrugged and rolled her eyes and raised the puppies to sell.

Except Gem didn't sell. She stayed around for ten months or so, either kept in a crate in the house or out in the big kennel run with the other dogs, waiting for the right buyer. It wasn't a case of neglect, it's just the way stock dog and bird dog breeders often do things. The dogs are not pets but rather working farm animals. They are cared for, trained, often times appreciated, and maybe even loved. But they are not pets. Besides, Pam intended to sell this dog. So she was kept at arm's length, given the rudiments of training on the sheep and goats, and passed around by word of mouth until someone decided to take a look at her.

That someone was a lady we'll call Kathy. She had about a hundred goats, all living in the acreage around her house, and she decided she needed a good stock dog to help get them where they were supposed to be when they were supposed to be there. It was a good idea, but like most good ideas it took some work, and that was something Kathy wasn't expecting. She was anticipating a pre-packaged, pre-programmed stock dog, fully trained, capable, and reliable. And that's something that you're not going to find in a ten-month-old puppy.

Whether Pam didn't realize Kathy's expectations, or whether Kathy simply wasn't honest with her I don't know. But one way or another, Gem ended up in the cab of Kathy's pickup, headed for a new home.

It was a disaster. Gem wasn't pre-packaged and had only basic stock dog training. She had all kinds of instinct and, in the beginning, all the want-to in the world. But she needed guidance, training, and a firm but patient hand to mold all that drive and desire into a competent stock dog. Things quickly began to break down. She had no bond with Kathy. These goats were not dog broke, meaning they had never been taught by a seasoned stock dog to respect and take direction from a dog. And goats are sassy. They discover and take advantage of weakness very quickly. And this dog, as well as her handler, was weak.

Gem rapidly lost confidence both in herself and in her human partner. Kathy even more rapidly became frustrated and disgusted. It was more work wrangling the butt-headed dog than it ever was bringing in the goats without her. So more and more often, Gem was left behind and left out.

At least at that point she was still in the house. That is, until she began pottying and ripping things up. It probably didn't help that Kathy was an ER nurse who worked twelve-hour shifts and left the dogs in the house for that entire time with no company or access to the outside. It probably also didn't help that the other two resident housedogs were a couple of dominant Dobermanns who didn't mind throwing their weight around.

So, Gem slunk away and hid in corners. She tried to stay as unobtrusive and as out of the way as she could. She was bored and stressed, and she needed to pee. No one was there to stand up for her or to let her outdoors. No one took her out to work stock anymore. So she wet the carpet and jumped on the counters and plundered the kitchen table. Papers were always good to rip up. She would find two or three good sheets of paper or pieces of mail, scuttle back to one of her favorite corners, and shred them.

Then Kathy would come home and find the puddles and the desiccated envelopes on the floor, haul Gem out of the corner and begin to hit her. She liked using the horse whip. And she would yell. She was good at yelling.

Eventually, Gem was no longer welcome in the house. Instead she was thrown out into the yard, which doubled as a pasture for those one hundred goats. Left to her own devices, she was eventually pestered enough by the goats to begin looking for escape options. The wire fencing was easy enough to finagle. She was soon roaming the neighborhood, reluctant to come home and, not surprisingly, staying just out of Kathy's reach when she attempted to get Gem safely back on the right side of the fence. Kathy was exasperated. Gem could find any tiny hole in any stretch of fence and make the most of it. And she never came when she was called.

Within a few weeks she was put on a chain and kept in the yard by force. And now the goats really sensed weakness. I don't know how long the chain was, but it was at least long enough to keep Gem from serious bodily harm as they chased and slammed her, running her as far as the chain would allow for hours every day. As time passed, she became more and more skittish and frightened. She was terrified of the goats, most of them bigger than she was, all of them totally aware of the fact that she could not get away from their bullying and harassment. She was always on edge around the other dogs—the unstable Dobermanns when they came outside, and the large, intimidating guardian dogs who were also in the pasture. She was isolated from all but the barest human contact. She was desperately lonely.

If I have anything good to say about Kathy, it is that she at least recognized that Gem needed a different situation. After about eight months, she returned Gem to the breeder, griped about not getting her money back, swung up into her truck and wished them good riddance. Pam gave Gem a rub under the chin and put her back in the kennel run with the other dogs. That was how she spent the next four months of her life.

"He has only one thing on his mind," said Pam, once again

wrenching Happy's head away from Gem's back end and rolling her eyes. "He needs to be snipped sooooo bad."

As we piled back into the car and rumbled along the dusty rural roads headed for home, I began the mental wrestling match that always consumes me when the decision to get or not to get a new dog is on the line. In this case it was doubled. Which dog did I want? Or could I find room for both of them. THREE border collies? Did either one of them really have the potential and talent to be an obedience or agility hopeful? Would neutering Happy really bring about a total transformation, or would it just tone down who he had been allowed to become over the past eighteen months of his life? And what about skittish, sensitive, smart little Gem? What could still be salvaged after the neglect, trauma, and lack of direction that had accompanied her basically since birth?

Come to think of it, was I so sure that I actually wanted either one of them?

If anything, I am too slow and cautious when it comes to bringing in a new dog. I had told Pam that I would need a couple of nights to sleep on the decision, but that I'd let her know either way. Two nights became three, and then five, and still I just didn't feel quite right about Happy. Instead, it was Gem who kept putting in an appearance. Her sleek head, her determined front paws on my pockets, her eagerness, her need. Her searching, commanding gaze touching more than just my face. I remembered something Pam had said about her, "Most dogs just look at you. This dog looks into your soul."

In the end, of course, she came home with me.

From the very beginning I knew we were embarking on a rough-and-round-about road. She was not going to be an easy dog. It was a conclusion drawn more from intuition and long-time dog experience, rather than from actual problems. As introductions go, Gem's acclimatizing herself into the household was uneventful. She took the other dogs and the cats in stride.

She joined in on our walks with joyous abandon, running almost desperately at times, always ready to go and never unhappy to come back home. She was friendly to everyone who met her, never tried to escape the back yard, content in her crate when I had to be gone for a while.

On the surface everything was smooth sailing.

But underneath. Underneath she was still shaking off the cobwebs and shadows of her past.

Most of the time I'm pretty unsentimental about rescue dogs and their past. That's not to say I don't want to know where they come from and what they may have come through, but I don't dwell on it or make a big issue of it. Neither do they. Dogs live in the moment. That's one reason humans have such a connection with them. Dogs are constant, available and unhindered by grudges or guilt or worry. So when I bring in a dog that has a history, I salt that history away, chalk it up and just start from square one.

But Gem wasn't quite that simple.

She hid in dark corners. For hours and hours at a time. One of her favorite retreats was the old shower in my laundry room. She would stay there sometimes all day, coming out when it was required—for a walk, for food, for a couple hours in her crate if I had to leave—but she would always slink back to that same hidey-hole. I would find her there, curled in a tight ball, her back to the shower door, on freezing January evenings. The wind, icy and bitter from the north, came funneling up the drain in frigid drafts, soaking her in freezing wafts of air. I would crouch down beside her, rubbing her cold back and talking to her, "Gem, honey, what are you doing way back here? It's absolutely freezing, babe, why don't you come out and be in the warm house with everyone else, okay?"

Then I would take her gently by the collar and lead her into the living room or computer room, sweet talking and encouraging, and try to keep her with me. She would come along dutifully, put her head under my hand once or twice, maybe even lie down if I was really paying attention. Then as soon as my back was turned or I got busy with something else, she would click quietly away, and I would hear the rustle of the shower curtain as she crept back to her dark corner.

Sometimes she would huddle in a corner of the computer room. Again, she chose one particular corner in which to hide. Curled up in a tight ball, her back to the room, she would stay there perfectly still for hours at a time. And once again she picked the coldest, draftiest corner, up against the northwest angle of the wall. She arrived in early November, and as the winter closed in and the vicious winds cut in from the northwest outdoors, even my snug, warm house couldn't keep out all the icy seeps of air. I found a thick, fluffy rug to put in her spot, folding the edge up against the wall in an effort to smother the draft. It worked pretty well, when she would lie on it. Sometimes she did—it was in her spot, after all—and sometimes she would lie right next to the rug, or more likely, I would find her camped out in the shower stall again.

As the months passed, I also began wrestling with the hard truth that Gem seemed to have no attachment to me whatsoever. A year went by, and although we shared the same house and the same schedule, although I continued to walk her, treat her, train her, and generally love her, there was little if any reciprocation. Those of us who live with dogs just know. There's a rapport that develops between a dog and its person. More than just physical routines and habits, there's mutual enjoyment of each other's company, satisfaction in seeing each other after being apart for a while, seeking each other out for attention or affection. None of that happened with Gem.

She remained distant and disinterested in me. She kept to her corners, almost never venturing out to find me or request anything. In fact, many times she would leave the room when I came in. I began talking to people about it.

The first person I went to, of course, was the breeder. Pam laughed most of it off. *It's the genes,* she assured me. Gem's grandmother, Dare, had gone so far as to earn the title "the closet queen" because of her tendency to hole up in secluded corners. *Don't worry about it. Border collies are quirky. Just keep living with her, working with her, getting her out as much as you can. But realize that, at the end of the day, you might just be stuck with what you're stuck with.*

She did suggest making Gem work for her food every day. *Nothing in life is free. If you want her to value you,* Pam said, *teach her to associate you with her daily rations. Mix her kibble with something yummy, like chicken or deli meat, and start some serious training.*

Gem still showed no interest in working livestock. I let Pam take her into the big training corral at her place, but even with a group of running, very dog-broke goats, and some encouragement, she just stood by the fence, tail tucked, making no eye contact.

We went home, I, a little more enlightened and eager to try a new plan, Gem, nonplussed and unruffled. Even seeing Pam again had brought no spark of happy recognition. I'm sure that Gem remembered Pam. And, in typical fashion, she greeted Pam enthusiastically, then turned away to do her own thing. Just like she did with everyone. Mom, Dad, friends, the cashier at Petsmart, the furnace repair guy, the man from the phone company—she was happy to see each of them but had no attachment to any.

She liked everyone and loved no one.

At the suggestion of another trainer, a gal who had been an obedience mentor to me at one time, I also used the tether trick for a while. This is a system I've occasionally used when bringing in a new, usually un-housetrained adult dog, but I had never attempted it as a method to get a dog bonded to me after she had already lived with me for a year. One end of the leash snapped to her collar, the other end secured around my middle, we went everywhere together. We folded laundry together, did dishes together, typed emails, cleaned cages. I kept her with me while I read, tethered her outside the shower, and took her with me when I headed out front to do chores. She came along, put up with it all, willing but disinterested, there but not present.

I put a little more faith in the work-for-food program recommended by Pam.

Up to this point, I have to admit that Gem and I hadn't done much training together. I felt like she just needed to detox for a year or two, just get her confidence built up, run out that pent-up, neglected border collie energy, learn to trust new people and new situations, and just generally get back to a normal canine existence before I asked for much more. But maybe that was the wrong approach. It didn't seem to be working anyway, so I took a deep breath, strategized about how to get started, and took Gem out to train.

We began with basics. Simple heeling patterns, turns, pace changes, teaching her to automatically sit when we stopped in tandem. I taught her to lie down and stand on command, taught her to wait as I walked across the training area and then to come to me and sit in front of me when called. We began experimenting with low jumps, and she slowly learned to retrieve a dumbbell when it was thrown a short distance. But the sparkle, the drive, the want-to that every competitor hopes to see in an up and coming performance dog just wasn't there. From the very first I had discovered that Gem was not motivated by food. She would take treats. Sometimes. But she did not work for them. A lot of times I would praise her for doing something right, pop a treat on her nose, and she would completely not register that it was there. Cubed ham, sliced deli turkey, chicken, Vienna sausage, it didn't matter. Sometimes she took it, other times she totally dismissed it or, what was even more aggravating, she would take a treat just because she knew I wanted her to, then let it fall out of her mouth and forget about it. She also cared absolutely nothing for toys. To me, the easiest dogs to train, whether you're talking about teaching goofy tricks, competitive agility, or precision obedience, are those with high drive and enthusiasm for both food and toys. Gem didn't care about either. And she didn't appear to care about me. She was lackadaisical in her response to praise. Sometimes she would respond happily, jumping up on me or shoving her head under my hand. At other times she would ignore it and look the other direction.

I was discouraged and frustrated. But through the daily struggles, setbacks, and intermittent successes, I gradually began to learn more about my dog.

First of all, she was smart. And second, she did not know how to learn.

Of course, dogs naturally learn about their environment, and the physical, mental, and social skills required to navigate that environment and its routines and odd surprises. But learning from a human, how to take direction, intuit what we want in particular situations—in other words, understanding how to understand us—is something different. And Gem didn't have it. Until she came to me, and even perhaps for a few months afterward, she had largely been left to her own devices. One might even argue that she had actually been taught not to learn, or at least, not to learn the good things people asked of her. She had learned to get attention by jumping up on people. She had learned that people are not consistent and either don't mean what they say or can't call her bluff and insist on it. She had learned not to stay in a fenced area or close to a person when outdoors. She had learned that the best thing to do when she was called was to turn tail and slink the other way, or to hover just out of reach and see what happened.

But when it came down to working with a human partner, learning teamwork and anticipating what that partner might want or ask, she had no clue or desire. And as I had discovered, she also had no motivation.

Gem, however, was no dummy. She could open cabinet doors. She may not have been motivated by treats to do something I wanted her to do, but if there was something in the trash that really caught her fancy, it was the work of just a few seconds to flip open the door to the cabinet under the sink where I stash the trash and dig in.

She was extremely observant and took stock of every little thing in her familiar area. Every time I would leave the house, she would get up and take inventory, especially scrutinizing the kitchen table. If there was one thing added or out of place—for instance, a piece of mail brought back from the mailbox that morning, or a different placemat—she would remove it, carry it to one of her corners and nibble on it.

And perhaps most impressive of all on the brainiac scale, Gem could undo zippers. I once came in to find my backpack pulled off a high bookshelf. It was on the floor, one pocket neatly unzipped, and the lunchbox that had been shoved into that pocket gone. On further exploration, I located the lunchbox on Gem's favorite dog bed. It had also been deftly unzipped and everything even remotely edible had been pulled out and devoured or shredded. The backpack and lunchbox themselves were unscathed. I mean, who needs to chew and rip and make a mess when you can just jimmy the zippers?

A final strike that Gem had against her was the one and only character trait she seemed to have inherited from her sire, Butch. It didn't appear that Daddy had gifted his daughter with any of his loyalty, confidence, or work ethic. But he had given her a lovely dose of don't-care. This dog had a hard streak in her. Cut through all the crud and ugliness she'd had to live through, slice away the insecurity and shyness of her mother, Shot, and brush aside the superficial friendliness, and there is a part of Gem that just doesn't give a rip. Some people call it stubborn, farm folks call it pigheaded. Herding people usually call it "hard" as opposed to "soft" which refers to a dog that is very submissive, easily shut down or discouraged, gentle and maybe even timid. A hard dog just gets something in its head and does it, regardless of verbal reprimand, a pop from a training collar or longe whip, or being kicked by a cow. Hard. Hardheaded, some might say hardhearted, hard to handle, hard to train, and sometimes even hard to love.

So I had a dog who had been neglected and abused for most of her life, relegated to a crate or a kennel run for extended periods of time, unmotivated by food, disinterested in toys, and unattached to me; a dog with lots of brain power but with no coaching or desire to learn, skittish in new places, and with a hard streak in her personality to top it all off. She needed patience, gentleness, and constancy. She also needed a firm, determined hand and someone who wasn't going to take *I can't* and *I don't wanna* as acceptable answers. She needed a cheerleader and she needed a tough-butt drill sergeant to get in there and tell her, *Yes you can, and I'm going to make sure you do.*

I realize that there are some people reading this who are shaking their heads and lavishing loads of sympathy on Gem. In the minds of these well-meaning readers, I am the demanding and totally unsympathetic, old-school obedience trainer who has to be "alpha" no matter what and who has no time for compassion or empathy. But there will be a few readers, probably lifelong dog people or maybe people with challenging children, who recognize the desperate need Gem had for direction. To have left her where she was—a messed up, traumatized dog who had been allowed to get away with being both timid and pigheaded—would have stunted her even more than she already was. This is a disservice to any dog. But to a super smart, working breed like a border collie it is a travesty. This is a breed that thrives on mental exercise just as much as, if not more than, it thrives on physical exercise. They love to work. They love to learn. They need to learn.

I knew that dog was in Gem somewhere, and I decided we were going to find it. Sometimes you don't get the dog you want, you get the dog you need. And sometimes you get the dog that needs you.

When we had worked with basic obedience skills to the point that I felt she was ready, I entered Gem in a Canine Good Citizen test. This is an evaluation compiled by the American Kennel Club, intended to replicate real-life situations that a dog out in public might encounter. It includes skills like walking through a crowd on a loose leash, meeting an unreactive new dog, and allowing interaction with a friendly stranger. The dog must also demonstrate that she can sit, lie down, and both stay and come on command.

Pretty rudimentary stuff for most well-socialized dogs. But for my little girl, it would be asking a lot. It would be a good opportunity to determine where we were and how much progress we had made.

The CGC is a pass/fail test. The team is not scored—you either make it or you don't. And we made it. Barely. At the completion of all ten exercises, the evaluator congratulated me and said we had done it. "She was just very timid," she said, glancing down at Gem who was plastered against my shins and staring in the other direction.

"You don't have to pass us if you don't think we were quite there yet," I said, feeling slightly embarrassed. Maybe I really had jumped the gun on this and asked too much of my challenge-child. Maybe my impatience had reared its nasty little head again and we needed to take things slower, be more realistic.

The evaluator shook her head. "No," she said, smiling, "she did everything you asked her to do. She's just a little shy, but she did well for you."

And so, Gem and I earned our first AKC title.

I wouldn't say that this was necessarily a turning point for our relationship, but it was a milestone. It was a successful experience in which both of us could put our confidence. I was getting through to this tough and timid little dog. And she had proven that she could and would work for me under unfamiliar circumstances. We were beginning to trust each other.

I began taking her to more and more shows. Not that she was anywhere near being ready to get in the ring herself, but she rode along whenever one of the competition dogs was entered, just for the socialization opportunity. Between warming up and working other dogs, I would get Gem out of her crate and let her slowly soak in the atmosphere and surroundings of a dog show. Strangers walking past, usually with at least one dog in tow. The banging of crate doors. The judge calling out a heeling pattern in the ring beside us. Applause. The barking of an unfamiliar dog somewhere close by. The clanking and scraping of folding chairs. The doors of the building clunking open and whooshing shut again.

It was all new and scary and exciting to her. She vascillated between thrilled enthusiasm at the chance to meet new people, and skittish uncertainty about walking through such different and unpredictable surroundings.

We didn't just hang out ringside in the quiet obedience competition areas at shows. We ventured farther afield, wandering through the grooming tables and crates of the conformation rings where there was much more activity, louder applause and cheering, and many barking and excited dogs.

The first few times we headed into these new situations, Gem literally wrapped herself around my legs. She shied and spooked, velcroing her sleek body against my shins. Her eyes were wide and darting, her mouth shut tight in panic. So we walked slowly, or just stood and let her work through it, making light of the situation so she knew I wasn't worried about it. And then we went on. One literal step at a time. One psychological and emotional step at a time. A day at a time, an hour at a time, I kept asking, supporting, reassuring.

And little by little, Gem gained confidence. She began loosening her mouth and tail. She assessed things instead of just taking one furtive glance and reacting. She walked beside me as we passed through a door or between crates, flinching but not cowering. She smiled when we met new people.

Maybe a year, I thought. *Maybe a little more.* And we would try for our first show.

Gem was still afraid of the goats. Two or three times each spring, I would take her out to the corral where the new babies lived. The big, inquisitive adults were way too intimidating for her. So we would visit the kids, much smaller than her and eager to follow me. I always kept her on a loose leash. We would stand outside the fence for a minute or two, Gem's tail tucked and her head turned away from the kids. Then I would open the gate and gently tug her in, encouraging her to come get the goats. All being bottle babies, the kids would cluster around us, pushing moist noses against my knees and nibbling hopefully at various hems, pockets, and articles of clothing. They never showed much interest in the dog—after all, they had never yet met a dog that kept bottles of warm milk on hand—but Gem couldn't get far enough away from them. She usually bolted, then, brought up short by the leash, she would freeze, tail clamped, and head turned away.

It was heartbreaking to watch. This purebred border collie, descended from generations of dynamic, dependable stock dogs and herself once a working dog, was too afraid and demoralized to even look at baby goats. If I dropped the leash and walked away, drawing the kids with me to encourage Gem to gather them, she would turn tail and slink to the gate, begging to get away and find one of her favorite, dark corners. No coaxing or sweet-talking would stir any flicker of interest. Neither would getting the goats up and running. That was another trick I tried, trotting from one end of the corral to the other with the perpetually hungry babies galloping eagerly around me. My hope was to jump-start that herding instinct. Maybe if she saw small livestock moving quickly right past her, that border collie-drive to circle and control would overpower the learned behavior of fear.

But it didn't happen. Spring after spring kids came into the world, ran and jumped and cried and grew, eventually were sold or moved into the big pasture with the older does, and Gem showed no interest or instinct of any kind. After three years or so I just gave up and let it go. She would never be a stock dog. That was okay—I hadn't gotten her to work the goats anyway.

One April morning when Gem bolted out the dog door as I went to the corral to bottle feed, I didn't really think much about it. I mean, she's a border collie. And she's strange, even for that breed, which is saying something. But the next morning it happened again. And the next. And then that afternoon. By the third or fourth day I was finally taking notice.

The north side of the babies' corral is a shared fence between their area and the dogs' domain in the back yard. Most mornings, the kids hang out in their little shed at the total opposite end of the corral from the gate I come to when it's time to feed them. What that translates to is a pell-mell, top-speed sprint from one end of the corral to the other as soon as they see me. Or more accurately, as soon as they hear me. The slamming of the front door and the jingle of the dogs' tags as they come through the dog door to meet me on the other side of the fence are the signals for the kids to come pounding out of the mini barn, feet flying, bells tinkling, and screaming at the top of their lungs. Breakfast time is a pretty exciting occasion around here.

I'll never know exactly what the trigger was that lured Gem out of the shower and into the back yard. Maybe it was the two or three other dogs that went out to keep tabs on me. Maybe it was hearing the desperate calls of the running babies. Maybe it was just coincidence and she was out in the back, going potty or just looking at the scenery the first time. But however it began, once she saw the little goats running and realized they were on the other side of a fence, the stock dog drive began to kick in.

The behavior terminology for it is "barrier frustration." It's why dogs on chains often bark and lunge and act ferocious, and why dogs in vehicles or behind fences often put on world-class Kujo routines. They know they can't get to the target, and whether that makes them feel safe or simply frustrates them as the term implies, they usually act out by lunging, running, vocalizing, and challenging the barrier that restrains them.

My best guess is that Gem, who ordinarily shied away from any contact with the goats when she knew they could get to her, put the pieces together and figured out that, on the other side of a fence, they were safe from her and she was safe from them. So she began running the fenceline whenever they ran. I would go out the front door. Gem would go out the back. The babies would see me and come tearing down the length of the corral, and Gem, safe in the confines of the back yard, would race along with them, crouched low, gaze riveted. Time and again it happened. At first, I just shrugged, and made some snarky comments about how weird dogs are and about how exceptionally weird this particular dog was. I didn't think it meant anything. I had seen, and even provided, many opportunities for Gem to work goats. She had seen them run, she had seen them worked by other experienced dogs and had shown no inclination to work them herself. She had been given chance after chance, both inside and outside of corrals and round pens. And she had refused to engage or show any interest. And that was fine. I hadn't brought her home to be a working stock dog. She was damaged goods, the product of neglect and abuse, and essentially ruined for stock work by her past.

So I just let her do her weird fenceline thing every time I went out to bottle feed.

Then she started herding Meg on our walks. Almost overnight, she took to racing in circles around me and whichever dogs happened to be close as we trotted down the road. Most of them didn't care. But Meg, a fellow border collie, got it. They would be up ahead of me, playing their little mind games and trying to outrun each other, and then there would be a subtle shift and Meg would slow down and begin to drift back to me. Within another hundred yards, Gem would have her in orbit. She would put pressure on Meg, gradually pushing her closer and closer to me, never touching her but posturing and crouching, always in constant motion, giving her that intense stare for which the breed is so famous. And Meg, always the one to dash ahead and be the first one to get anywhere, would acquiesce.

Gem pressured her back to me, not letting up until Meg was within ten or fifteen feet of me, and then she would begin to circle. It was nearly always counterclockwise, her favorite direction as I would soon come to learn. She would get Meg where she wanted her, then race around and around me, keeping her there, panting hard, crouching low, the picture of border collie concentration. It could last for half a mile, or just a hundred feet, and then Meg would get fed up, wait until Gem was behind me, then flip her off and rocket forward. It was all part of the game. Gem would gallop after her, catch up, and usually the whole thing would begin all over again.

There are some sheepdog people who would have instantly quashed this behavior. Border collies especially can get obsessive about herding, circling, nipping, even to the point of becoming true bullies. They are incredibly fast, smart, and intense, with inexhaustible energy and work ethic. But in this case, I was so thrilled to see Gem come to life and begin acting like a sheepdog that I didn't stop it. And it never morphed into bullying. If Meg didn't want to play the game, they wouldn't play, and when she got tired of it she would break away. I also discovered that Gem would stop if I told her to, and things would lapse back into a regular walk if I put my foot down and forced the issue.

So most of the time I didn't. And as the weeks passed and Gem continued to run the fenceline whenever I fed babies, and kept herding Meg on nearly every walk, I began to think about trying again. Maybe it was time to take her back into the corral and see what she could do.

I tried it one spring afternoon. At first I held her collar, the kids bunched up on one side of me and Gem on the other. I could practically hear the wheels turning in her brain, trying to figure out this new, and yet not so new, situation. She was still, watching, alert but not afraid. The kids began to shift in her direction, curious as ever, sniffing, then nibbling the hand that held her collar.

I let go. She stood there, stock still for a moment, head and tail low. I eased away from her, the kids skipping along with me. They crowded against my legs, pushing and bouncing, ringing their bells, deciding that the strange new dog didn't have any bottles of milk available and so was therefore not important.

I kept walking, slowly, quietly, ignoring the dog irresolute behind me. She hadn't run to the gate. She was still interested, not shut down or refusing to make eye contact. She was thinking, sensing, and weighing her options.

And she decided to try.

The kids danced around me, still close but not quite as eager anymore since no bottles had materialized. They were beginning to spread out and wander, all moving in the same direction but in a much looser group than before. And that's when magic began to happen.

Gem came up so fast I didn't even know she was moving until she dashed counter clockwise to block the group. They startled, drawing back to my safety, and I immediately turned around and reversed direction. Now we were heading back toward the corral gate, the goats bounding along with me, glancing uncertainly at the dog. She came around again, with more purpose this time, fast and furtive. The goats bunched, wary now.

Again, I sheered off and changed direction. The kids came with me, Gem blocked them, and we turned again, this time sharp to the right.

I am not a herding trainer, but I had just enough knowledge to understand that Gem needed above all else to have confidence in herself. She needed to believe she could manage and move those goats. Even though they were really following me, I was maneuvering in such a way that every time she blocked them, I moved away, bringing the kids with me. So as far as she was aware, Gem was moving them by her own authority. She scurried around, again counter clockwise, and as she came up on our right front I veered away to the left rear. The kids followed. She came back around, quick as thought, pushing them toward me from the left, and I shied away to the right rear, the kids rushing with me.

I walked faster. The kids ran. The dog crouched and circled, her eyes intense. She was starting to pant now, a rapid, open-mouth sound that I would come to associate with her being in the zone. She was truly working now. She was in the moment, not in the past. She was quick. She was smart. She was confident. She was in control. She was a border collie, doing what she was born to do. And I was absolutely blown away.

"Good girl," I said, quiet but cheerful. "Good girl. Go get 'em, babe. Good job!"

It was an amazing moment. The whole atmosphere had changed. This was a dog I had only met in my imagination, that place where faith encounters dreams. It's hard to describe the dynamic of watching, of feeling, a herding dog bringing livestock to you. It is something so ancient and yet so present, a depth of relationship, yet almost completely driven by instinct. It's primitive—the wolf hunting and driving the prey—yet it is sophisticated, a uniquely dog-to-human, human-to-dog interaction. Both parties are working toward the same goal, and both must learn to think not only like each other, but also learn to understand the minds and motives of yet another party (the livestock) in order to reach that goal. It was humbling and magical, and I think I felt the prickle of tears for just a second. But it was also such a rush—seeing, feeling, the transformation—the sheer joy and power of a running, darting, working sheepdog.

I didn't let her work much longer that day. End on a good note. Keep her wanting more and take her out of the game while she's still winning and confident. But over the next few weeks, we went out to work the kids every two or three days. Most of the time it was a repeat of that first remarkable session. Every once in a while, something would go wrong and set her back. Sometimes I didn't even know what it was, and she would just quit working, lose heart and either find a corner to hole up in or go to the gate and wait for me. At those times, I would always try to bring her back in and encourage her to work again. I didn't want her to walk away without a last success, or to learn that she could walk away whenever she chose to, just by shutting down and deciding not to work anymore. But it never succeeded. If something had scared her or discouraged her, she was done for the day. It didn't matter if I got the goats up and running or called to her with lots of upbeat praise, or if I put her on a leash and tried to fake herding by keeping her on the outside of the circle while bringing the goats along with me. She wasn't doing it. Still, within a week or two, Gem had progressed to taking the kids out of the corral and into the front yard. From there, I opened the front gate and we were experimenting with hiking up and down the driveway. That was more challenging, and some personalities started to come out as the goats got the chance to interact with a new environment and new forage. The old saying about the grass being greener on the other side of the fence is totally true. In the corral and front yard, the grass had been familiar and boring. Out along the driveway it was fresh, new, and so much more delicious. Plus, there was way more than just rotten old grass. Along the driveway there were weeds, saplings, vines, cedar trees, and occasional patches of poison ivy, which goats absolutely love. And if somebody didn't want to stay with the group because she found a really yummy patch of weeds, then who was going to make her?

Gem tried and slowly learned to succeed. Sometimes when two goats went one direction, one went another and three more stayed with me, she simply didn't know which way to run. I wasn't much help. I tried the traditional "come by" and "way to me" herding commands, one cuing the dog to circle clockwise, the other counter clockwise, and she didn't respond at all. Bringing the longe whip along to help signal her was a catastrophe. Herding trainers will almost always start a dog out with the help of a five-foot horse whip trailing a five-foot cord. It serves as an extension of the handler's arm, allowing her to reach over the backs of the livestock and visually signal the dog to stop, swing right, swing left and so on. It's rarely if ever used to physically correct a dog, the only exception being if the dog gets too assertive and begins nipping the livestock.

But it had been used incorrectly on Gem many times. She knew exactly what that whip could do, and the first time I carried it with me and held it out to cue her direction change, she turned tail and fled. I was left with all the teenage goats to grab and drag back to the corral. After that I wasn't sure if she would work for me again. I waited a week or so before attempting anymore herding, then took her with me back to the corral, leaving the whip behind. And she was okay.

Another time as we trekked up the driveway, I made the mistake of reaching over to slap one of the goats, who was crowding me and tromping all over my feet. By this point we had gotten to where the kids definitely respected Gem. Even along the gravel drive with its tempting vegetation, they had learned that she wouldn't put up with any nonsense. The silliness and boundary pushing had disappeared. Now the problem I had was that they pressed and cowered up against my legs as she worked very close to them on the narrow lane. That afternoon I was tired of having my toes trampled and let one of them know it with a mild smack.

I didn't even think Gem had seen it. But next thing I knew, she had vanished. I never did figure out where she had tucked herself away. After penning the naughty goats back up, I searched all over the yard, the corral, the mini barn, the carport. I crawled under the rabbit cages and the Gator, reached behind the trash containers, walked the whole length of the driveway. I called and chirped on my whistle and even brought Meg out to try and entice her back.

Nothing. No skittering paws, no jingling tags. No dog. So I just left it alone and decided to wait her out. All I could think about was the memory of her time at Kathy's, and how Gem had been so scared and bullied there that she had run off at every opportunity. The years that Gem had been with me up to then, I had never seen that tendency in her. She had always stayed close to home, never challenged any fences, and loved being in the house. So I stuffed down my fear, prayed, and went on with the regular routine.

And eventually she showed up, about half an hour after I had given up searching. I was afraid to try anything with the goats for weeks after that. Maybe this dog wasn't very attached to me, but the fear that she might have bolted and run away, as brief a fear as it might have been, had shown me that I had gotten quite attached to her.

After each one of these episodes where she would have a failure or a shut-down, I would always question whether or not Gem would ever work with stock again. And each time, with a couple days to recoup and debrief, she would always come back and do it. That pigheaded hard streak from her daddy did have its merits after all.

Meanwhile, I started considering when to enter her in an easy rally class for our first show together. Rally is a good place to start dogs if the goal is to get them into competitive obedience someday. It requires a lot of heel work, turns, pivots, halts, pace changes, and recalls. But at the novice levels it's all done on-leash. And unlike formal obedience, in the rally ring you can talk to the dog, repeat commands, and cheerlead all you need to. It's good for any young or green dog to introduce them to the show ring, but for Gem it was exactly what was needed.

We earned our Rally Novice—the first rally title a dog and handler can achieve with the AKC—in three trials, and even landed in the ribbons a couple of times. To say that I was a proud mama was putting it mildly. That prickle of tears was back, threatening behind my eyelids every time we were called forward by the judge and I heard the applause of the onlookers and the other exhibitors. If they only knew what this little girl had come through and what it had taken to get here.

My journey with Gem is ongoing. But sometime in that third year together, things changed between us. It was subtle, but gradually I began to sense that our hearts, which had for all those years beat from opposite sides of the room, were drawing together and starting to synchronize. I would walk into the computer room, and instead of jumping up from her bed and slinking past me, she would look up, then stand and come to me, putting her nose in my hand. She would seek me out, coming to me at odd moments—while I washed dishes or folded towels or changed the radio station—and touch my knee or ankle, or my backside, which will always get someone's attention. She would check in. She didn't spend as much time in corners. She discovered how comfortable dog beds could be. She lay facing the room, relaxed on her side instead of coiled into the tight ball of one or two years before. And every so often, if I was really lucky that night, I would step out of the shower to find her curled up on the rug, waiting for me.

There was warmth between us now. Purpose. History. We had both come a long way.

The Topeka dog shows that August were what I determined would be our next step. She was ready, I felt, to try for her Companion Dog Novice obedience title. The novice class is pretty basic. Exercises include on-lead and off-lead heeling, a stand for examination, a recall, and two stay exercises.

It's basic, but it isn't easy. Even for a well-socialized, confident dog, working in a ring setting can be a game changer. For a dog like Gem, it might be asking too much. It would certainly be asking a lot.

"You never know till you try," I told Gem, and I signed the entry form and mailed it.

"Where there's a will there's a way," I reminded us both on the morning of the show, pushing away my half-eaten breakfast and wiping my sweaty hands.

I hate showing. The training beforehand is fun. The titles and hit-or-miss ribbons afterward are amazing. The show itself is like a slow nightmare.

But we were going, so I put my game face on and went out to load the van.

When we arrived at the show building, Gem bounded out of her crate, smiling all over herself and lashing her tail like a Labrador. We checked in at the steward's table, brought in the other crates, brought in the other dogs, then settled in for what's probably the worst part of any show day. The waiting.

As we waited, my dad and another friend with me noticed a striking black Belgian sheepdog warming up in our area. You don't see many representatives of the breed, so we asked about him. In a strange twist of fate, we discovered that the dog was one that Pam, Gem's breeder, still trained for herding. She was not the one showing him today in obedience, but the connection to Pam, someone Gem and I had not seen for two or three years, was uncanny at this precise moment.

Our class was called. My fickle tummy flip-flopping, I got Gem out of her crate and began to warm up. We worked on simple heeling steps, about turns and halts, then I would release her and goof around with a few free-style tricks. She spun around me, twirled in circles, first left, then right, lay down, leaped up and put both front paws on my knee, on my arm. These little quirky extras brighten up most dogs and keep them focused and motivated before they enter the formal setting of the obedience ring.

The other dogs in our class weren't giving me much encouragement. A little shih tzu got distracted on the off-lead heeling and wandered away from her handler, pottering up to the ring fence and gazing out at everyone. A golden, overwhelmed by the new surroundings, bolted from the ring and fled to the security of her open crate.

Gem and I kept working. My goal was to keep her alert, ready and focused. This is working time, not social time, not freeze-in-the-corner time. But still, keeping things light and rewarding enough that she maintained her exuberance.

The Belgian went in right before us, and he did not qualify. They came out of the ring, the handler shaking her head, the dog shaking his entire body and looking for treats. The butterflies gave their wings a mighty flutter in my stomach. I pasted on a smile, squared my shoulders, and stepped into the ring with my dog right beside me.

We stepped out again with a first-place ribbon. And we did it three days in a row. To achieve the Companion Dog title, a dog and handler must earn qualifying scores in three separate trials. They don't have to do it three trials in a row, and many dogs don't. Most of mine haven't. I'd say four or maybe five trials is typical for most teams. But this little shocker wowed everyone. She stood far and above the competition. A perfect score in obedience is 200, and you need at least a score of 170 to qualify. While most of the other teams trooped out with scores in the 170s and low 180s, Gem landed each first-place ribbon with a working score of 193 or higher.

On our very last day and the very last ring exercise—the recall—I thought she was wavering a little and losing some heart. So on the judge's signal, I called her with a bit more enthusiasm than usual. Gem came racing across the ring, grinning like a goofball, rushed straight to me, leaped up for one brief moment to put a paw on my stomach, then jumped back into heel position. Not what you want from a dog on a recall, but at least she was with me and glad about it.

The judge's comment, delivered with a chuckle, summed up the entire experience for Gem that weekend. "Exercise finished," he said, and then with a big smile he pointed out the obvious, "she is just so happy to be here."

At a much more recent show, I had Gem with me again. She wasn't entered, but I brought her along anyway to keep her thinking and socialized. We walked into the show building and Gem, in her typical observant fashion, understood in one border collie sweep what things were all about. She saw the ring gating and matting, saw the rows of crates and chairs, heard the familiar obedience commands, both from judges to handlers and handlers to dogs. And without any signal from me, without even having her working collar on, she put herself in heel position, sat down, and stared into my face. Those intense eyes of hers looked into my soul, and our hearts synchronized. "What are we doing next, Mom?" I could almost audibly hear her ask. "I'm ready to go to work!"

Not long ago, I went out to the barn on a quick errand, carrying a bag of pellet bedding to spread out in one of the pens. The bedding was heavy, my back was bugging me, and the weather was smoking hot, so I was a bit lazy when I shuffled into the pasture. I pushed the gate closed behind me but did not chain it shut. The goats would follow me anyway. They'd be curious about the bag I was hauling, and as soon as it was dropped in the barn, I would trot back out to secure the gate.

Except I didn't. It happens all the time. You go out to the barn to do one simple task, and you find five more that need instant attention. And while I was taking care of all those little addendums, the wily goats, who always notice more than you think they do, pushed the gate open and began raiding the alfalfa supply in the mini barn.

Actually, some of them raided the alfalfa supply. A few others decided the grass in the corral area around the mini barn was much better than what they had in the pasture, and two or three more figured out that the corral gate was also open and that the grass outside was amazing. Anyway, by the time I got it, they were all over creation and running wild.

I rolled my eyes and stomped out the gate. Seriously? Well, if they thought they were so smart, they had another thing coming. I had a Plan B. Weaving my way through the just-out-of-reach escaped convicts I went to the back door, leaned in and hollered.

"GEM!"

She came dutifully, shaking off the coolness of the shower stall. I grabbed her braided leather collar and started marching.

"Let's go get the goats!" I told her. "You ready? You wanna go get the goats?"

She came along with me, uncertain what I was asking of her, until we reached the backyard gate and she locked in on them.

"Go get 'em!" I said, and she was away like gunfire.

It took roughly ninety seconds for my secret weapon to do its work. These were big goats now, not the dinky little bottle babies she had worked with a year before. But they all remembered each other. I had worked Gem on the kids a little through the late winter, but not recently. It didn't matter. She scorched around them, a Hellfire missile, eyes burning, absolutely confident and determined. She raced for the farthest stray, charged between the goat and the fence, peeled around and brought the entire herd thundering straight for the pasture gate. They were practically knocking it down before I could get the chain unlatched.

I flung the gate open, told the dog to lie down, and let ten very intimidated, very grateful goats back into the fence where they belonged. They stampeded through, I slammed the gate shut, yanked the chain into place, and turned back to the dog, crouching behind me, staring and panting.

"Good girl, Gem," I said, and I gathered her in my arms. "What a good dog."

CHAPTER 3

WALKS: THE PULL OF THE OPEN ROAD

As far as I'm concerned, there is nothing in the whole world you can do for a dog that is better for the dog than to walk the dog.

That's even more true if you live with a group of eight dogs in the same house like I do.

I didn't start out walking that many. I started with two, and it was because of one in particular, that I decided to make walking my dogs a lifelong commitment.

Her name was Storme. She was a pound hound from an animal shelter in Missouri. As a little, mostly scared, seven-week-old puppy we thought she was a smooth border collie. Black and white, wedge shaped head, bushy tail, prick ears, and tons and tons of energy.

She was the first dog I had ever brought home with the specific intention of training to be a competition dog. And the first step in that long journey was to give her the exercise she so desperately needed.

My other walking buddy those many years ago was Chai, a cunning American Eskimo with a true talent for escaping any fence or enclosure. Because he was completely untrustworthy off-lead, Chai accompanied me on a retractable leash, eagerly sniffing and peeing on everything within about a fifty-foot radius. But Storme ran loose. And run she did, blasting through the brush and tearing across the pastures and crop fields along the rural roads we traveled.

We soon realized she was more German shepherd than anything. There was border collie in there for sure, but she wasn't the purebred dream dog I had so hoped for. Still, she was part of the family, and she introduced me to miles and miles of gravel roads and exercise. She taught me the pleasure and adventure of walking with a group of dogs in all seasons.

Fast forward about fifteen years. Now there are eight dogs, all at one time, all wound up and ready to run. The walk is the high point of their day, and there's a lot of preparation that goes into it.

Lacing up my hiking boots and unlocking the front gate are the first signals that a walk is on the way. The two border collies wait, watch, then start to pace. The two Aussies start to whine. The tension builds. But it's not time yet. I still have to do one more thing.

When I scoop the bells off a shelf out in the utility room and bring them clanking and jingling into the house, then they know it's real. That's when dogs come racing from every direction and we teeter on the brink of pandemonium.

To avoid complete chaos, I have made it a house rule that dogs have to be calm before exiting the front door. Most of them have assigned places to wait until it's their turn to go out. A few don't need that safeguard, but the majority are expected to sit and wait in their specific places until the appropriate name is called.

When Meg is called, she comes dashing to sit in front of me and eagerly lets me put on her no-slip safety collar and her own specific bell. Then we head for the front door. If she wants to get out, she has to sit, lie down, or stand on command, and she has to remain in that position and remain calm until I give the release word that lets her rush out into the utility room. Now there's only one more door between her and freedom. Another sit, lie down, or stand—another wait. I open the door, say the release word, and then she's flying up the driveway like an arrow from a bow.

With Dundee it's the same thing. And with Brio. And Tassie. And so on until everyone is calmed down, belled up, and headed out.

I never let them out in a predictable order. It's whoever is the calmest and quietest that gets the green light first.

And then it's all wild, joyous freedom and they are loose on the world.

We walk the roads year-round, at least five days a week. Winter, summer, spring, and fall we're out. Conditions I definitely don't walk in are excessive heat, ice, heavy rain, thunder, and wind gusting more than thirty miles per hour. Any wind higher than that makes it very difficult to hear vehicles approaching.

Walking the gravel roads means, of course, that there are no sidewalks, and cars have the right of way. I am always alert for them. As soon as I hear one bearing down on us, I chirp on the referee whistle hanging around my neck and start cataloging dogs.

The three dogs who stay on retractable leashes are easy to corral. The five who run off-leash all wear bells, each a unique sound that I learn to associate with that individual. Meg and Gem are always out in front. Being true, stereotypical border collies, they are obsessed with competition and are always trying to outdo each other. Who can run the fastest, turn the sharpest, nip the other the quickest, and stare the most intensely? That competitive, calculating energy propels them out in front of the main group. And it also means that, when I chirp on the signal whistle, they compete to see which of them can get back to me the fastest. Meg usually throws herself down in the ditch beside and slightly ahead of me, and Gem whips around to face the direction we're heading and begins slinking back out into the road before I can snag her collar. After all, she needs to have a head start on Meg.

Dundee and Brio are closer to home. Brio would much rather sit out in the middle of the road, positioned in such a way that she keeps the border collies contained during their inevitable sprint back down the road. Her idea of a good time is to stand directly in their path, get flattened by their rocket-launch charge, and come up screaming and snapping as they fly by. However, over the years I have persuaded Brio that the best place to be when a car goes by is actually in heel position at my left knee, and there she sits like a statue as we wait. Dundee, solid, reliable dog that he is, stands in front of me at my knees and simply waits.

While we walk, Tassie shuttles between Meg and Gem out in front, Dundee and Brio walking more at my pace. She's still young and hasn't totally decided yet who she is or what her style should be. She's moderately competitive and driven, so she likes to prove that she can keep up with Meg and Gem if the need arises. She also likes to prove that she can not only keep up with, but also control, even the single-minded border collies. At least twice on every walk, she'll start zipping in and yapping at Gem. Meg will hardly look at her, but Gem, who has more herding instinct than Meg ever will, can be bought. She and Tassie understand each other. Gem will waffle and shillyshally, letting Tassie get in her space, and Tassie will take the bait and start darting and yapping, blocking her in, dashing and nipping and pestering. Then at some unknown signal, Gem will just decide that enough is enough and will neatly dodge around and go streaking forward, kicking gravel in Tassie's face.

But as much as Tassie loves the competition and the thrill of the chase, she might love the forbidden world of road kill even more. This is where she joins forces with Dundee. Thanks to his expert tutoring, she can now hunt down dead possums, squirrel skeletons, and smashed snakes with the best of them. She once came up with an entire deer leg, complete with hair, hinged hock joint, and two-toed hoof.

So when a car approaches, I never know if Tassie will be way up ahead or dragging surreptitiously behind. Fortunately, I do carry a secret weapon. When it comes to training dogs, I firmly believe in bribery. In this case it takes the form of Vienna sausage. It's greasy, easy to cut up, and it has a smell that will get just about any dog's attention. I carry it in a Ziplock baggie stuffed in the bait bag belted around my waist. Even Gem, who is not into treats, will usually take Vienna sausage on a walk, and the other dogs will do practically anything to earn some.

When I break in a new dog, it usually starts out on leash, unless it's a very good-natured and submissive puppy who is perfectly happy to stay with the group. In either case, it doesn't take long for a new dog to learn that two tweets on the whistle and an authoritative shout of "Come on, guys!" means there is food coming. Again, competition is my friend. Usually whoever gets to me first gets the sausage first, so a new dog given the chance to earn such a high-value treat figures things out pretty quickly.

We cower in the ditch as the vehicle whooshes by. I make sure everyone comes when they're called, and I also make sure nobody leaves until I say so. That way they stay calm and continue to focus on me.

But once the coast is clear and everything is quiet, I give them the release word and they're free to run. Meg and Gem bolt, each trying to bite the other as they meet. Brio and Tassie are right on their butts. Dundee veers off to start combing the area for stinky stuff, and Pixel, Cinder, and Kola, who are on-leash, take up their positions and come with me. Kola plods patiently to my left, Pixel trots to my right, and Cinder scampers as far ahead as his retractable leash will allow.

Walks are essential, not just for the exercise and energy outlet they provide, but also because they allow the dogs just to be dogs. At home, wild running, yapping, chasing things and being rowdy is generally discouraged. On walks they can operate as a pack or as individuals and they can sniff, dig, swim, and run like maniacs with much more freedom. It gives them space and opportunity to either stay away from each other or to form alliances. If Dundee wants to get away from Cinder for a couple hours, although they are good buddies in the house, he can. If Meg, Gem, and Tassie want to have a hundred-yard dash and see who gets to the top of the hill first, they can. Once they've had the freedom to run and rearrange themselves on the road, they live together much more peaceably at home. In other words, they don't get on each other's nerves quite as much.

Of course, there are a few rules. Chasing cars, cattle, horses, and chickens is strictly prohibited. We do not bark at random strangers that we occasionally meet. We stay out of people's yards when we do pass a house. Come when you're called. Never get involved with any nasty neighborhood dogs we might encounter, no matter what trash they might talk. And don't eat road kill. Yeah, right. They know the law on that last one, but there are always loopholes. One of Dundee and Tassie's favorites is to trot calmly along with me as we pass something icky that they want. They let me keep moving ahead, check to be sure I'm concentrating on the other dogs, then they slow down until their bells quit ringing. Bing, off my radar. From there it's a simple matter of a neat 180 and a plunge into the brush, and *haha*, Mom never knew until she was a hundred feet up the road. I can't stop them from doing something that I don't know they're doing, and without the ringing bells to help me, they pull that little prank on me more often than I'd like to admit.

The bells help me keep track not only of who everyone is

and where everyone is, but oftentimes what everyone is doing. I may not be able to tell whether a dog is chasing a cow or just having a joy run, but I can tell that the dog is running. Then I have to fill in the pieces. Whether Dundee has paused to sniff a weed or to pee on a bush I might not know, but I know that he's paused.

I'm picky about bells. They need to sound very different and distinct from each other. They need to be loud and clear-ringing, and ideally, they should be very live, meaning that they ring decisively with very little motion. I've learned where to look to find bells like that. They come from pet supply stores, farm supply stores, from an online seller who gets them handmade and puts them on Ebay. And I always keep my ears open for new bells. Some of the best I ever found were a string of cylindrical sheep bells which I happened across in a little shop in Israel. Tassie currently wears one of those.

Another adaptation I've mastered is the trick of walking multiple dogs on-leash while still always managing to have one hand free. Right now, there are three dogs who stay on-leash. Obviously too many for just two hands. So around my waist I wear a bait bag—a big pouch where I stash treats, keys, extra leashes, Kleenex, and other essentials. I run the belt of the bait bag through the plastic handles of Pixel and Kola's Flexi leads, hold Cinder's Flexi in one hand, and there you go. I can switch Cinder's lead from hand to hand as needed or clamp it between my knees if there's a reason for two hands at one time.

Meg, Gem, and surprisingly Cinder, are the ones who love water the most. Brio, Dundee, and Tassie will splash into a creek or overflowing ditch if one is handy and if the weather is warm, but they aren't crazy for water like the other three. Kola will wade in if we walk right past water and she's hot, and Pixel won't get anywhere near it.

One of the border collies' favorite stops is the huge, round horse trough about half a mile from home. It's set right beside the road and it's almost always brimful. The weather doesn't have to be anything like hot for Meg and Gem to nip through the fence, bound over the side, and cannon-ball in. Even in forty or fifty degrees they're soaking themselves in it.

Cinder, the ankle-high, wavy-coated Russian bolonka is about as far removed from a border collie as you can get, but for whatever reason, he adores the water. After a heavy rain, he splashes and paddles in every ditch and puddle we pass. There have been a handful of times that I have stopped and ducked through the pasture fence myself to dip Cinder into the horse trough, on days that have gotten warmer or muggier than I think he's comfortable in. Cinder absolutely loves those times. He's a typical bolonka who never forgets anything. Days after his last dip in the trough, each time we pass it he still hesitates, looks at me, looks longingly at the wallowing border collies—*Come on, Mom, pleeeeeeease?*—then finally moves on reluctantly. With a half mile remaining between us and the air conditioned refuge of the house, the horse trough has proven very helpful at times. It gives the dogs a refresh and the cool-down they need to make it safely home.

Each season brings its own joys and challenges to the road. Summer is the hardest. Put simply— it's just stinkin' hot. On a day when the temperature overnight doesn't drop below eighty degrees and the humidity is running at eighty percent, there is no cool time to walk. Even at six in the morning I'm sweating by the time I reach the end of the driveway. And when the sun arrives, it gets steadily worse. On many summer days I curtail walks to only two or three miles and leave as early as possible. Kola and Pixel stay at home on those days, and they don't seem to mind. I'm soaking wet by the time I've walked a mile. So are most of the dogs. There's that horse trough after all, and they know every ditch, creek, water hole, and pond we encounter on our regular route. As long as they're wet, I don't worry about them too much in mild heat, but summer walks are always ones to watch.

Winter is far more enjoyable for them than it is for me. The rule of thumb is that anything in the single digits is just too cold. Not that they agree with me, but in bitter temperatures like those I start to worry about their ears and toes, especially when you factor in the perpetual, biting Kansas wind. Bundled up in my down jacket, fleece-lined jeans, warm hiking boots, alpaca socks (and scarf if it's breezy), and deerskin gloves, I'm warm enough as I tromp down the road. Often times on those walks I'm moving so fast that I can pull off the gloves after a mile or two. In the cold the dogs run more—faster and farther. Many times, we go for seven or eight miles. Sometimes we go ten. The road is hard as iron underfoot, the sky thin, blue steel overhead, slate-gray clouds whisping across it. A skim of two-day-old snow glistens, fine icing across the fields, slick and treacherous in the tire tracks on the roads. Sometimes the sun shines pale and crystalline, its warmth hardly reaching the frozen earth. Other times we never see the sun, buried behind banks and brakes of sullen clouds. The wind cuts across the fields, rushing through the shivering stands of timber, their skeletal branches and bony trunks only half-heartedly sheltering us as we trot past, their limbs creaking and squeaking in the never-ending freezing tide from the northwest. On those days especially I hurry, tucking my chin into my coat collar and determining to get this business over and done with as soon as humanly possible. Wafts of woodsmoke catch me on the fly, then the fresh, keen scent of cedar, then the pungent smell of old horse manure from the neighbors' corral. Home is just around the corner. Almost time to close the door against the buffeting wind, dole out salmon brownies to the dogs, and click the thermostat up at least three degrees.

Spring and fall walks are the best. Cool and comfortable, enough breeze to keep us fresh—from the south in the spring, northwest in the fall—and with miles and miles of sweet air beginning to smell good again after summer's dust and winter's killing cold. Every so often a spring thunderstorm will pop up and chase us down. At least once I've taken refuge under the bridge we cross on our northern route, huddled way up underneath its curve and as far away from the creek as we could get, hanging onto Meg, who is terrified of thunder. Several times I have turned tail and raced the storm home, alternating between cheerleading the dogs and praying that the storm would slow down or change course. We summit the last hill, fat raindrops beginning to splatter, and then we're slewing around the corner, careening down the driveway, and the first rumble of thunder shakes the sky. I hit the front gate with key in hand, and we gallop, all nine of us, steaming and panting, into the house just as the heavens crack and dump buckets of rain.

The mud lies thick in the spring—heavy, Kansas clay. It tracks into the house with what seems a life of its own, shedding from the dogs' paws in crumbs and clods and peeling from my boots in chunks. Meg and Cinder, with their wavy coats and propensity to get as wet and filthy as they possibly can, bring in the heaviest loads. Brio stays remarkably clean, even with her competitive running and swimming, and is back to her regular, clay-free self within hours.

Then there are the autumn walks with the restless breezes and the cinnamon smell of leaves, the honking of a small V of geese overhead in a deep, clear sky, the tang of frost still lingering in the low places, the revving of a chainsaw off across the woods, and the feeling that you could go on like this for half-another day. The dogs run and run, crunching and cavorting through mounds and drifts of leaves. The blue jays jeer and scold, and the sassy little chickadees are starting to titter and chatter in the cedar brush. Those are the good walks, the ones when you don't want to end up back at the safe, smothering shelter of the house, but instead you long to follow the road and meet all of its moods and surprises. When I take the pack out nearly every day, no matter the weather or my own feelings and the kind of day I'm having, it can be easy to drop into the dog-walking doldrums and brave the road only to discharge a duty. But those autumn walks remind me of the deeper reason that we walk. It's not just for the exercise, or the required number of miles, or so that I can check it off the list. We do it to get outside, bond with each other, meet the world at our doorstep, and come home truly tired and content after our long foray into that world.

However, by that same token, the walk for me is also the hardest and most stressful thing I consistently do. It's not for the risk of getting lost. These are Kansas gravel roads, mapped out in a reliable grid pattern. North, south, east and west, with an intersecting road every mile or half mile. Because of the fact that I can see light and dark and shadows, I'm also able to stay on the road by following its lighter gray surface contrasted with the darker, rougher appearance of the ditches and grass to either side. There are few houses and fewer vehicles, and as long as I keep a good accounting of how many hills we've climbed, which driveways we've passed, and any other noticeable landmarks, I very seldom get disoriented.

The one exception is walking in wind and snow. Anything like two inches of snow or more can be very confusing, not only because it whites-out the contrast between the gravel and the roadside grass, but also because it dampens and distorts sound. The wind is a more obvious hazard, since it also tampers with the hearing of anyone who relies on their ears to navigate. Put those two components together and you have a nasty combination that can turn me around even on a familiar road. Snow and wind definitely shove me out of my comfort zone.

And that's precisely why every single day, the walk is such a tough assignment for me to complete. No matter the weather, in one way or another, it always shoves me out of my comfort zone. Once I step out on that first stony road, I have left the safety of my little corner behind. Winter or summer, I'm the weak one in a treacherous, complicated, and very sighted universe. And I have eight other living and unpredictable beings that I'm bringing out into it and for which I am completely responsible.

Anything can happen. Lots of things can go wrong.

People drive too fast. They don't expect to meet a crazy blind lady and eight dogs looming on the horizon.

On many occasions we have startled wild turkeys and deer, and most of the dogs will chase both. My heart always does a little somersault when they shoot forward into a dead run like that. I'm never quite sure if they've spotted something or if they're just having fun. We've met joggers, other walkers, horseback riders, even a horse-drawn wagon jingling and rumbling along the road.

I've been accosted by a stalker. I've been run off the road by a deer poacher. I've been chauffeured home in the sheriff's squad car, dogs included, when a man with a gun was spotted on the road. I've been slashed on barbed wire, fallen and hurt my back, skinned my hands and knees, and once plunged six feet down into a culvert. One dog was bitten by a copperhead, and all of them, as well as myself have been threatened and/or bitten by other dogs.

Did somebody say, "Out of my comfort zone?" Serious dog walking is not for the faint of heart.

But even apart from any of those adventures, the stress of the walk is a low-grade constant, nurtured by all the tiny but real insecurities of stepping out into the world on my own. For me, freedom and fear are never far apart.

Still, freedom always wins out. I can trek ten miles in a morning, just because I choose to, and take joy in my own endurance and confidence. I could walk all the way to Nebraska if I wanted to. Meg and Gem would love that. But you know, I won't do it without my dogs. Okay, I wouldn't do that even with my dogs, but then again, I won't walk even one mile on these roads without them. The dogs are the motivation, the responsibility, and the reward that gets me out of my house, out of myself and into real life. That is a debt I can never quite repay. If it weren't for my crazy, high-energy dogs, I would be stuck in the house. I'd be missing the wind and the weather, and all of their moods and mysteries. I would never know the taste of summer dust or the flavor of fall frost. Because of the dogs, I know what it is to stand in the shadow of cedar trees and hear the wind caress their boughs. Did you know that the wind sounds different in the cedars than it does in the cotton woods? I know how deep the woods can feel, how high the sky can feel, the difference between the feel of a winter sky and the feel of a spring sky. I know when the birds come back and when they leave, and I know when my neighbors decide that it's cold enough to fire up their woodstove. Half the time I even know what kind of wood they're burning.

I know how good it feels to travel, and afterward, to be tired. I know what it is to get out of myself, to get away from myself.

It is a great debt that I owe my dogs.

But when I pause at the top of a hill, the fresh wind cooling a sheen of sweat on my face, and I listen to the dogs racing ahead, charging down the other side of the hill, bells ringing loud in the crisp air, and I catch the sharp taste of their ridiculous joy and the love of speed and the anticipation of just what might be around the next corner—then I don't think about debts or fear or worry or comfort. I just smile. And I think how lucky I am, and how I want to be more like them, and how I'm just glad to be with them, out on a good, long, country walk.

CHAPTER 4

PIXEL: IN THE WAY YOU LOOK AT THINGS
GOLDENGREENE'S BIG PICTURE

It's funny how things work out sometimes. Pixel joined the family exactly one week after Gem arrived. And whereas Gem's story is a shadowy road, full of ups and downs and twists and turns, Pixel's is simple, sweet, and straight forward.

It all started when I finally decided to make good on one of my long-time dreams and begin training a dog for agility competition. Dog agility, a fast-growing sport that really took off in the 1990s, is the iconic obstacle course for dogs. Almost everyone has seen it on TV and has enjoyed the super-fast action of dogs flying over jumps, streaking through tunnels, scrambling over A-frames, swaying on the teeter-totter and zigzagging through weave poles. If you're lucky, you've been to an agility trial live and in person, and you've gotten a chance to experience the adrenaline rush of intense energy, yapping dogs, yelling handlers, and the applause after each blazing fast run in the ring.

Agility is just plain fun.

And I have wanted to do it for about twenty years. There's only one little problem. The American Kennel Club, the organization which holds the most trials and with which my dogs are registered, does not allow visually impaired handlers to compete. It's too much of a liability. And yes, pun intended, I can see their point. There are tons of ways for a blind competitor to trip, fall, get caught on equipment, and to compromise her own safety as well as that of her dog on an agility course. The rules also do not allow a sighted runner to come into the ring with a blind handler and guide the blind person around the course. So while those who are deaf or in wheelchairs can compete in official agility classes, people like me are still not allowed.

The only way the situation is likely to change is for an enterprising, courageous blind person to train a really good dog all the way through agility, and then sue the AKC when they are barred from running their dog at a trial.

I'm not saying that I had such a grand ambition as to be that enterprising and courageous blind person. But I did want to give serious training a try. I've messed around with agility for years. Most of my dogs have been on an A-frame or a dogwalk at one point or another, and almost all of them know what a tunnel is really for. But I had never pursued focused and intensive agility training.

There had been a brief period where Meg and I had taken a few private lessons, but it didn't take me long to realize that she was way too fast for me. Even a sighted person would find it a challenge to match strides with Meg on an agility course. For me it was impossible.

So the gears in my head began turning and working through the problem. If not a lightning-fast sheepdog or athletic retriever type, then a dog I could keep up with would have to be either very large or very small. Big dogs are usually set to a slower speed than other breeds. And while that would translate well to my ability to keep pace, it wouldn't work so well when you consider the wear and tear on a large dog's anatomy that would result from all that climbing and jumping. Agility dogs are true athletes. Navigating a course, and doing so at a snappy pace, requires tight turns, steep climbs, all kinds of posture changes, and multiple jumps on every course. Large and giant breeds just don't physically tolerate that kind of hard-core workout like the smaller, more nimble dogs which usually dominate agility competitions.

So I turned my attention to toy breeds instead. They are still fast, but they don't cover as much ground in as short a time as the regulars. Maybe if I found something really small with short little legs, I could keep up and make my agility dream come true.

And so I turned to my constant resource when it comes to searching for a new dog. I thumped down at my computer and pulled up the pets page of Craigslist.

That was where I first met Pixel.

I don't intend to get into the whole, sordid debate about the best method and place to acquire a new dog. It's enough to say that I have at times done everything by the book, researched the breed, chosen an ethical and reputable breeder, talked to the person, met the dogs. At other times I have followed the rescue route and walked past kennel after kennel at the local animal shelter. I've acquired dogs through breed rescue groups and from private individuals. And I am not going to commend or criticize any of those methods. Suffice it to say that I have been both totally satisfied and bitterly disappointed in dogs over the years, no matter where they have come from. Craigslist is a good resource. It's amazing what breeds and what needs you can find there on any given day. If you have a good idea of what you're looking for, if you're patient, and if you're smart enough to ask the right questions, oftentimes you can find the right dog.

Pixel's ad certainly looked appealing.

"Six-year-old papillon," it read. "I adopted him from the shelter a few months ago, but my health situation has changed, and he has too much energy for me to keep up with."

Yes, he did sound like a possible match for an agility home.

A charming, athletic, and trainable breed, the papillon was already on my agility candidate short list. The perfect size, the right temperament, and in the case of this little boy, tons of energy that probably wasn't being used appropriately.

I was right. The ad went on to describe his tendency to bolt through any open door and roam the neighborhood. This guy definitely needed exercise and a job to do.

But there was a problem. The price tag was set at four hundred dollars.

Apparently, Pixel had racked up some major medical bills. He was found on the streets of Kansas City, running at large, no owner, no collar, no ID of any kind. Based on his habit of door dashing, the most logical theory is that he had just run one too many times, and when he didn't return home, no one had gone looking for him. The animal shelter held him the required amount of time, waiting for an owner to claim him. But nobody ever did. So he was put up for adoption.

However, as is the case with many toy breeds, his teeth were so decayed and rotten that at least half of them had to be surgically removed. I heard later that they were so bad his putrid breath could be smelled from the other side of a room.

So out the teeth came, leaving Pixel with a lopsided sneer and an adoption fee that was a bit more than I was comfortable spending on Craigslist.

After some heavy mental debate, I dropped the owner an email. I told her I was interested, a little about myself and my agility plans, and said very clearly that I thought this little guy had real potential. However, I did add that, in my opinion, he was priced way too high, and that I wasn't willing to put down that much money.

We exchanged a few emails. The upshot of it was that we came to a stalemate. I wanted the dog but wasn't willing to pay the price. She wanted me to have the dog but given the money she had already spent on him with the shelter adoption fee and the medical bills on top of that, she wasn't willing to lower the price.

So I said thanks but no thanks and moved on. Six was a little too old anyway. True, a papillon at six is a lot younger than a mastiff at that age. But still, if I was serious about agility, my goal should be to get a dog that was maybe two or three years old and start there.

And then I heard about Gem, and my attention diverted that direction instead. Agility was only a pipe dream. I didn't even have the big contact equipment on which to train an agility dog. And it's not like the AKC was going to let me waltz in and do it at all, regardless of the dog, its age, or what equipment I had available.

So. . .whatever. I quit checking on Craigslist and turned my focus to welcoming Gem into the family. I forgot about Pixel.

And then about three days after Gem came home, I got an email from Pixel's mom.

It had been about three weeks since we had last corresponded, so this was totally out of the blue. She wrote that she had no one else really interested in him and wondered if I still might be. She had been thinking about the adoption fee, and because the shelter where she had acquired Pixel had covered a lot of the dental expenses, she had concluded I was right and that she needed to substantially lower the price. If I was willing to pay the new sum she was asking, he was mine if I wanted him.

Now what was I supposed to do? I had essentially put my agility dream back on the shelf, confident that it would happen someday, but okay with the fact that this wasn't the day. And there was Gem, the already-new dog, to consider. It might just be too much at one time.

But you know, there are two things that I rarely if ever shy away from. One is a challenge. And the other is a gift dropped right in my lap. Whether or not this would actually prove a challenge I didn't know. But I was pretty certain that Pixel was a gift. So I decided to take him.

He rode home in my lap, never seeming suspicious or uncomfortable. My policy when introducing a new dog to the existing pack is to just bring him in. Throw him into the mix, let everyone hit the ground running, and deal with things as they happen, if they ever do. Pixel was so little that I carried him into the house and set him up on the back of the couch right beside the front door.

And it was a nonissue. He was fine with everyone, and everyone was fine with him. All the other dogs were larger than he was, and he was completely unintimidated by any of them. Even all ninety-five pounds of slobber and shag presented by Kola didn't faze him. He just checked things out, decided he liked what he found, and determined to stay.

What I find most interesting about Pixel's story is how well-adjusted he already was when I got him. Most dogs will have some sort of baggage they arrive with. This is especially true of a rescue dog with an uncertain history. And beyond that, it's almost always the case with rescue toy breeds, tiny dogs who have often been allowed to get away with all kinds of nonsense. But Pixel was very stable and well socialized. He was not only fine with the other dogs, no matter their size or idiosyncrasies, but he was fine with the cats, ferrets, and rabbits. He didn't fuss about the goats on the other side of the fence. He was perfectly house trained and knew how to use the dog door. He was comfortable with men, women, children, people in hats, guys with beards, wheelchairs, walkers, loud noises, heavy traffic. Nothing really daunted him or dampened his bright, cheery spirit. He was totally leash-trained, even on the retractable leash which I used when he came for walks.

And he did come for walks, every day. He was undeterred by any of the unfenced and unfriendly dogs we met along the road. He just trotted in front of me, head and tail up, calm and confident.

The question I kept returning to over and over was how such a charming and stable little dog, a dog that someone had obviously put a ton of time and work into, had ended up as an unclaimed stray at an animal shelter. He had only lived with the lady I'd adopted him from for a few months, so it was unlikely that she had made such a difference. Toy breeds that act like Pixel are almost always molded as puppies. That kind of training and socialization begins early and continues throughout a dog's life. So what had gone wrong? How had his life, which must have started out in a very caring and responsible home, taken such a dark turn that he had ended up on the streets of Kansas City?

There was the problem of bolting out any open door, and that could indeed explain how he had gotten away and been picked up by animal control. But why hadn't that caring and responsible owner ever come searching for him?

As is so often the frustrating situation with rescued dogs, we will just never know. It's a case of "take it and be thankful." But I still wonder.

That first night I let him sleep in my bedroom. The lady who gave him to me had told me he slept just fine on the floor of her room and seemed very content that way. The first night or two with a new dog is always a little tense. With puppies, of course, you usually have to accommodate potty trips at ungodly hours, besides putting up with wailing and ear-piercing, heartbreaking howls of loneliness. With an adult dog brought into a new setting, things can be even more awkward when the lights go out. Especially a dog not accustomed to sleeping in a crate who finds itself restrained in one for a number of hours, you could be looking forward to barking, scratching, thumping, and other things that totally disrupt a good night's sleep, both for you and any other household pets.

So that first night I doused the lights with some trepidation, climbed into bed and settled in to see what would come next.

I think I was the only one surprised when, after about three minutes, there was a sprightly tinkle of collar tags and something small and furry landed on the foot of my bed. Yup, everyone except me knew that was going to happen.

Let me just pause here for a moment to outline my position about dogs on the bed. In my house, it doesn't happen. The first reason is pretty obvious. In a structured, obedience-oriented household like mine, everyone has their accepted and expected place. And dogs don't belong on the bed. Dogs sleep in crates, or on dog beds, or on the couches if they want to. They do not sleep on the bed. People sleep on the bed.

I know there are plenty of folks who share their sleeping arrangements with at least one dog, and the dog has absolutely no behavior issues and is sweet and dependable. But many times that isn't the case. Dogs who sleep on the bed, and again especially toy breeds afforded that privilege, can turn into real brats. They can get possessive, nippy, and difficult to deal with. Dogs are very aware of status and hierarchy, and there is something about sleeping on the bed that is a definite status symbol in the canine mind. Some dogs just can't handle it. Or to put it more bluntly, some owners just can't handle it. To these folks, sleeping on the bed is a right the dog was born with, not a privilege that has to be earned. And it doesn't take long for the dog to decide the same thing.

That's when you run into behavior problems. And it's not going to happen in my house.

Besides, if I were to start reversing on this decision, which dogs would I allow on the bed? All of them? Would I play favorites and only take certain ones? The "no favoritism" rule has always been another of my standbys. It has to be when you live with multiple dogs. Added to that is the simple fact that some of my dogs have absolutely no desire to sleep with me. The border collies especially are very uncomfortable and anxious if invited up on the bed. Even with clear encouragement and lots of sugar from me, they just don't want to be there. Brio is the same way. Kola would love to get up on the bed, but yeah, I don't think so.

Anyway, in the complex relationship between humans and dogs, my opinion is that it's just better if the people sleep on the beds and the dogs sleep in another assigned place that everyone is okay with.

The second reason dogs don't sleep with me is thanks to my own personal weirdness. I just don't like sharing my bed. With anyone. It doesn't matter if it's a big dog, a little dog, a cat, a baby goat, or another human being. The answer is no. I can't tell you why, but I don't relax or sleep as well with bedtime company, and that's final. I just don't share my bed well, okay?

And then Pixel showed up. He bounced onto the bed by my feet, paused, then made a few turns and settled down. He stayed beside my feet, just barely brushing his back against my toes, and within about sixty seconds I heard him snoring.

My heart went out to him. For once in my life, I swatted aside all the training talk and behavior workshops and just looked at it for what it was. Pixel wanted to be near me. This sweet, cheerful little boy, who had been left on the streets, endured the stress of the animal shelter, the pain of all those rotten teeth, and betrayal by at least two owners, was still courageous and trusting enough to try again. He was reaching out to me, gently asking permission to be my buddy. And apparently, that meant even at bedtime.

I let him stay. To this day, Pixel is the only dog that has ever shared my bed.

One thing we did need to work on was his weight. Tiny, athletic, and elegant, the papillon should tip the scales at seven or eight pounds. When he came to me, Pixel weighed a whopping fifteen. For a toy breed that is extremely overweight, nearly double what he should have been. But that was an easy enough problem to fix. It just took time. And after months of steady exercise and strict diet, he was down to about eight and a half pounds, an ideal weight for him since he was on the tall side for a papillon. By the end of the process I had tightened his collar by almost two inches, taking up the slack where all that excess body fat had been.

As sweet and social as he is, one glitch does still flare up from time to time. Pixel has never been totally trusting about getting groomed or having his nails trimmed. He's not nasty about it, just tense and very nervous. He stiffens up and flinches, no matter how slow and gentle I am. He pulls away when I carefully brush him, then briefly snuggles back against me, seeking reassurance, then flinches away again. He has occasionally growled if he perceives something as very startling or scary, but he has never gotten nippy or naughty. Even when it comes to trimming nails, I can hold him in my lap and coax him into letting me gently do all four feet, one toe at a time. He's not relaxed, but we just take it slow and work it out.

When Pixel had shed those extra pounds and we had settled into a good routine and relationship, I began looking for opportunities to get involved with agility training. One of the local animal shelters offered semi-regular agility classes, most of them geared toward beginners, so my first step was to sign him up for one of those. As expected, he aced the basics of jumps, tunnels, and contact obstacles. After spending six or eight weeks that way, we progressed to running short obstacle sequences on our own. The class had been a simple introduction to each obstacle and piece of equipment encountered on an agility course. But the concept and skill of stringing together five or six of those obstacles in one, unbroken run takes more time than eight weeks for a dog/handler team to learn.

I stayed in loose contact with the class instructor and began putting together easy courses at home, mostly relying on jumps, tunnels, and a small, combination obstacle called a contact trainer. I didn't have the big obstacles yet—the A-frame, dog walk, and teeter totter—so we made do. The important thing was for us both to learn how to smoothly navigate, or sequence, a multi-obstacle course.

To up the ante a little and make running courses more realistic, weekends often found us dropping in at the same animal shelter where the original class had been held. Their agility equipment was permanently set up and was open to public use most Saturdays. So we took advantage of it.

It was good practice for Pixel, but probably even more so for me. At an actual competition, handlers are given a set amount of time to walk the course and familiarize themselves with it. They do this without dogs. So at our practice sessions, I would walk my mini courses over and over, trying to commit to memory not only the order of the obstacles, but also the spacing and angling between them. That was the biggest problem I came up against. I could pace off the course, plan my turns and cross-overs from a jump to the dogwalk or from the tunnel to the pause table. But when the dog was added everything changed.

For one thing, we were suddenly moving at a much faster pace. All at once my carefully planned spacing shrank as the speed increased and I took longer strides. The turns could also get whacky as two of us navigated the course rather than just me. And in the excitement of the run, my already blurry vision often let me down abysmally. A long tunnel could look very much like the long and narrow teetertotter. I would trip hard over the supporting feet of the dogwalk. I would crash right through the jumps and weave poles. And so many times, I would pivot wrong or cross behind the dog too wide and angle off to the incorrect obstacle.

It wasn't all awful. There were times that we would nail a course, and it was beautiful. I was fast, efficient, and gave my dog good verbal and visual communication. Pixel was quick, willing, and smart, and he gave me whatever I asked for. Sometimes it all came together, and a person standing on the sidelines would never have known that there was anything different about this particular dog and handler team. It was just another agility run, and a decent one at that.

But I knew, and I began to ask some tough questions. If it was this challenging for me to run a five-obstacle sequence in the familiar surroundings of my own front yard or the animal shelter's training area, how would I ever manage in an actual competition arena? The visuals, such as they were, would be totally different. Dirt instead of grass, or rubber matting, or sometimes wood shavings would be underfoot. The obstacles might be different colors, and although I don't see colors, the contrast of a different shaded obstacle against a different shade of running surface might be incredibly confusing. The sound dynamic would be completely different—a bigger building, or another team running in a neighboring ring, or even crowd noise depending on how large the trial was.

There was the possibility of recruiting a sighted person to enter the ring with me and guide me through the course as I directed the dog. But that raised its own set of questions. Who would the person be? Mom or Dad were not an option, since neither one could be counted on to be consistently available or to keep up with us. So did I hire somebody? If so, how would I find the right person? Did I just snag a brave volunteer at the actual trial? That seemed pretty risky, not only for me, but for them. You need to know each other a little bit to run an obstacle course together. They would need to know how I should be guided, how much to tell me, how to stay out of the dog's way; and I would need to figure out exactly how this person operated, how fast they were, how easy to follow, and even how smart they were as we navigated through a course that would have been demanding enough for a dog and just one person.

Maybe we could have sorted out all these questions and problems given enough time and practice. But two things eventually emerged that blocked any progress I might have been making.

As much as I love agility and have dreamed about doing it, my first love has always been obedience. We'll get into that in a later chapter, but it's just my thing. And as I floundered and faltered with our agility training, it became obvious that Pixel would be a talented little obedience competition dog. As I've already said, he was a quick study and had the want-to and willingness to succeed. And obedience was something I knew how to train. It would be easy enough to get him started in novice and in rally, and then assess where we might be able to go from there.

So we jumped in. Before I knew it, Pixel had a Rally Novice title, a Companion Dog title, and multiple public relations titles like the Canine Good Citizen. He was fun to work with, and he did me proud in each of those rings.

As we excelled at obedience, I began to worry about mixing my sports. Or rather, about Pixel mixing them. I've seen several instances of dogs who have gotten confused when transferring from one sport to another. I've seen a dog who was amazing at agility get on the rally course and be so freaked out that he couldn't complete it. I've seen a couple of other agility dogs put into the obedience ring who have raced over the jumps at the wrong time or have even cleared the ring fence (a definite no-no) because they were looking around for their familiar agility obstacles. I didn't want that to happen with Pixel. He was doing so well in obedience that I hesitated to muddy the waters by insisting on taking the agility route. Maybe we could focus on obedience for a year or two, get his Companion Dog Excellent title, and then back up and reconsider agility.

But then the second thing cropped up.

As those one or two years sailed past, it began to become obvious that Pixel was older than I had first thought. In fact, probably much older. The best guestimate when I'd adopted him was that he was around six years old. But his teeth had been so atrocious that it was nearly impossible to tell for sure. And again, there is the simple fact that toy breeds do not show their age as quickly or obviously as larger breeds do.

Pixel was getting stiff. He hid it well, but I could feel it when I picked him up. He wasn't as supple as he had been, and he wasn't as comfortable being held as before. He began to get tired on walks. He just didn't have the interest and liveliness of a year or two before.

But the final decision was made when he began to go deaf. As I write this, he is almost completely without hearing. He doesn't respond when I call him. He doesn't know when Mom comes over with groceries. He doesn't hear the crumb hit the kitchen floor which would have brought him across the room like lightning six months ago.

It may be that he can still pick up certain frequencies or types of sounds. But for the most part he lives in silence.

So he is now retired. No more training, and not very many walks. He spends his energy on the extremely important task of keeping my floors absolutely scoured and free of any kind of food residue whatsoever. That, and keeping tabs on me wherever I go and whatever I'm working on. Heaven knows someone's gotta do it. I always need supervision.

In some ways, it's tempting to view Pixel's story as a failure. Or at least as a disappointment. There are those who could use it as a shining example of why you should never get a dog from the internet or from an unknown individual. But I don't see it that way. My dream of having an agility dog has not failed. It's just been put on hold. Taking in a rescue is always a risk. Whether you get the dog from the Humane Society, a breed rescue group, as a rehome from a breeder, or off of Craigslist, there are always unknowns. Sometimes you get it wrong. But more often than not, you get it absolutely and wonderfully right.

Pixel is not an agility dog. He didn't make my dreams come true. But maybe I made his dreams, his needs, a reality. Maybe he needed someone to constantly follow around, someone who drops crumbs on a fairly regular basis. Maybe he needed all the exercise I provided him out on the open road and the chance to shine in the performance ring and learn more about the world. Maybe he needed a comfortable bed to sleep on.

And maybe I needed him, too. Maybe, just maybe, all the lessons he continues to teach me about loyalty, joy, resilience, adaptability, eternal optimism, and trust are lessons I still need to learn. And if I can master those characteristics, it will go a long way toward teaching me to navigate the obstacle course of life.

CHAPTER 5

KOLA: A GENTLE HEART
GOLDENGREENE'S DIVINE INTERVENTION

It really is possible to have too much of a good thing. By the time we got to autumn that year, I was loving my sheepdogs and definitely wishing for something else. Not instead of, but in addition to.

That year, I had three herding breeds in house—Meg, Dundee, and Brio—and the dynamic was getting a little intense. Pacing. Staring. Random rushes out the dog door. Frantic, ear-splitting yips and chirps. Hyperactivity, OCD, insecurity, neuroses of various kinds. All the typical behaviors and imbalances that arise from owning—yes—three, young, high-energy, high-drive herding dogs in one house.

It was time for a change of scene.

Enter Kola, the sweet, plodding, gentle Newfoundland who saved me from sheepdog solitary.

I had always liked this breed and had done the reading and meeting thing to find out more about them. And the more I found out, the more I liked them. Big-bodied and even bigger-hearted, the Newfoundland is a heavily-coated, water-loving breed from the eastern shores of Canada. They're probably best known for their unique work in water rescue, a task some still perform in certain places even today. Perhaps the only thing a Newfie loves more than the water is people. I've heard it said that the Newfoundland is the only breed which has an innate love for human beings, even as newborn puppies.

They're famous for their water work, but the breed has also served for centuries as the heavy draft animal of the dog world. They have been relied upon to pull carts, haul sledges, and carry packs. They are steady, stolid, and trainable. And did I mention that they love people?

In a nasty twist of fate, Kola's devotion to her first family was how she ended up with mine. The time or two that I met them, her owners seemed like nice, knowledgeable people. They had done their homework and knew what they were getting into when they chose to add a Newf to the household. The ample size, constant shedding, pervasive doggy smell, and persistent slobber were all part of it, and they loved her regardless. Things worked well for about three years. And then their bloodhound, younger and more enterprising than Kola, figured out how to escape from the back yard.

Let me just say right up front that, as much as I love and admire the Newfoundland, they are not the brightest lights on the Christmas tree. That's not to say they're stupid, and remember, this is coming from a border collie/Aussie person. But they are not sharp-as-a-tack smart. They are not cunning or clever dogs. The way I always say it is that their hearts are so big that their brains don't really have to be. They are sensitive, caring, and steadfast. They see a situation, or a need, or an absence, and they just step in and do what that situation, need, or absence requires to be done. And they do it with gentle joy and quiet dignity.

They don't look for ways to be clever or naughty. They learn the rules and live with the rules, not searching for ways through, over, or under them.

But one thing that was not quite right in Kola's simple

world, in fact, one thing that hadn't been right since long before the bloodhound arrived, was that her family was gone for so many hours on so many days. That just wasn't okay. She wasn't sure what to do about it, but the thing she wanted most in the whole universe was to be with them. And for fourteen or fifteen hours every day, most of them were away from home, or only there for short, drop-in periods of time and then gone again.

Much of that time the dogs were relegated to the back yard, and that's when the young bloodhound learned to dig out from under the fence.

Kola, who I may have mentioned did not like being alone, went right along with her, at least as far as bulldozing under the fence. But whereas from there the bloodhound would gallivant happily away to explore the neighborhood, Kola would turn her attention to the front porch and the driveway where she knew her family would eventually return. Sometime. One of these monotonous and empty hours, they would come home again.

When they did, they would find her waiting, loose, and monitoring the street. Neighbors began to complain. Animal control got involved. Something had to be done. Schedules couldn't be changed, jobs had to be held. So the dog was the one who had to go.

And she came to me.

My hope was that in a totally new situation, with lots of exercise and the freedom to come and go as she chose via the dog door, Kola would stay where she needed to stay at my house. Since her problem had largely been the result of unsupervised time in her former family's back yard, I was banking on that dog door. If she realized she didn't have to remain isolated outdoors but could return to the safety and comfort of the house, perhaps she would be content to stay at home even without me being there.

That illusion lasted for about two hours. She was a Newfoundland. She didn't care about the house or the yard or the cats or the other dogs. She wanted to be with me. All the time and end of discussion. When I dashed off to the barn and put the goats in for the night, it took Kola all of three minutes to galumph out the dog door, rush the six-foot chain-link fence and slam through the bottom of it. It bowed out and curled up like tin foil. She had that move down cold. She didn't dig. She didn't need to. She just dropped her broad chest to the ground and used that big, blocky head as a battering ram. It worked every time.

There followed an awkward six weeks or so during which we worked our way around the bottom of the back fence. My first solution to the problem was heavy concrete blocks. Just fasten however many were needed to the bottom of whichever section of wire she had busted under that time, and the bulldozing stopped. It would take maybe a day, maybe an afternoon, and she would expose the next weak spot, do her ramming routine, and come out on the other side to find me.

Because that was the thing. If I was indoors and with her she was at peace. I was the reason she forced the fence. It wasn't for the freedom or to chase the chickens or greet the goats or wander the roads. It wasn't even just because she could. It was because she wanted to be with her new and apparently very important person. Me. If I wasn't home at the time, she would camp out in the front yard and wait. As my vet put it, "Apparently somebody thought you needed a guardian angel."

But as flattering as that was, and as warm and fuzzy as it might have made me feel, the bottom line was that she was getting out. Outside the protection of my house and yard-fence she just wasn't safe. And when a few other dogs began going with her on these little excursions, it was time to pull rank and hold the line. I hadn't wanted to do it, but desperate times called for desperate measures.

For Christmas that year, my dogs received the gift of safety. It was called a hot wire.

For the uninitiated, a hot wire is verbal shorthand for a

strand of electrified wire fastened around the perimeter of a given area. In this case, we secured it on the inside of the yard fence, along the bottom about twelve inches above the ground. And it worked like a charm. Kola stayed where she belonged, and so did everyone else. In fact, nowadays the hot wire is usually turned off, and she has never even considered leaving the confines of the back yard. She knows now that she doesn't need to. I'm not going to leave her. She can always have access to the indoors, and even if I do take some time out for myself and occasionally leave the farm to be with people my own age, Kola understands that I'll always come back.

Still, she does wait for me. I may have proven I'm not going to leave her, but she's made the decision not to leave me, either. Most of the time when I return home, she's out in the back, watching for whoever it was that picked me up to bring me safely home again. It's not a timing thing, either, because I don't have a set schedule where I always come home at the same time every time. There have been occasions when I've hopped out of the car and come dashing indoors out of a downpour and find Kola slogging through the dog door to meet me, slinging heavy rainwater from her glorious, midnight coat. What's a little rain to keep a dog from her duty?

Not that Kola feels the wet. Or the cold. She could stay outdoors in any wintry weather in complete physical comfort. Warm and waterproof, she encounters winter with complete confidence. It's the heat that brings her down. Most warm summer days find her crashed out in the middle of the laminate floor in the kitchen or the dog room, passed out.

Besides rain and snow, she also doesn't worry about water at bath time. Kola loves baths. There have been numerous times when I've gone into the bathroom to fill up a bucket from the faucet in the tub, not quite latching the door behind me. Sometimes the door will suddenly and inexplicably snap shut, and I realize that Kola is on the other side, clumsily trying to shove her nose through the crack in the door and accidentally latching it instead. Or sometimes she'll get lucky. I'll be standing there, absorbed in the irritation of why exactly it takes so long to fill one five-gallon bucket of water, when the bathroom door will creak open. There follows the sound of heavy, shuffling footsteps and even heavier breathing. And there she is, standing beside me and leaning her big head over the edge of the tub to have a hopeful look.

One time my mom and I were having a discussion in the bathroom. I have no idea anymore what it was about, but the door had been left wide open. We were completely oblivious to it, involved in our conversation, and the next thing you know, Kola had materialized in the small room and was climbing awkwardly into the bath tub. She's the only dog I've had so far who will voluntarily step into the tub with no prompting or persuasion. She got all four furry feet and all ninety-five pounds clambered in, then swung her massive head and gentle gaze around to us as if to say, "Well, why doesn't somebody turn on the water?"

And if Kola can't have a bath herself, she enjoys watching others get theirs. Many's the time when I have been busily bathing another dog, and the door will once again squeak, and Kola will come happily blundering in, panting expectantly. Denied the possibility of getting a bath of her own, she's content to flop down on the floor behind me and soak it in, figuratively if not literally. Just a goofy Newfy.

Her real obsession, however, is with the hair drier. She adores the hair drier. Again, if I'm blow-drying another bath victim, Kola will come up beside us and wait in line. Hope springs eternal. And it's usually not disappointed. Because, seriously, who can say no to that kind of patience and sweetness? All she wants is a few wafts of that warm air.

Actually, she would like about two hours of it. When it's her turn for the hair drier, she flings herself down on the floor and stretches out, letting that hot, dry air work into her heavy coat. You can dry her feet, her chest, her ears, areas that most of my other dogs are uneasy about. You can flip her over to the other side and go to work on that one, too. No problem. She'll be here all day.

Kola is a dog of simple joys and loyalties. The dynamics, politics, and mental gymnastics of the sheepdogs are a foreign language to her. She has no need or knowledge of such a hard-scrabble existence. She loves the hair drier. She loves food. She loves her family. She loves her friends. And just give her a biscuit, a belly-rub, and a few blows with the hair drier, and you'll be one of those for the rest of your life. And life is good. Especially when you're a really big dog with an even bigger heart.

PART TWO

WINTER

I stand outside, midway between the house and the barn. The sun shines clear and brittle from a pale sky. Its warmth is far away, as if its fingers, brushing the frigid earth's face, are cramped by the cold. The sky is high, remote, and clean.

Around me the air is absolutely still. It crackles and crushes with cold. I can feel it pressing in on me, intense. The thermometer stands at minus six degrees. I breathe slowly, and the air crinkles the inside of my nose. Under my feet the thin coating of snow shrieks and squeals at even the slightest shifting of my boots, a sure sign that the mercury hovers near zero. It sounds the way cornstarch feels when you squeeze it in the package.

There is not a breath of wind. It's too cold for that. Our deepest freezes happen when the wind completely quiets and the skies are swept clean. The air carries no scent. It only smells of itself—cold, sharp, deep and pure. The sky feels so high and the earth so unyielding. It is so perfectly hushed, you sense that you could snap your fingers and break it. Or it could break you.

It is a bitter and beautiful winter morning.

And there's work to get done. More work than usual. Everything becomes harder in the cold.

Water tubs frozen almost solid. Bucket after bucket of steaming hot water to be hauled from the house out to the barn and corrals. The rabbits' water bowls to be filled with warm water and carried back out to the cages.

Once filled or thawed as the need dictates, the water demands regular tending. With a high temperature of only five degrees forecast for the day, even hot water freezes in a remarkably short time. In temperatures like this, the outdoor animals also require extra hay and grain. The goats won't want to go outside anyway, so I muscle two heavy bales of brome into their pens at the barn and pack the half-empty hay racks full. Another half bale needs to be carried up to the billy goats and Mocha in the corrals.

Heat lamps burn all day for the hens and the rabbits. At three p.m., the warmest part of the day, the thermometer registers four degrees. We never did make it to that forecast high.

The only animals who don't seem to mind the brutal cold are Mocha and the two Pyrenees. Mocha meets it with her typical, stalwart donkey pathos. She stands out in all weathers, placidly munching hay or gazing off into the distance. Driving snow, arctic wind, and subzero cold make no impression on her. She accepts and ignores them all. Turning her tail to the brunt of the wind, she stands beside her shelter hut and calmly eats her brome. Even if the double portion of fodder is tucked into the farthest back corner of the hut, she will usually pull it out and scatter the hay in the snow, foraging for the icy wisps. Her coat is so thick and insulating that in snowy conditions, ice freezes onto clumps of it so that she clinks when she moves.

Drifter and Snowstorm, the two Pyrenees guardian dogs, are comfortable in any cold. Like Mocha, their fur is thick and shaggy with amazing, dense undercoats. Ice crystals crust on their stand-off outer coats, shimmering on their backs and the heavy ruffs around their necks. They love the snow. They gambol and gallop in it, leaping alongside and sometimes even over top of one another. There's some good-natured growling and shoving as they see me coming from the house toward the barn and accompany me along the fence. In truly brutal weather, the Pyrenees either choose to hunker down in their huts, stuffed with fresh hay, or they dig into the big hay pile on the hillside. When I clean the goats' pens, all that extra hay they waste is dumped in one huge pile out in the pasture. As it ages and is soaked by rain and sun, it composts and holds heat. The dogs know it. They will often lie in the pile, curled up or stretched out in whichever hollow of hay takes their fancy, the gusting wind swirling over them as they snuggle into the deep bedding.

As bitter as the deep-freeze days can be, the worst weather comes with wind. Vicious, polar winds sweeping down from the northwest, they bring misery and fear on their deadly wings. I can feel brutality and death when I walk out into weather like that. Winds up to forty or fifty miles per hour, they roar through the shuddering trees in long, hungry gusts. Wind like that is not lonely or mournful. It is malicious and murderous. It comes in frigid fury, bent on destruction. It burns the skin of my face, clutches at the windchimes and hurls them away in contempt, driving the dry, powdery snow before it in white wrath.

There is no mercy in the northwest wind. In many ways I view it—not the cold or the dark or the extra work—as my arch rival in the winter. I have battled it bringing in temperatures of twelve below zero, blowing at forty miles an hour. Or blowing at fifty and heaping more than a foot of snow onto the freezing fields and timber. Wind chills of thirty and forty below zero, frightening and ferocious.

My house becomes a haven of light and warmth. Sleepy dogs and cats sprawl on the couches. I can hear Kola snoring as the wind roars overhead, creaking the house just a bit as it settles in the cold. The dryer hums and clicks, soothing. The kitchen smells like apple pie.

It's a good place to be on these black, windy nights.

The dark comes boldly in the winter. It falls swift and early, and by five in the evening I have every light in the house switched on. Because I can see light and dark, I do rely on lights turned on in my home to help navigate. In winter especially, the house is bright. Part of my need for light is the simple fact that it's a small house, and that my various tasks and chores send me into every room often enough that it's silly to turn the lights off. But at a deeper level, I just need light. I need to carve out a place of solace and strength for myself at this bleak and brutal time of year. If one way to do that is as easy as flipping a light switch, count me in.

Still, one bonus of living on the open plains is that no weather system lasts for long. They come barreling down on us, linger for a couple days, then blow out again and the weather moderates. Warming trends happen often. The white quilt of snow, stitched together with fences, roads, and belts of brush, is folded up and put away for a while. High temperatures in the thirties and forties. The pastures and crop fields brown and dejected. The trees, leafless and lifeless, except for the precocious cedars. They accommodate any season with resilient, prickly green, breaking the relentless wind, providing shelter to the chickadees, cardinals, and other little birds that stick it out all winter long.

Wood smoke wafts heavy in the mild air. I can hear the mournful whistle of the train, seven miles to the south, consoling in its loneliness. Little wedges of geese honk overhead, cheerful and comforting after that last cold snap. The eaves drip. The air and earth soften just a bit, and the sky loses that brittle, vaulted feeling. I can stand out in Mocha's corral with my gloves off, rubbing my warm fingers into her warmer coat and enjoying the blessing of the sun. The breeze might even blow from the south for a day or two, lifting my heart and giving me courage to face the next Arctic blast.

Because there will be a next one. Winter isn't finished with us. It's only breathing deep and gathering strength. And that means that so must I.

CHAPTER 6

GESTATION: THE CALM BEFORE THE STORM

Winter is a quiet time for the goats. It's filled with long, cozy hours in the barn, munching hay, or sunning themselves on the hill in the pasture. They eat well, rest well, and generally enjoy life.

In winter, all the activity is happening on the inside. Not just the inside of the barn, but the inside of the goats.

All the does are pregnant by now, and they have five months to get those little ones ready to enter the world. You can't rush these things. The best way to pass the time is to eat all they want and laze around the barn.

The barn itself is sweet with the good, grassy smell of brome. I keep the hay racks filled with it, a high-nutrition grass hay, all the time. Goats need hay all year round. Even in the summer when the pastures are tall and green and all kinds of weeds and leaves are on offer, dry hay is critical to their digestive health. Of course, in winter when there is little if any outdoor forage available, they need free-choice hay twenty-four seven.

Evening chores happen early in the winter. By about four in

the afternoon, all the does are standing in the corner of the pasture closest to the house, just waiting. They still have an hour or two to burn before I show up, and the longer they loiter the more impatient they get. They holler at me and comment on most things I do out in the yard.

It's a sunny corner, so on clear days they stand there soaking in the last warmth of the day. On cloudy days they stand there anyway. It has to be driving snow or drenching rain to force them into the barn at that time of day.

Goats do despise the wet. Even a light rain will discourage them from venturing out, and a heavy downpour is like poison falling from the sky. They stay as far away from it as they can get.

I've been outdoors when a thin shower decides to patter down while all the goats are out in the pasture. There comes the first splattering of drops on the grass or gravel around me, then a sigh as the shower strengthens. Then the music of bells. The goats rush for the safety of the barn, a few dramatic bleats and wails thrown in for good measure. Collar bells tinkling, feet pounding, they dash for shelter as if a nuclear bomb has just been dropped. Three minutes later the shower clears, and the first tentative survivors poke their wrinkling noses out the barn door.

By the end of the year I've quit milking. The rule of thumb is that a dairy doe should be "dried up" a minimum of two months before the kids are born. Most of the kids on my farm arrive in early to mid-March, so it works well to dry the does up by the end of December. Producing milk demands a lot of the doe's body resources. If she isn't being milked anymore, her body can capitalize on those freed-up nutrients and use them for healthy kid development instead of milk yield.

So the does munch their hay and scarf down their grain, and get fat and furry. By February they're looking quite rotund. Most of them are carrying twins. Some will be working on triplets. All of them are getting uncomfortable. Lying down has become a chore, and let's not even talk about getting back up again. They grunt and groan and even wheeze sometimes as they try to find an easy position to breathe. You try taking a deep breath when you're stuffed to the gills with triplets. Goats can even have litters of four or five, although I haven't yet experienced that on my farm.

By mid to late February, I can stand quietly beside a doe and, firmly pressing my palm against the right side of her bulging belly, I can feel the kids doing acrobatics. With only a couple of weeks before they make their grand entrance, the babies are often very active. Pebbly little hoofs thunk against my hand. Jostling, sliding, bumping. On lucky days there will be a broader, stronger, and more insistent nudge against my flattened palm. The butting of a tiny head.

It's magical. Even though I have never wanted children of my own, I stand there captivated. Snow swishes against the sides of the barn, an impertinent chickadee chatters somewhere outside, a plane rumbles far and frosty overhead. The world goes by, and I forget it all, lost in the wonder of new life.

Then my quirky pragmatism crops up. I mean, what are they doing in there? Playing? Practicing their circus stunts? Having an argument? As grumpy as goats can be, it wouldn't surprise me if they started tussling before they're even born. Then again, they're even more curious than they are ornery. Maybe it's driving the little things nuts that they just can't seem to get beyond this fleshy wall. What is out there, anyway?

The placid doe fidgets just a little, then goes back to business at the hay rack. We're almost there, ladies. Just a few more weeks and your work will be done. And mine will just be getting started.

CHAPTER 7

THE GUARDIANS BEHIND THE SCENES ON THE FRONT LINES

There's a lot to consider when you're preparing to welcome a new baby. That's especially true when you're preparing to welcome four or five new babies.

My biggest concern as I sidled into the whole goat-raising thing and began to plan for my new babies was their safety.

In northeast Kansas, our main predators are coyotes. There have been confirmed reports of cougars passing through on rare occasions. But the primary antagonist for anyone raising small livestock around here is the clever, quick, and cunning coyote.

I admire coyotes. They are incredibly smart and adaptable. They know more than we think they do. They watch us—those of us who live on the land—and although we rarely get to see them, it's a guarantee that they are present and accounted for. They see us. I know they monitor my farm, my animals, and even my routine, skulking in the brush on the fringes of my territory. They're smart, and they know better than to invade far enough to take a chicken from the coop by the carport, or to harass the adult goats in the pasture. But baby goats might be too much of an opportunity to pass up.

I needed a helper—someone who could keep eyes and ears on my stock at all times—what people have labeled a "livestock guardian." This refers to an animal of a different species integrated into the main species a farmer raises. The guardian animal lives with the livestock and so is on duty to protect them around the clock. It's a perfect, built-in security system.

The most common livestock guardians are dogs. People also use llamas, donkeys, and occasionally mustangs. For several reasons I decided at first not to go with another dog. Instead, I brought home the long-eared, long-haired little donkey we've already talked about. Mocha first signed on with me as a goat guardian.

Most people don't realize how protective donkeys can be. They are suspicious of anything new, and they're very alert without being hyper-vigilant, like dogs can be. Because they are fellow grazers, they naturally join up and hang out with other livestock, calmly moving along with the herd until danger shows up. They also have a natural dislike of dogs or anything resembling dogs. Again, coyotes are the main predator problem here, and stray dogs are another thing to worry about. So an animal that instinctively disliked them and required no real training seemed like a good idea to me.

Mocha was turned out with the goats and left to her own devices.

And it didn't go well. She began to chase her own goats. Several people saw her do it. She would wheel around, ears clamped back, teeth bared, and go pounding across the pasture hot on the heels of whichever goat had looked at her the wrong way. To my knowledge she never caught one, but she didn't really need to. Obviously, Mocha was not meant to be a livestock guardian. It's likely she would have eventually killed a goat if she'd been left with them long enough. I never truly understood why her behavior took such a dangerous turn. The best guess is that the smaller goats especially, might have appeared dog-like enough that she just took exception to them and decided they didn't need to be in her pasture. Mocha is a pretty dominant personality. It could be that, dog-like or not, the goats were too nosy, too pushy, and just plain too annoying for her to tolerate.

Whatever the reason, she ended up in her own personal corral with no way to reach the goats.

Of course, goats being what they are, they still have the gall to torque their heads through her cattle panel fencing, craning their necks as close to her hay or water tub as they can get. But she can no longer mess with them even if they mess with her. She has her own space to get away from their shenanigans.

Thus, once again I was left without a guard animal. For several reasons, I just wasn't interested in trying the llama or mustang options. And so I found myself toying with the ever-tempting prospect of adding another dog to the mix.

My initial reluctance to go with a dog was due to a couple of uncertainties I still had to work through. Guardian dogs can be aggressive. That is, after all, what they're paid for. Did I really want a big, mostly unsupervised dog on the place who would be territorial enough to worry about? What if I had to be gone for a day or two and an unfamiliar person had to take care of the goats? How would a dog like that react, and could it be trusted? A dog would need a little more tending and do a little less blending than a guardian animal that was a fellow grazer. A dog would need better monitoring, stronger fencing. A dog was just more responsibility.

But I began asking around. And as it happened, the first person I asked brought me to the perfect dog.

His name was Glacier. A huge, stout-hearted Great Pyrenees. Like all members of his breed, he was winter-white, and like many Pyrs he also sported large, badger-colored body patches and mask. He was seven years old. His coat was an absolute disaster. And he was the best livestock guardian dog that I have ever met.

Glacier isn't with me anymore. He was almost twelve years old when, one scorching July, his health rapidly began to deteriorate. I had him put down before he could truly start to suffer. But as my first guardian dog, and as I've said the best that I've yet known, I'd like to be allowed to share his story with you.

The year I met Glacier was the same year that Gem joined the family, and as fortune favored, he, like Gem came from Kathy. She had owned him his whole life, and for most of that time he had been kept on a heavy collar and chain. Glacier, like many Pyrenees, was naughty about getting over fences.

The Great Pyrenees is an old French breed. For centuries they have been the protectors of large flocks in the remote areas of the Pyrenees Mountains along the craggy border between France and Spain. They were developed long before the advent of fenced pastures and next-door neighbors. They followed the flocks year-round, moving as the grass and the human shepherd dictated. The sheep and goats under the dog's care grazed the high, mountain meadows most of the year, oftentimes without the supervision of a shepherd at all. In those isolated, mountainous areas, wolves were a real threat, along with bears and wildcats.

For that reason, the Pyrenees is a giant breed. Males tower up to thirty-two inches at the shoulder and tip the scales close to 130 pounds. Females are a little smaller but still very formidable. The dogs' abundant coats were ideal for their harsh, high-elevation homeland.

The Pyrenees' bark is just as impressive as his body. They are the least aggressive of the big guardian breeds, and they try to use their bark effectively enough that the bite is not necessary. That was one reason I chose the Pyrenees as the dog I wanted for my hobby farm. They're just a little softer and less edgy than the other guardian breeds. Being as how my farm is small, with people stopping by fairly often, a barky but less aggressive dog on duty seemed like the right choice.

The Pyrenees' ancient history as a flock follower does not always translate well to modern-day life. They have a strong desire to patrol, to wander and cover large areas of land. Fences have only been around for a couple hundred years, and as far as the Pyrenees is concerned, they mostly just get in the way. A dog bred to look after three hundred sheep in thousands of acres doesn't always understand the restrictions of watching over a hundred goats in an area of about ten acres.

Not only are they huge, Pyrs are also athletic. They can dig, climb, chew through, and crawl through just about anything if they figure out how. Glacier had learned as a puppy that he could get up on his hind legs, hook his front paws and claws through the welded wire of Kathy's pasture fences, and just start climbing. As he got bigger and heavier, the fence would obediently bow and scrunch as he leaned on it, so that by the time I met him, he had perfected the art of crab-crawling over any wire or panel fencing put in front of him.

Glacier was an unneutered and territorial male, and his idea of a good time was to bust out of the goats' area, lope down the road, and start thrashing the neighbors' outdoor dogs. Naturally the neighbors complained. And so Glacier found himself staked out on that chain twenty-four/seven, barking at the wind and whatever else caught his attention.

We pulled up alongside the shed where he had been secured.

"There he is," my driver informed me. "He looks just like Kujo."

Indeed, the comparison was very compelling. Glacier reared up on his back legs, standing a good six feet tall. His shaggy, matted coat ruffled in the wind, and his huge mouth gaped wide open, strings of slobber flying every which direction. His bark rattled the windows of the van. Deep, challenging, and impressive. He lunged against the chain, pawing the air with his mighty front feet, straining to get as close to the vehicle as he possibly could.

We got out to say hello.

Kathy came straggling out of the house to help wrangle him. She talked and talked, while Glacier pleaded for attention. He quieted down once we were within reach of his jangling chain, plastering himself against both my driver and me. His need for human contact was palpable. He pressed against our legs, butting his huge head under our hands and wrapping the chain around our ankles. He panted and drooled, breaking away every three minutes or so to rush over to his water bucket and take a noisy, very sloppy drink. He was delighted to have visitors.

I found out as much of his history as I could. He had been with goats his entire life. Born in a goat barn up in Michigan, he had lived with goats and learned about them ever since. When Kathy relocated to Kansas, Glacier rode along in the stock trailer. He knew goats. He knew how to do his job. But, Kathy said, he was so unreliable about staying home. And she had the other two guardian dogs, and the Dobermanns, and honestly, she didn't really need him, especially with him having to be tied up all the time.

"I'll take him," I told her. "I think he's just what I've been looking for."

We unsnapped the chain and loaded him into the van. He trotted right up to it, bounded in, flopped down on the floor like he owned the place, and then proceeded to vomit about half a gallon of water all over the floor.

Kathy recoiled. "Glacier!!" She slammed the van door and shook her head, "I better let you guys go!" she said, and we were on our way to Glacier's new home.

We had talked it over beforehand and concluded that the best permanent solution to Glacier's escaping fences was to fall back on the ever-effective hot wire. We would run a strand of electric along the top of the pasture fence, arching it over the top of each gate, and hope that the charge would deter him from climbing. But the hot wire hadn't been installed yet. So I went old-school. Until we could get the wire up, I employed a bit of livestock guardian wisdom called a tire drag.

It's a pretty simple solution. Take an old car tire, attach a short length of chain to it at one end, then snap the other end to the dog's collar. The chain should be long enough to let the dog stand and walk without the tire hanging from his neck, but short enough that when he rears up to start climbing, it drags him back to earth and makes climbing virtually impossible. It's not pretty, and it's not something I necessarily recommend. But when you're in a pinch, it works extremely well. I needed my new guardian dog to stay where he belonged and not to wander and get shot by the neighbors until we got that hot wire up. So I wheeled out the tire drag and attached it to Glacier's collar.

We brought him into the pasture, and he went happily trotting along the fence line, the tire alternately dragging and rolling beside him. He didn't seem to mind. He examined a section of wire fencing, tilted up his massive head, put an experimental paw on the wire, and started climbing.

Within about fifteen seconds he had somehow flipped over the top and landed on the wrong side of the fence, where he was brought up short by the resisting tire. It hadn't made the journey with him. So there it hung, swaying slightly, and Glacier on our side of the fence, stuck tight. He turned to us, his big eyes full of questions.

"I think you got the chain too long," I told my hapless driver. "We need to shorten it up at least a foot."

We led the panting, wagging dog back in with his goats, shortened up the chain, and left him again. This time it worked. He returned to the same spot of his previous success and tried to rear up and go over. The tire brought him up short. And that was the end of it. He stayed with the goats.

Glacier was only on the tire drag for a couple of days. As soon as we got the hot wire up and running, I took the tire off and pitched it behind the barn. I also exchanged the heavy collar he was wearing for a much lighter one, gave him an ID tag, and set him free. He was a working dog with two acres to cover and a fence that would hold him in.

He never got out again. Almost certainly he challenged the hot wire and tried to climb the fence, but no one ever saw him do it. It was like he knew. This was his place. These were his goats. It was almost like he breathed a sigh of relief. At last he understood what his boundaries were, where he belonged. And he was okay with it.

Glacier took his job seriously. Not only did he have impressive size and an even more impressive voice, but he had presence about him. It wasn't tough-guy attitude. It wasn't cocky or macho or aggressive. It was a strength of body and power of personality, and a happy, unshakable confidence in both. He was a strong, watchful dog, steady and brave, devoted to all things under his care. He was a true and trustworthy guardian.

For the first two weeks that he lived on the farm, I heard absolutely no noise from the area coyotes. Until he came home, the coyotes had been vocal, yipping and yammering at least every other night. But as Glacier established his territory, patrolling the fences and voicing his presence every night, there was complete silence from the coyote population. I could feel the undercurrent of surprise and respect out there in the wilds. Just who was this new, very big, and very assertive dog anyway? Exactly what was he capable of, and how far did his territory extend? They were quiet, waiting, weighing him, and watching.

Eventually I would hear coyotes again. But never in the whole time that Glacier lived with me did they venture close, at least not to be seen or heard. And never did Glacier's animosity toward them waver. He hated coyotes. Even one, far-away howl would bring him charging out of the barn or jerking his head up from his food bowl or galloping headlong from one end of the pasture to the other. He was on guard, and coyotes were enemy number one.

As a general rule, livestock guardian dogs are nocturnal. This is because prey animals, like rabbits and deer, are most active at dawn and dusk. That means the predators which hunt them are also most active at those same times. By necessity then, the dogs who defend against those same predators are most alert and vocal overnight, when the predators are moving and hunting. For most of the day, Glacier would sack out in a comfortable spot, shady in the summer, sunny in the winter, and didn't seem to be paying much attention to things. He would snooze the daylight hours away, getting up groggily if I came out to the barn or if a car rumbled down the driveway. But mostly he dozed. The goats would browse the area around him, or sometimes they would lie down, too, scattered loosely around him. It was a peaceful, ancient scene—the vulnerable flock secure enough in the presence of their quiet guardian that they could lie down and relax. It was a picture thousands of years old, something that dogs and goats have experienced down through the ages.

But by about five in the evening, Glacier would begin to stir. He would get up, shake the hay and grass from his woolly coat, and survey his domain. He would check on things—the barn, the driveway, the corner of the pasture closest to the house. He would bark experimentally a few times. As the sun faded and the shadows gathered, his barking became more purposeful and persistent. Glacier was a moderate barker for a Pyrenees. Some of them can be downright obnoxious, barking apparently just for the thrill of hearing their own voices. Glacier was never like that. If he barked there was a reason. It might be only a plane flying overhead or the neighbor starting up his truck, but Glacier never barked wantonly or without purpose.

He was what dog people refer to as a "proven guardian." He

was trustworthy. With anything. I could rely on him to be calm, gentle, and responsible around pregnant does, bucks in rut, newborn kids, and even does in labor. It's a nasty and not very talked about fact that this is not true of all dogs supposedly called guardians. Some of them can get into ugly habits. Some will chase and chew on the stock they're employed to protect. They will gnaw on ears, udders, and legs, and the more the animal bleeds the more the dog picks and pesters. Some will actually kill and eat members of their own flock. In my experience, these are usually dogs that have not been introduced to and supervised with the livestock appropriately. Occasionally there is a special, very instinctive dog that can simply be turned out with the flock and left to its own devices. Those dogs somehow just figure things out. But most dogs need some teaching and structure. Learning what is and is not acceptable around livestock is a process. And some dogs, although they might be a guarding breed, just are not guardians by nature.

Glacier was. He was responsible, reliable, and always behaved flawlessly around the goats. One of the sweetest things was to see him in the spring, surrounded by bouncing baby goats. An enormous white dog, sprawled out in the midst of six or seven dancing kids. They would race around him, trample his paws and tail, and sometimes even jump on him, and he gave no reaction. If it ever got a little too rough and tumble, he would simply stand up, shake off, and walk away.

Glacier is perhaps the only dog I have ever had who I know without doubt would have laid down his life for me. The dogs in the house fill a different role. They are my companions, my kids, my students. I am their undisputed leader. I'm their protector, not the other way around. But Glacier was my partner. He was my right hand, my ears and my eyes out there on the front lines, and I knew he could and would take care of not just his flock, he would also take care of me.

The only thing in the world he was afraid of was loud noise.

Thunder was especially scary to him. Even distant booms and flashes would send him slinking into the barn where, for some bizarre reason, his coping strategy was to tip over any bucket or tub of water he could reach. Even a twenty-gallon tub, filled to the brim and extremely heavy, was no match for him. He would work and work at it until it was flipped over, and then he would frantically paw the mud it created back into the empty tub. I never did figure that one out.

After a few sessions like this, I learned to bungee-cord the water tubs tight to the pen fences in the barn, and that solved the problem. Denied the chance to dump over water containers, Glacier's next best plan was to furiously dig into random corners of whichever pen he decided to hide in. He would scrabble desperately, his huge front feet throwing chunks of hay and clods of soil all over the pen, panting and shaking as the storm grumbled closer.

Most of the time, though, he was a rock. His work ethic and personality were so exemplary that I began pondering the idea of breeding one litter out of him. He was still unneutered. And he wasn't young. If I could get a male puppy out of him who would carry on Glacier's guarding ability, Glacier could then mentor the puppy for the next three or four years. Pyrenees are a slow-maturing breed which doesn't reach full potential until individuals are three or four years old. By the time the puppy would reach that age, Glacier would be close to twelve, old for such a big dog. It would be a natural thing for the younger male to step into the role of chief guardian when his dad could no longer do the job.

So I thought about it. I began asking around and putting out feelers. I even posted a want ad. And after a few weeks, Snowstorm came to the farm.

I would have my work cut out for me with this one. It was a lesson yet to be learned that not all Pyrenees come pre-programmed as ready-made guardians. It might be buried somewhere deep in their DNA but drawing it out and teaching them who they're meant to be can be a challenge.

Snowstorm was the casualty of a divorce. As I understand her story, the couple she began her life with split up, and Snowstorm ended up with the woman. Then things went even farther south, and that person felt she could no longer keep the dog. Snowstorm was passed off to a friend who promised either to give or to find her a forever home. I'm not sure how that worked, especially since, when I met her, she was attached to a tree in the back yard by a heavy chain. There was no shelter available to her. She had lived that way throughout the winter. I don't know if the people provided shelter when the weather turned nasty or not. To be honest, I didn't want to ask. It was obvious they wanted to get rid of her. So guess who she ended up riding home with?

She was not a fan of the van. The three-hour ride home was a bit dicy as she panted, pawed, and when her energy and anxiety hit the boiling point, flung herself onto either my driver or myself and clawed her way into our laps. I should have brought a crate but making room for one would have been a chore; plus, assuming she had never been confined in one before, I decided the lesser of two evils was to just hang onto her and ride it out. Better to keep my hands on her and soothe her than to force her into a crate and have her totally panic.

Things got worse on arriving home. Snowstorm had never seen a goat before. She had been a house pet for the first year or so of her life, then she'd been relegated to being yard art. Now she had no idea of where she was or who she was with. Because I didn't know how she would react if let loose with the goats, I closed her into one of the pens to let her acclimate more gradually. She was not at all happy about the arrangement.

She barked and lunged at the goats on the other side of the fence. They shied away from her and her barking was so loud in the metal building I could hardly catch my breath. Within a matter of minutes, my peaceful, idyllic farm had turned into a breeding ground of fear, stress, and violence. My stomach flip-flopped and I wanted to turn around, throw her into the van, and hightail it back to that junky little house in Missouri. The people would take her back. At least, they said they would. They could find her another home, a good home. She was a beautiful dog, friendly with people, even with kids. A unique breed that would catch someone's attention. They hadn't charged me anything for her. It's not like the money would be an issue.

My driver left. Snowstorm barked and fretted in the pen. The late winter evening darkened, pressing in around me, ominous and unfriendly. I felt sick.

I went to the house, tried to toss supper together, tried to restore my usual routine. I could hear Snowstorm barking. Chores that evening were a miserable affair. Snowstorm was miserable. So was I. The goats were spooked and afraid. The night was cold and black. I wished I had never brought her home.

The only bright spot in the gathering gloom was Glacier. He absolutely adored her. No doubt some of his infatuation had to do with the fact that she was an unspayed female. But beyond that, Glacier was just plain sociable. He liked company. And when the companion selected was another Pyrenees, and a cute little girl at that, he liked it even better. He hovered near her pen as I tucked everyone in for the night, grinning all over himself.

"I'm glad you like her, buddy," I told him, snapping off the lights. "Personally, I don't know what I'm going to do with her."

I headed for the house, heaving a sigh of relief. Snowstorm started barking. I rolled my eyes and broke into a jog.

By the third day I had contacted her former owners. Or tried to. After exchanging one or two emails I didn't hear back from them. And after that chilly response, I was reluctant to try their cell number. It was obvious they didn't want her back. And I didn't want her myself. I had at least begun to let her out overnight with Glacier. The goats were locked in for the night anyway. The fences were secure and Glacier was in hog heaven. So the frantic barking had subsided and she could stretch her legs and get out of that pen for nine or ten hours.

However, I hadn't brought her home to be just another pet. She was supposed to be not only Glacier's companion but his working partner. And if she wouldn't work, she wouldn't stay. She had stopped lunging at the goats through the fence, but I knew I still couldn't trust her with them. I had no idea how to integrate her with the flock if she wouldn't come in on her own. I was beginning to suspect that she just didn't have the flock guardian instinct. And once again, if she didn't have it, she was out. I could not keep her if she wouldn't work.

So as a last-ditch effort, I contacted Pyrenees rescue. If I couldn't keep her, she certainly deserved better than she'd had before. Even if those people had wanted her back, I don't believe I could have returned her to them in good conscience no matter how desperate I was. Pyrenees rescue was the way to go.

And that's how I got in touch with Dianne.

Pyrenees rescue is a nationwide network of volunteers. They love the breed, and they are committed to helping Pyrs who need homes find homes. These dedicated people specialize in locating, evaluating, fostering, and adopting out dogs that owners can no longer keep. Many times the dogs who end up in rescue are "owner surrenders," meaning that the dog's original owner chooses to relinquish it to the nearest rescue group. Rather than putting an ad on Craigslist or sending the Pyr to a shelter, these owners realize that a rescue group is the most responsible way to find a new home if it becomes necessary. If I had to part with Snowstorm, I wanted her to be handled by a group like that.

Dianne was the coordinator for Great Pyrenees Rescue of Iowa. The local Kansas City rescue group referred me up to Iowa because that group specialized in evaluating and placing Pyrs as reliable guardian dogs, not just as pets. Since Snowstorm was already somewhat accustomed to goats, the consensus was that Dianne was the one to call.

She took me in hand. By the end of the conversation, I had laughed a lot, learned even more, and finally had a sense of hope. The fear, the heavy dread that had taken up residence somewhere between my quaking heart and queasy stomach, was tucking its tail and whimpering. I love making fear afraid. And I love having a plan of action.

"Remember," Dianne told me, "Snowstorm is in the middle of complete culture shock. She's been a yard ornament. She's never seen a goat before. She's very confused, lonely, and upset. And you," she sternly informed me, "are going to have to step in and be the leader. Show her that it's okay to be where she is and that you're happy with her. And then get her out with the goats and see if she's got what it takes."

I waited two more days, as Dianne had suggested. During that time Snowstorm calmed down and began to settle in. Dogs are suckers for a routine, Dianne had reminded me, and this breed loves routine even more than most. Once she understands the routine and the expectations, she'll be much more comfortable. Take it one step at a time.

The step after allowing Snowstorm to acclimate to her new surroundings was to begin evaluating whether or not she might make a guardian. Following Dianne's precise instructions, two days after talking with her I went out to the barn, clipped a leash to Snowstorm's collar, and gently led her out of the pen.

The goats were there, of course, milling around and just hanging out. I brought her in among them, keeping the leash loose while maintaining a death grip on my end of it. Snowstorm was quiet. She stood beside me, processing, thinking.

She had passed test number one. "What you're not looking for," Dianne had told me, "is a dog that stares at the goats, a dog that lunges or snaps at them. Probably not going to be a guardian if she has that as a reaction."

The goats had gotten used to her by now, and after we had stood there a few seconds, one of them came right up to her and pressed in to say *hi* to me. Snowstorm sniffed lightly, then backed up a little.

"Here's what you do want to see," Dianne had continued. "it's okay for the dog to be curious, but you want her to stay calm. Sniffing is fine. Curiosity is fine. If she gives the goats space or turns her head away, that's good, that shows that she respects them. And if she sits down, that's amazing."

Another goat wandered up to us and bleated softly, then nibbled my jacket sleeve. The whole group of them lingered, unconcerned. One of them crowded in for attention, brushed past Snowstorm, and stepped on my foot. Snowstorm, still beside me, gave the doe space, eased back, and sat down.

My whole heart warmed to her. I took a breath and smiled, really big. The fear that had remained cowering in a corner of my mind turned tail and fled. I knew she was going to make it. Snowstorm was in.

It took time, and there were a few hiccups. But gradually, Snowstorm earned the right to stay out with the goats full-time. She started on a long line and with my constant supervision. Again, following careful instructions from Dianne, I would keep her out in the pasture for fifteen or twenty minutes, dragging the long line just in case I needed to rush in and grab her. I would clean the barn or refill water tubs, doing little chores that needed doing, keeping tabs on her without upsetting the natural balance of what was going on. After that allotted time, I would bring her back to her pen, give her a hoof or a chew bar as a reward, and go back to the house. Then we would try it again later in the day.

As the days passed and she proved herself trustworthy, I extended her free time. She got half an hour or forty-five minutes loose in the pasture, and I would take short trips away from her while still keeping my ears on what was happening. I would check on the rabbits or set up training jumps for the house dogs, or collect the eggs from the chicken coop, all while listening for any ruckus or distress sounds from the goats. If I ever had any question, I would put her back in her pen and we would try again the next day.

Within a couple of months, Snowstorm was spending all day every day out with the goats. More than either of the other two guardians I have used, she is a dog who really keeps track of her stock. She knows who is in heat, who is pregnant, and when that doe is close to kidding. She loves new babies. If I ever bring in a new goat, she will take time to assess it. She isn't pushy or assertive about smelling or body blocking animals. She just knows. She watches and listens and sniffs judiciously. She studies and knows each of her charges.

Since adding her to the pasture, I have concluded that the best way to work guardian dogs is in male-female pairs. On a small acreage like mine, I really only need one dog to look after things. But I believe the dogs benefit from having a partner. It gives them someone of their own kind with whom they can play and engage, and that usually keeps them out of trouble with the livestock. They can wrestle, run, and patrol together. They have more confidence as a team. There's strength in numbers for dogs just like there is for people. Many times, I have seen how one dog will rush forward to bark a challenge while the other dog stays behind with the goats. One goes out to block a threat, the other stays back to watch the flock. Sometimes one dog will go out to patrol the farthest boundary of the north pasture, while the other dog remains in the barn, keeping an eye on the goats.

Almost every time, Snowstorm is the one who takes the initiative and goes forward to issue a challenge or check the boundaries. She is intuitive, calculating, and always watchful.

That doesn't just translate to her responsibilities with the goats. She notices everything in her environment. All Pyrs are keenly aware of their surroundings, but I think Snowstorm mentally processes things more than many do. For a long time, I didn't realize that there was a gaping hole in one corral fence. Apparently neither did the buck who lived there, because he stayed right where he belonged in his corral. But Snowstorm knew. My corrals are situated along one side of the pasture, so that the gates open on the inside fence and access the pasture and the barn. The outside fence of the corrals borders the driveway, and no one from the pasture has access to those outside fences. The fence with the hole was an outside fence. The dogs don't have access to the bucks' corrals. They patrol the inner fence and the gates that open into the big pasture. But those gates always stay closed, so the dogs don't get in with the bucks.

However, one evening while I was cleaning this particular corral, I did leave the gate open. The buck was tethered so he couldn't get out, the other goats were locked up, so they couldn't get in. No worries. I pushed the wheelbarrow in and out and didn't bother to shut the gate. I didn't think I needed to.

This was the opportunity she had been waiting for. Snowstorm went quietly, quickly, and was gone for hours. Not that she went far. She visited each of our neighbors, wallowed in the pond to cool off, then sat up in the green fringe of cedar trees along the driveway and observed.

That hole got patched, and never again did I allow the corral gates to stay open. But that was okay. Snowstorm's next great escape was so cunning that I never would have figured out how she did it if I hadn't been there to catch her in the act. Once again it involved a corral gate. This time it was Mocha's. Like the other corral gates, hers is improvised from a small section of cattle panel, cut to size and hinged at one end. The other end is secured with a double snap which snugs it up tight to the fence and keeps it closed. Only if you really study it do you realize that the bottom corner of the latch side isn't quite as tight as the rest.

Snowstorm figured out that she could shove her nose between that bottom corner and the fence post. From there, it was a methodical process of working her nose through the gap, then wedging her head through, and then worming the rest of her body through. With that obstacle behind her, she loped across Mocha's corral, slipped through the bars of the metal pipe gate, cut a neat turn out in the front yard and dashed up the driveway, free at last.

The most annoying part of this whole scenario was that she could also do it in reverse. When she realized that I had a visitor with me in the corrals a little later, she came back into the front yard, bounded through Mocha's five-bar gate, sprinted across the corral, and squeezed back between the post and the panel just barely breaking stride. The panel slapped shut behind her, and there she was, all smiles and success to greet my friend. It was disgusting.

But I had to admire her ingenuity. Another double snap added to the bottom corner of the cattle panel gate sorted her out. Snowstorm is not a dog who searches for ways to escape. She's content to be at the barn with her goats. But she studies things, constantly gathering data and information and filing it away for future reference. If the chance for a fling presents itself, she always accepts the offer.

Another thing she notices is turtles. The first summer I had her, she found more turtles on that little patch of pasture land than I thought possible. All kinds of them. All colors and sizes, and quite a few different species. Not just the cute little box turtles that go trundling along roadsides and across back lawns. She also found snapping turtles with monotonous regularity.

The first one was a common snapping turtle, larger than a dinner plate and not thrilled about the state of the world. After that it was an alligator snapping turtle. They are native to this area and grow to enormous size. Snowstorm's first find was about eighteen inches long, its spiky shell stinking of pond mud and fetid water. I can almost always smell when it's a snapping turtle she's found. The alligator snappers especially are aggressive and lunge at anything in front of them, mouths gaping and ready to latch on.

Snowstorm has a special turtle bark. It's higher-pitched than her typical, deeper, ringing challenge. Sharp, staccato, rapid barks, squeaking at the top of her register. When I hear her making that noise, especially June through August when the turtles are most active, I get a dog crate ready, pull on my boots, grab a shovel and go stumping out to see what she's discovered.

She stands about two feet away from her latest quarry, barking and squeaking frantically. She's crouched, head down, eyes blazing, and occasionally leaping backward as the cranky turtle takes a bite out of the air. I slowly sweep the shovel back and forth in front of her until, sure enough, it bumps up against a hard shell. If it's a gator snapper it will lunge and grip onto the blade of the shovel, sometimes even hissing its vehement outrage. My job then is to cautiously ease the shovel underneath its irate shell and scrabbling legs, deposit it in the wheelbarrow, and from there transport it to the prepped and waiting dog crate. Stowing it in a crate keeps it, and everyone else in the area, safe until my dad arrives on the scene and relocates it. I don't know how many turtles entered the Snowstorm relocation program that first summer. I lost count after a while.

The great day came when Glacier suddenly realized there was more to his new companion than just a working partner and a buddy to hang with. Let's just say that he thought she was beautiful and spent every waking moment making sure that she knew it. I remember one unfortunate episode when the UPS truck lumbered down the driveway and my two spirited guard dogs, *um,* did not have their minds on their work. Or at least, not on that particular job. There they were along the pasture fence for all the world to see, somewhat incapacitated. I pretended not to notice and hoped the UPS guy would be just as polite.

The puppies, all ten of them, arrived one cold November afternoon, the day before Thanksgiving. Six girls and four boys. In keeping with the winter theme established by Glacier and

Snowstorm, I officially christened my pick of the litter Snowdrift. But because that name shared its first syllable with the name Snowstorm, to avoid confusion I switched it, unofficially, to Drifter.

Drifter was the most laidback and submissive of all the males. That's what I was looking for. In a breed as protective and powerful as the Pyrenees, I didn't need a super dominant dog, especially a male. Drifter was sweet, easygoing, and steady. Not timid or unsure, just not as outgoing or exuberant as his brothers.

And that's who he's continued to be. Steady, watchful, and more reserved than his mom and dad, Drifter has slowly stepped into his role as full-time flock guardian.

Perhaps the most interesting thing about Drifter's story is that, for the first year of his life, he did not bark. Odd for most dogs and downright unnatural for a Pyrenees. With Glacier and Snowstorm to mentor him, I had just assumed that he would find his voice and learn how to use it within the first few months of life. But month after month went by and he remained silent. He wasn't goofing off out there; he did pay attention when his parents sounded off, staying right with them and very alert to whatever they saw or heard. He just wouldn't comment on it himself.

I waited and hoped and tried to be patient. But by the time he was ten months old, I was getting a little peeved. Part of a guardian dog's strategy is to make enough noise to send a clear message to any area predators. "I am here. Don't mess with mine and I won't have to mess with yours." It's part of the plan to avoid trouble. The best defense is a good offense. Make enough noise and the coyotes will naturally steer clear and go in search of an easier meal. Stop trouble before it even starts.

But if Drifter wasn't going to bark and declare his territory, half the battle was already lost. Once again, I reached for the phone and called Dianne.

"He'll figure it out," she assured me. "I mean, he's a Pyrenees. If he has two older dogs in with him, right now he's just letting them take the lead. But he's watching and following along. Give him another six months or so. He'll find his voice. Or maybe," she added as a laughing afterthought, "maybe he'll turn out to be one of those Pyrs who just sneaks up behind an intruder in the pasture and bites them in the butt."

So I gave it some more time. His first birthday came and went, and he was still mostly silent. A few uncertain woofs and wavering barks here and there, but no challenge barking, no territorial vocalization. And then, just a few days after he turned one year old, I heard him barking. Just for a minute, but it was him. It was big, loud barking. For a minute I thought it was Glacier, but the voice was different, unique. Definitely Drifter.

And little by little, he really did find his voice and learn how to use it. Now he barks more than Snowstorm does, she still being the prudent and judicious barker as which she started. More than either of my other two Pyrenees, Drifter has a very wide range of sound and vocabulary. His vocalizations vary from the falsetto, wavering woof which means he's heard something unimportant but is alerting to it anyway, to the deep-chested, very aggressive challenge bark. That sound is heavy and ferocious and makes me glad he's on my side.

He's also the only dog I have (and this is downright embarrassing) who howls. Not at coyotes or sirens or opera music, either. Nope, the thing that makes Drifter howl is when Mocha lets off one of her air-horn, window-cracking donkey brays. That will set him off. One hideous noise to outdo the other.

What I value and appreciate about Drifter the most is his true desire to be with his goats. Nine times out of ten—where the herd is—that's where Drifter is. If they browse along the driveway fence, he flops in the shade of the nearest tree. If they wander up to the south end of the field, he hangs out in the hay pile, the highest vantage point in that area. If they sun themselves in front of the barn, so does he. And at night when they're penned up, often times Drifter will camp out in the aisleway or in the milk room. He enjoys Snowstorm's companionship and he's bonded to me. But when the chips are down, Drifter likes his goats.

With the passing of Glacier, Drifter truly is the alpha male of the pasture. He is more serious, more watchful, and interestingly enough, more social now that his dominant daddy is gone.

My guardian dogs have never done anything amazing or heroic that I am aware of. I've heard stories of incredible things that livestock guardian dogs have either accomplished or intuited, and I just kind of shake my head and make peace with the reality that mine will never have the smarts or the chutzpah to do anything like those dogs. But just about the time I've given up on them and begin questioning exactly why I keep them around, I'll catch them doing something that gives me pause and reminds me.

One afternoon as I worked out at the barn, I noticed that all the goats were browsing out in the north pasture quite a distance away, while both Drifter and Snowstorm lazed noncommittally under the hedge trees on the complete opposite side of the building. *Wow,* I thought sarcastically, *they really do take good care of their goats.* So much for staying with the flock at all times and always keeping their attention on their animals. And then the neighbor's bratty little dogs showed up and began running the fence line nearest to the goats. Like white lightning, both Pyrenees were on their feet and flying down the hill, around the barn, across the north pasture, and straight to that fence. Both growling and barking, both making it very clear we'd had quite enough of such nonsense. I stood up and cheered them on. And I chided myself sharply for doubting them. They see, hear, and understand more than they appear to.

Another evening during chores I had fed both dogs and was finishing up everything else for the night when Snowstorm began barking. Not the squeaky, annoying turtle bark, but a loud, assertive challenge letting me know something was in her territory. Because she and Drifter are both tethered when they eat, I thought at first that maybe he had looked at her the wrong way and she was telling him to back off and mind his own business. They are tethered at opposite sides of the milk room and cannot reach each other's food, but maybe he had given her the stink eye and she was just laying down the law.

Still, that was unusual for these two, and when I returned to the barn and Snowstorm was still fussing and carrying on, I decided there must be more to it. I picked up the dishes and stowed them in the feed room. She had calmed down at my return to the barn, but she was still tense and wanted to be out and back in the pasture. She sat as I asked her to so I could unsnap the tether. Then as soon as she was free, she raced out of the building, took a hard right, dashed through the open gate into the north pasture, and galloped hard all the way down to the farthest fence. I let Drifter loose, shut off the lights, and then stood outside the fence to see what happened.

Snowstorm was standing at the far northeastern corner of the pasture, her barking fierce and formidable. The neighbor dogs were making noise, too, so I knew there was really something out there beyond the fence. Then Drifter came out of the milk room. He moved at a long, ground-eating trot, growling ferociously, went a quarter of the way down the north pasture, and stationed himself between his goats in the barn and Snowstorm on the far fence. I hadn't often heard the kind of serious, aggressive barking I heard from him that night.

Both dogs kept at it for several minutes, the intensity of their defense never faltering. And then they quieted, and I heard the dogs much farther to the north of us begin barking. I desperately wished I could have seen what they had seen and heard what they had heard. That was true guarding behavior, true teamwork. I'll never know what they scared off, which might otherwise have waltzed right across my land and maybe even detoured into the barn. I'll never know the myriad other times that they have stood in the breach, leaped to the defense of their goats and their home, perhaps even averted death and disaster. Most of their work takes place after hours, unseen and unsung. They are truly the behind-the-scenes heroes of the farm.

I slept well that night. My guardians were doing their work. I could rest secure in the knowledge that they were my ears, and my eyes, even through the watches of the night.

Note: During the final edits of this book, Snowstorm passed on to run in greener pastures. She will always be missed, and she will always be loved.

CHAPTER 8

CINDER: LITTLE BY LITTLE MAGIC'S CHIMNEY SWEEP

As Pixel really began to show his age, I started to consider bringing another toy breed into the picture. I always want my dogs to be accustomed to little dogs. Because we attend shows and other events where there are lots of other dogs, my own dogs need to be as dependable as possible. A dog and handler team never knows who they might end up next to at a show. If you're beside a toy poodle and your big dog doesn't know how to behave around tiny dogs, you both might get into some trouble. I didn't want to put my own bigger dog, or someone else's little dog, in that situation.

So my solution, of course, was to get a tiny dog of my own and make sure my other dogs knew how to be gentle with it. Not treating it as a chew toy or an animal of another species which needed to be chased, grabbed, and tasted. *This is a dog*, even though it only weighs five pounds, and it must be treated with calm respect.

My current little dog was aging, and while I was in no hurry for another furkid underfoot, it was time to begin putting my ear to the ground, considering breeds, and talking to people.

Eventually, I heard of a lady in the Topeka area who bred and showed Russian tsvetnaya bolonkas.

Bolonkas are a new breed on the American scene. The name loosely translates to "colored lapdog." About the only thing they have in common with my traditional papillon is that they are also classed in the toy group. Bolonkas are compact, stocky little dogs with big, furry heads, drop ears, and mustaches. Their coats, which can be any color except solid white, are long and wavy. There is minimal undercoat and very little shedding. Whereas the papillon is the flitting, charming, social butterfly of toy breeds, bright and adventurous and quicksilver smart, the bolonka is a more docile, more reserved teddybear. Slower to warm up to strangers and utterly devoted to his person, the bolonka looks different and acts different than the perky papillon. And I wanted something different.

As long as the breed was fairly athletic and reasonably trainable, I was interested.

The breeder and I met at a local dog show and sat down to talk. She told me one of her females had a litter due sometime in November, and she was eager to let me sponsor a puppy. She would give me the puppy free of charge if, in return, I would agree to get him out in the community and compete with him at shows. Her primary goal was to get these dogs out into the public so people could become familiar with an unusual, new breed and perhaps want to learn more about it. She knew that I did companion events with my dogs, so she was excited to get a puppy going with me and see where we might take each other.

As promised, by mid-November three puppies had arrived, two girls and a boy. It appeared that this new addition to my family was actually going to happen.

By Super Bowl Sunday, they were all at my house, scampering around on the computer room carpet. I crouched on the floor, too, evaluating and trying to make the right match. It was a tough decision.

The breeder sat in my cushy swivel chair while I tried to corner puppies. They were shy and skittish. They scuttled around the room, hugging the walls. They hadn't been socialized at all, and were even reluctant to go to the breeder, the one person they'd known all their short lives.

I hesitated. Not all puppies are Labradors, and I was willing to accept that. Some breeds are just more reserved with new people in new places, and I knew bolonkas were one of those breeds. The puppies were healthy with beautiful coats and bright eyes. They were clean and cared for. They were just very timid.

One of them, though, seemed a little less flighty. It was the little male, coal black, and shaggy. He seemed a bit more stable, a little more curious than his nervous sisters. He sat on a dog bed as I eased slowly over to him, scooting sideways on my knees. He didn't sniff or interact with my hand, but he didn't flinch or shy away, either. I felt drawn to this one.

"The boys are all about you," the breeder told me. "The little girls tend to be much more independent, just kind of doing their own thing. But the boys are totally devoted to their person."

Well, if I was going to do obedience, rally, and maybe even agility with a bolonka, I didn't want one who would just be doing her own thing. A male would definitely be a better choice. Decision made. I scooped my little boy, Cinder, up in my arms as the breeder stuffed the two females back into their carry crate.

"Yeah, I think this little guy will do well here," I said, grinning like a proud new mama. "I think he's the right one."

Cinder had never worn a collar before. He had no idea how to walk on a leash. He had never been on grass before. As far as I could determine, he had never even been outdoors. To me, this is not the right way to raise puppies. I strongly believe that even at a young age, puppies need to be introduced to tons of new people, lots of different stimuli, and many unfamiliar environments before they're placed with new owners. But some breeders don't agree. To some, the risk of a puppy picking up germs and parasites precludes the idea of heavy socialization. This can be especially true of those who raise toy breed puppies, which are easy to start indoors with puppy pads and play pens. These breeders feed and care for the puppies well, but they leave it up to the new owners to decide and provide however much socialization they deem appropriate.

That's how Cinder had been raised, and I had my work cut out for me.

At my house, dogs live like real dogs. They potty outdoors. They learn to use the dog door. They go for long walks, thrive on hard exercise, and learn to play with toys. They get out and about and meet people. And they are all given the opportunity to work.

This was a brave new world for a not-very-brave little dog. The first day or two he lived like a feral animal in the house. If he was indoors on the floor or outside in the yard, I could only catch him fifty percent of the time. If he was placed on the couch or on my lap he would simply freeze. He was shell-shocked and completely confused. He hardly made a sound, even overnight when I tucked him into his little crate with a warm blanket. He was like a stuffed animal, staying where he was placed, never soliciting attention.

Bolonkas are one-person dogs. They pick their human, and then nobody else matters. I wanted first to ensure that I was that human. And I wanted as a close second to make Cinder tolerant and social with other people. His strongest tendency would always be to nurture a bond with only one person. But as a future competition dog, and one expected to be an ambassador for his breed, he needed to at least accept other people, even if he didn't care about them.

The first goal was the easy one. After all, it wasn't like he had many options. I was the only human in the house. I fed him, brushed him, held him. Unless I did something really consistently nasty, it was only natural that he would attach himself to me. However, I did take it one step further. For the first few weeks of his life with me, Cinder often rode in a carry sling draped around my neck. Because he was initially hard for me to find and catch, the breeder and I agreed on the sling as a game plan to teach him to trust and stay with me. Similar to what I had done with Gem years before, I kept Cinder close until a true bond could be forged between us.

We did lots of things together. We folded laundry, washed the dishes, cut up sausage for training treats. When I cleaned cages, he watched from his sling. When I read, he was installed at my feet. And while I worked at the computer, Cinder got to cuddle in my lap.

It took most of a month, but I still remember the evening that we passed the first milestone. I had just plopped down to check emails and dash off a few quick responses, when I heard the jingle of Cinder's collar bell. He had followed me voluntarily into the room and came right up beside my chair. When I reached down to him, he nudged his blunt muzzle into my hand. And there was no looking back. That became his trademark greeting to me. He would trot toward me, tail wagging and fur falling into his eyes, and as soon as I crouched and dropped a hand, I would feel that wet, mustachioed muzzle tucked gently into my palm.

When I get a new dog, my strategy is to integrate him as quickly and completely as I can. That means walking with me and working with me from week one. But Cinder was his own unique challenge. He was so tiny and so timid that neither of those things happened immediately. Leash-training didn't happen overnight, either, and I wasn't about to let this scared baby run the roads without one. So we worked on the leash at home, in the yard and on the driveway. When I felt he was ready, I clipped a light retractable lead to his collar, slung an empty backpack onto my shoulders, mustered the rest of the pack, and headed out for a walk.

Cinder was so small, so shy and so short-legged, that I

wasn't sure he would or could keep up with me for all those miles. The backpack was a safety net. If he got tired or discouraged, I could stow him in the pack with the top partially unzipped to let him rest and regroup. He had plenty of room to get comfortable in the bottom, and the arrangement let him come with everyone the full distance even if he didn't walk the full distance. He could still get acquainted with the concept of a walk.

The first leg of the journey went better than expected. Cinder trotted along, staying right in my shadow but not as apprehensive as I thought he might be. After about a mile, I picked him up with lots of praise and petting and stashed him in the backpack. He settled uncertainly at the bottom, I slung it carefully over my shoulders and we went on. No biggy.

After about five minutes I felt Cinder stir. He shuffled and reoriented himself, then I felt him stand up on his back legs. Reaching one hand over my shoulder, I found his furry face peeping through the gap where I had left the pack unzipped a few inches. Apparently, he didn't want to miss anything.

After another half mile I dug him out and set him on the gravel again. He was eager to go, so we did another couple miles, Cinder scurrying along beside me, taking in the big wide world. He wasn't confident but he was curious. A good sign.

"Okay, buddy," I told him, scooping him into the pack again. "Let's give you a ride one more time, then you can be a big boy and walk the rest of the way home."

He seemed a little more reluctant this time, but Mom said to do it, so it must be okay. He settled down at the bottom and I picked up the pace. This backpack thing sure was a pain. Anything to help my dogs however they might need it, but still, if he got comfortable with walking in the next day or two, that would be okay with me.

His nose was at the unzipped slot again. He whimpered, then scratched, and pushed his front paws against the confining nylon sides. Now his whole head was out in the open.

"Hold on, baby," I told him. "Almost. We're almost there."

But Cinder wasn't waiting. The other dogs were on the ground, and he had been, too, up until about ten minutes ago. This backpack thing was stupid. With a flip of his head and a final push, he launched himself upward and outward and tumbled to the gravel. Bolonkas, the breeder had told me, were thinkers. Cinder had been thinking this through. And he didn't think he needed to be babied anymore. His little legs and his big heart were up for the job, *thank you*, and he was walking from here on out.

He never went back in the pack. I carried it on a couple of subsequent walks, just to be safe, but he didn't need it or want it. He still trots way out in front on walks, retractable leash pulled as far as it will go. He'd really like to be running with the border collies.

My second goal for Cinder was much harder. Getting him comfortable and friendly with other people remains an ongoing project. Not having heavy socialization as a young puppy, combined with the fact that he had no desire to meet new people because he had already chosen his person, meant a steep uphill battle for me.

The first challenge was simply getting him places. Cinder was so shut down and shy in unfamiliar settings that even walking on a new surface was enough to freeze him up. For several weeks that was all we worked on—going to a new location and rewarding him for stepping from rubber matting to slick floor, or from grass to concrete, or from tile to carpet. We worked on approaching objects—chairs, agility equipment, unfamiliar corners of the room—all of which were things and situations from which he shied away. We worked on stepping up, stepping down, walking over things that tilted or rocked, eventually jumping up onto hay bales.

I took him to the usual places where I start new dogs. We

went to pet supply stores, farm supply stores, training buildings, and dog shows. At first I carried him in the sling. Not an ideal solution, but when he was too scared to put one foot in front of the other and so shut down that he wouldn't take treats, the sling was my ticket to get him into places. I would carry him in, shaking and pulling his head away from everything we passed. Then once inside the store or camped out at the show, I would take him out, clip the lead to his collar, and set him on the ground to soak things in at his own pace.

Gradually he began to blossom. He became inquisitive enough to start watching things and smelling stuff. He began to take treats. First from me, then from other people. I tried to let as many people as I could hold him and feed him.

It's a process, and there haven't been any overnight miracles. But at a recent training event, he surprised me by going right up to a stranger who reached out to him and wagging his tail. Like so many things in life, like so many things that are worth doing, with this little guy it has been one baby step at a time.

It has also been baby steps with obedience work. He was so hesitant and shy for so long, many times not even comfortable taking food, that I didn't start formal training with him for five or six months. But as he matured and gained some confidence, I took more serious action and launched him on the work-for-food program. Translation: if you do not work, you do not eat. Like everything else with Cinder, we started small and worked up to things. At first it was enough that he sat on command, walked beside me through various turns, and stayed in one place when told. Then we progressed to things like off-lead recalls and some rally work, which required multiple tasks in one exercise. At this point in time, Cinder is working at jumps, retrieves, go-outs, and hand signals. He hasn't arrived, but the journey is well underway.

When it comes to competition in the ring, I invariably start my dogs in simple rally events. As mentioned earlier, rally is a less formal sport than competitive obedience. It's ideal for young, untried dogs, or for dogs who are especially skittish or unsure.

Cinder was all of the above. So to get him going, and to evaluate how far we'd come already, the rally ring was the place to begin.

I knew we would qualify, but I didn't think it would be pretty. Cinder had reached the point where he loved working, but he was no border collie. He was not as accurate or as driven as Meg or Tassie always were. Sometimes during training he would sit crooked, or sit off-center on his recalls, or stray too far to my left on heeling. He does not have the hawkish attention of a sheepdog, and he isn't a flashy, super precise working dog. But he does have the want-to.

And as I was to discover at our first trial, want-to made all the difference.

I got him out of his crate and clipped the lead to his collar to start warming him up. My dad, standing nearby and ready to help, said with perfect sincerity, "I don't think I've ever seen Cinder work before."

And my snarky comeback: "You know, I'm not sure I ever have, either."

Well, did I get told.

There were fifteen dogs in Rally Novice B that day. A big class, and Cinder came out on top. A perfect score in rally is one hundred, and that's what my little man earned. A perfect one hundred and a second-place ribbon, since there was one team whose time was faster than ours. No crooked sits or crooked fronts, no random tugs on the leash or refusal of any command. And no nervousness, either. He was unruffled by any of the rally signs, cones, or unfamiliar people in the ring.

He just went out there and aced it. It was a big brag for a little dog. It was a big step forward on this long journey.

A few weeks later at our third trial he did it again. Another large class, and Cinder brought home another ribbon. This time it wasn't quite perfect. Ninety-nine out of one hundred, and a fourth-place ribbon. The first working title to put behind his registered name.

When Cinder knows it's time to work, he is all in. He rushes the door, spins and chortles, leaps on the back of the couch, and will hardly hold still while I buckle the training collar around his shaggy neck. He also forms habits very readily. That's the breed talking. If a bolonka does something twice in a row, that's the way he'll do it forever after.

My job, then, has become doing my utmost to be sure this boy learns a skill or an exercise right the very first time. He has made me a better trainer, more concise and deliberate, with stringent attention to consistency. No half-hearted attempts or cutting corners. I take my time and never push, but I make sure the introduction to a new skill is solid and correct the very first time. And after he's learned it, we still don't rush or cut corners. He demands solid, careful consistency.

Cinder has also taught me to be a better trainer in the sense that with him, I must always remember to bring a big smile and a soft hand to the work. Cinder is a soft touch. Easily overwhelmed or discouraged, it doesn't take a lot of stress or new information to make him shut down and quit trying. My job is to keep things fun. I have to strike the balance between keeping Cinder pumped up, boyant, and believing in himself, while still stretching him a little, asking for more, and correcting when he gets it wrong. It's a tricky line to walk. But part of the beauty and reward of teaching dogs is that they usually have almost as much to teach you. Cinder's lessons for me have been in gentleness, patience, and persistence. He has helped me to once again see the simple joy and fulfillment that come with gradual learning, small victories, and the process of building up a little dog to make him bigger.

Still, before and after everything else, Cinder is a born lapdog. He is a wonderful representative of his breed, whose purpose is, first and foremost, to provide comfort and companionship. He is a true snuggle bug. He always has to be touching something or someone. Either another dog, or if they won't cooperate, then a dog bed or a piece of furniture. He cannot lie alone; he has to be in contact with something. I've learned to be cautious when moving my rolling chair at the computer, since one of his favorite cuddle spots is the angle of the wheels. They jut from the base of the chair at just the right degree for him to curve his back into the angle and rest his head on one set of wheels.

The best place to be, though, is in Mom's lap. He would stay on me for hours, curled against my tummy and with his furry face resting on an arm or a hand. If I'm not available, Dundee and Kola make good substitutes. He will cuddle himself into the curve of whichever body he can reach, often dropping his head onto a back, a flank, or a front leg.

Cinder is a day-at-a-time dog. I have lots of hopes and plans for him as we begin our journey together. But as we walk these baby steps and achieve each tiny victory, my greatest hope is that I will never shut out the comfort or stonewall the joy he so naturally shares. After all, there is nobody's lap he would rather be in. And as warm and sweet a thing as it is to hold him close, it's an even better thing that I get to hold him tightly in my heart and that he also holds me in his.

PART THREE

SPRING

Thunder. The sky shudders with it, and the ground itself seems
to shiver. The air is thick with humidity and heavy with tension.
It hangs over the hills and fields, smothering, stifling. Not a
breath of wind.

I've been waiting for this storm all day. Ever since last
night, actually. Ever since I checked in with my trusty weather
radio before bed and it promised there was an eighty percent
chance of thunderstorms the next afternoon. Switching it on
hopefully, early this morning, I learn the promise still stands. A
near certainty of thunder, the radio assures me, and, it adds with
what I take to be a note of excitement in its mechanical voice,
"some thunderstorms may be severe in the afternoon."

That's all I need to give me an energy boost and
anticipation for the rest of the long day ahead. There are few
things I love as much as a spring thunderstorm. Out here on the
Great Plains and with Tornado Alley right nextdoor, storms are
often rowdy and spectacular.

By 3:00 in the afternoon the watch boxes are going up.
Nothing on the ground yet, but "conditions are favorable for the

development of severe weather." I hover and pace, trying to concentrate on busy work, pretending attention to the chores for that afternoon, and snatching every excuse possible to dart back outside and listen.

When I finally hear it, the thunder is far off to the southwest. It's more of a sensation than a sound, almost intrasonic in its depth and intensity. I stand there, rigid, facing the southwest. I can feel the thrill and the threat of the grayness. I can practically taste the humidity, the ominous edge to the air. I forget to take another breath.

Long, long pause. I freeze there like a dog on point, willing it to come closer and rejoicing in the waiting.

Then the sky quivers again, and so do I. Yup, it's coming closer. And suddenly my focus clicks back to real time, and I remember everything that has to be done before the rain and wind arrive. Training jumps to dismantle and stow; baby chicks to be gathered up and bundled into the coop; potted plants to bring under shelter in case of hail; baby goats who need to be herded into the snug safety of the mini barn; and I had wanted to finish cleaning the pens in the big barn, then corral all the adult goats and lock them in before the worst of the weather wallops us.

Back in the house and the weather radio is jabbering ecstatically. Three severe thunderstorm warnings all going at once, and one of the storms definitely appears to be heading right for us. Meg is nervous and fidgety, shadowing me wherever I go. She's smart enough and scared enough to have figured out years ago that the weather radio's warning siren means thunder isn't far behind. I put her in her crate where she feels most secure, switch off the weather radio, and crank up the fan and some music to try and mask the scary thunder until the noise gets too close to cover up.

Outside again. The air is heavy and dark. The rumbling in the southwest is almost constant now and much closer. I wish I could see the flashes that slash out ahead of it. But not in the daylight. That's one thing I love about storms after dark. Then the brilliant stabs and starbursts of lightning are vivid and bright even to my limited sight.

Now there's a subtle change. A slight breath, and the chimes along the west side of the house clink, and all the trees along the quarter-mile driveway breathe deep, brace themselves, sigh, and bow before the storm.

It comes with wind. With wild and furious joy. It strides across the low hilltops, unfurling its wings and sweeping into the pastures and creek bottoms. It revels in its strength, in its violence, cracking the sky with thunder so loud and sudden that it's like hand grenades. It hurls hail against the northern slopes, against the windows, icy exultation. The wind roars. The rain comes in drenching, dizzying sheets, blown almost horizontal, overflowing the gutters. Its own torrential thunder on the metal roof of the barn is deafening.

I stand in the doorway of the front porch, delighting in the raw power and gladness of the storm. The door is open wide, buffeting in the gusts, and rain and hail spatter against my face and arms. I'm chilled and I'm thrilled. It was well worth the wait. The kind of storm that does Kansas proud.

But it doesn't last. Booming along at about sixty miles an hour, the storm sweeps past us, shoulders us aside, and moves off, banging and grumbling away like a two-year-old after a tantrum. The wind has blown itself out. The sun smiles and clears the sky, sparkling clean and spacious from west to east. Bright drops patter from the tender, new leaves of the trees. My neighbor's rooster crows, and a meadowlark whistles somewhere up the driveway.

These storms are the fullness of spring. They come in April and May when earth and sky have already warmed and moistened, fostering the fronts and pressure changes that clash and condense into thunder. However, the season really begins with frogs.

They show up around the first week of March. I usually hear them one at a time at first. A tiny trill, ascending the scale, like the sound you get when you run your finger just right along the teeth of a comb. Short, experimental, twice, three times. Then silence. Maybe it's still too chilly. It will freeze again tonight. Better wait until warmer weather has really arrived.

But no, there's another trill. It's down in the marshy area at the northwest corner of the property. And then there's another trill, this time from the edge of the pond along my east pasture fence.

I have to smile. It may freeze tonight, and tomorrow night, and most of the overnights for the next few weeks. But as far as I'm concerned, when you hear those little frogs tuning up, spring has truly set down a tentative foot in our corner of the world.

Day by day the frog song increases. By the end of March, practically every pond, marsh, creek, and ditch along the road is trilling. Even late in the evening, long after the sun has tucked itself in for the night and the temperature hovers at thirty-five, the frogs keep singing. The sound slows as the mercury drops, each trill taking twice as long to crest the scale. When I finally follow the sun and tuck myself in long after dark, I still hear them, now only trilling way down in the creek bottom where it's most sheltered, their sound slower and colder each hour.

By sunrise they're completely quiet. The temperature finally dipped into the twenties, too nippy for cold-blooded frogs. But by nine or ten in the morning, cautious trills have started up again. Spring is here and nothing's gonna keep it down for long.

Birds begin to come back. Blackbirds and bluebirds have been singing for a month or so by now. But the meadowlarks are joining in, and the cheerful phoebes, whose call sounds just like their name with a distinct question mark at the end, as if someone is looking for her and wants her in a hurry. "Phoebe?" And then with more emphasis and impatience, "Phoebe?!"

The crazy killdeer are swerving and winging their way across the open country. They fly in long, low arcs, skimming the new grass and calling in high, sharp piccolos. I love killdeer, unassuming and happy. On warm evenings you can hear them chirring even as late as eleven o'clock.

The doves' rich cooing fills the edges of yards and woodlands. Swamp sparrows and cowbirds and flycatchers, the rusty-hinge call of the prairie warblers, the intricate melodies of the song sparrows, and the orioles are back again this year.

Then one day as I turn onto the road with dogs in tow, I grind to a halt, delighted. The dickcissels have completed their long migration from South America and have found their way back to my mailbox. Or at least two pairs of them have. They nest in the high grass around that mailbox every year, and every year I welcome them back with unbridled joy. From dawn until dusk, from May until August, they sing and chatter in the prairie grass along the borders of pastures, crop fields, and roadsides.

Last to arrive are the darting, chatty barn swallows and the yellow-billed cuckoos, clicking and cooing in the highest treetops of the deep woods.

The first crickets announce themselves with busy, soft chirping as the grass really takes off. And the first grasshoppers pop up, too, whirring through the hay fields and pastures.

The smell of roads and woods and fields becomes fragrance. Damp, dark earth, churned up by the harrows; the freshness of new leaves in the sun; deep drafts of cinnamon, or cloves, or something sweeter drifting from some secret place in the brush; and best of all, the scent of just-cut grass, as heavenly as incense and as earthy as the roads I walk.

As the land greens, another ancient prairie tradition begins. The farmers burn their fields. They wait for calm days with no wind and preferably high humidity. Firing the fields eliminates last year's old growth, makes room for this year's fresh growth, and enriches the soil so that the new grass gets a head start. It's a practice that goes back centuries to the American Indians. And it still works today, even in the age of genetically modified corn and megabucks-combines.

Smudges of smoke lie heavy on the fields and crawl along the roadsides. The smell eddies in the low pockets of the land and lazes on the flats. It smells darker and dirtier than woodsmoke, not unpleasant, but laden with the remembered scents of rank grass and rotting sticks and animal dung.

Then the next day the wind gets up from the south and brushes the smoke away. The day after that, soft, green velvet covers all the scorched land.

I welcome the south wind the same way I welcome the frogs and the dicksissels. It's an old friend that I spend a lot of time with in spring and summer, but which I haven't encountered much throughout the winter. Whereas winter's northwest wind personifies death and brutality, the south wind of spring is a whole different presence. It embraces and laughs with whatever it meets. It rushes and romps, open-handed and joyous, flinging its favors to all, scattering its gifts abroad. It brings warmer days, longer days. It stirs up the storm fronts, breathing its power and joy into their creation. It brings sweet, lingering evenings when the sun just doesn't quite want to go down, and I just don't quite want to go indoors, not just yet; and the south wind stays awhile, breathing gently, laughing softly, tugging at the wind chimes on the front patio. A cow lows in the distance, the frogs trill down in the creek bottom. I catch the scent of clover, and mowed grass, and hope.

There's one more herald that cries spring has truly arrived. That's when I clank out to the barn with the stainless steel milk pails, and put the goats up on the milking stand. No matter how chilly those early March mornings might be, when I'm milking moms and feeding babies, spring is really here. The drama and delight, the heartbreak and the happiness of new life on the farm, have just begun.

CHAPTER 9

BIRTH: NEW KIDS ON THE BLOCK

The baby monitor squawks, and I jerk awake, my heart thumping. My first emotion is a charge of excitement, because I know what's about to happen. That charge lasts for about two seconds, until I reach over and slap the talking clock beside my pillow. One forty-seven a.m. *Nice.*

I heave a sigh and swing my feet, which are already cold in anticipation, over the edge of the bed. The monitor wails. Actually, it's Keiko who wails. Keiko is the big, black Nubian doe due to drop kids any day. She's the one I've been watching hour by hour, and by the sound of it, the kids are now going to drop any minute. She's definitely in labor, and I need to yank on some warm clothes and get myself out to the barn on the double.

So begins the rush and the new life of spring. It's exhausting, exhilarating, and never quite expected. Oh, I prepare for it beginning in February. I stock up on medicines, make sure there are probiotics and vitamin B in the cabinet, run the baby bottles through the dish washer for a thorough cleaning. I deworm the goats, clean out the snug pen in my utility room, throw down a bale of fresh, crackling straw. I hang the baby monitor out at the barn and start carting the receiving unit around the house and yard with me. I listen and check and count down the days.

But somehow, when the first moan of a doe in labor jabs into my consciousness, only then does it all become real. It isn't fun and games and anticipation anymore. It's now the stress and reality of the struggle to bring living beings into a harsh world, and the challenge of sustaining those new, fragile beings when they arrive.

My first brush with the tragedy and triumph of birth came the very first year kids were born on the place. That spring I only had two does pregnant. One decided to be traditional and have twins. The other went rogue and had triplets. At least it was rogue to me. Twins are the norm for goats, and this was, after all, only the first year I was doing goats. *Come on. Triplets?*

Yes, it was triplets. Three little boys, of course, which is not what breeders of dairy animals want. This was back in the Stone Age days when I still let the moms raise their own babies. I did not bottle feed. I had never bottle fed anything before in my life. She'd had the triplets, and I assumed she could raise them, on her own, and with no help from me.

By the second day it was obvious that not all of them were either well fed or warm enough. Temperatures loitered in the twenties and thirties. I know now that's too cold for newborns. But back then, I had no experience and no one to mentor me. Most baby animals with good shelter and a good mom thrive. I had yet to learn the pitfalls and challenges specific to raising goats.

By the end of that second day, I had brought the first of the triplets indoors. I had tracked down a bottle from a neighbor and was struggling to get whatever nourishment I could down the little guy's throat. He was weak and disinterested.

The next morning found us driving him up to the vet clinic. By afternoon he was dead.

Stunned and horrified, I bolted out to the barn and dropped down in the pen where his two remaining brothers crouched in the straw bedding. The bigger one lurched to his feet and toddled manfully over to mom. He started nursing. He seemed healthy, hungry, and warm enough.

The other one, though. I reached out to rub his back and was shocked at how cold he felt. Cold and unresponsive. My heart bounded into my mouth. It couldn't be. Not another one. I dragged his limp body toward me. Legs and ears icy. His head flopped in the straw.

My stomach clenched. *No. . .*

But cupping my hand over his nose and mouth, I felt faint, warm breath. I tucked my palm under his left foreleg, against the tiny chest, and there was the heartbeat, faint, so faint and so, so slow. But it was there.

And with that I flipped into mommy mode. No way was I going to lose another baby. I scooped him into the front of my toasty down jacket, strode out of the pen, and sprinted to the house, praying even faster than I was running.

Slamming into the house, I pulled up short, breathless, and not sure what to do next. We were out of the cold, but I knew that wasn't enough. This baby needed some major extra warmth. My mind flickered desperately, trying to pin down the best option. The oven was too dangerous. I didn't have a heating pad or an electric blanket. Hot water seemed possible, although I wasn't sure about the repercussions of getting him wet.

Then I remembered the clothes dryer, full of towels and blankets from a load of animal laundry waiting to be folded. Maybe if I restarted the dryer, got those items good and hot, then wrapped him up in that warm, fleecy fabric. . .

I slugged the on button, listened to the comforting hum of the machine, and tried to take some deep breaths. With the baby still draped in one arm, I settled down on the rug in front of the dryer to wait for the blankets to really get hot. I laid the limp, chilly body across my lap and began to rub. Again and again I rubbed my chapped hands over the velvety sides, across the empty belly, and down the spindly, satiny legs. I talked to him. I talked to God. I tucked one finger into the cold, moist mouth and got no sucking response.

But he was still breathing. The slow, labored heartbeat trudged on. He hadn't given up, and I wouldn't, either.

The blankets must be warm enough by now.

I jerked open the dryer door and bundled the baby inside. The blankets were hot, and within seconds, I had wrapped him up to his icy nose in their steaming folds. Then I clunked the door closed, pulling the corner of one blanket through to keep it open just a crack.

It went on like this for more than an hour. I would warm the blankets, snuggle the baby inside, run to do a couple other little things. Then come back, my heart sinking, until I reached into the dryer and felt his soft breath on my fingers. After a few minutes when the blankets began to lose their heat, I would cuddle him in my lap again while the dryer warmed once more, and I would rub his sides and legs and tell him what a good thing life was and how he needed to try, how he needed to hang on. Then wrap him back up in the dryer again.

After a bit he began to hold his head up. His skin lost that cold, lifeless feeling. His long, Nubian ears and the inside of his mouth weren't frigid anymore.

Then one time when I stuck a finger in between his gums to make sure his mouth was still warm, there was a definite tug at my fingertips. He was sucking. He was hungry. Small miracles. I folded him back into his cozy blankets and dashed to get a bottle started on the stove.

A little while later he was standing. Shaky and uncertain on the laundry room rug, but definitely on his feet and looking for vittles. I was only too happy to grab the bottle and introduce him to it.

That was my miracle baby. He not only survived, but he thrived. I named him Panicum. But everyone who knows the story remembers him as "the dryer baby."

After that year I made it a strict policy to bring all babies indoors and bottle raise them. This is how most serious dairy breeders raise their kids each spring. As counter intuitive as it might seem, it is a safer and healthier way to bring up babies. Goats are accident prone and surprisingly fragile, especially as newborns. Keeping them in a clean, climate-controlled environment with regular feedings guarantees their health much more than does leaving them in the barn with the adults. Feeding on a bottle with pasteurized milk also prevents the spread of any milk-passed diseases that mom might be carrying unawares.

And lastly, bottle-raising babies makes them incredibly tame and friendly. Because these animals will most likely be purchased as milkers, being friendly and easy to handle is a plus.

I'm a pretty good hand now at bottle feeding, but it was a learned skill. It seems reasonable to assume that hungry baby goats would take right to the bottle and start sucking down their milk immediately. I mean, they suck on everything else. My fingers, my wrist, my chin when I bend over, the hem of my sweatshirt and the cuffs of my jeans, even on each other's ears. But pop a rubber nipple into that vacuuming mouth and you can never quite be sure what the response will be.

Some babies do take right to it. They taste that warm milk, realize exactly where it's coming from, and latch on. Other babies take some gentle persuasion and I have to work with them and be patient for a day or two before they understand. Over the years I have developed a soft but firm touch. I've learned to be quick. Get them sucking on my fingertips, good and hungry, then sneak the nipple into that questing mouth and tip the bottle up before they know where they are. Give the bottle a light squeeze so the baby tastes some milk, and usually the sucking reflex will take over from there. Once they figure out that sucking on this tasteless rubber produces sweet, warm milk, they're on board. Getting them to that realization is the trick. Sometimes you just have to be stubborn and not take no for an answer. They get it eventually.

And once they do, look out. They never forget where the food comes from. Not only do baby goats suck on everything they can reach, they also have an aggravating, totally endearing habit of nose-bumping everything they can reach. When a baby goat nurses on mom, they instinctively bump her udder, which stimulates her mammary system to let down the milk. The more the kid bumps and nudges, the easier it is to get the milk. Kids raised on a bottle do the same thing, with slightly different results. The milk does indeed come down—bottles go flying and land all over the ground, nipples squirt milk in every direction—and meanwhile the babies are even hungrier and more impatient than when the whole fiasco began. But as they get older and more confident with the bottle, they know what to expect, and so do I. By the time kids are two weeks old, I can feed them two at a time, a bottle in each hand, and a ravenous kid attached to each bottle. With my bottles lined up on a storage tub in the utility room, I pull kids out of the pen two at a time and just let them go to town. I can feed a pen of eight or ten kids in ten or fifteen minutes.

As mentioned earlier, one goal of bottle feeding is to make the babies friendly and people-oriented. At this age, they never meet a stranger. In fact, a stranger can hardly get away from them. They operate under the assumption that every single human being has a warm bottle of milk stuffed in a back pocket somewhere. If you're brave or foolish enough to squeeze into their corral, you'll be fighting them off for the entire visit. They mob anyone who comes into their space. Think big, unruly puppies meet Mary's little lamb. They shove, they jump up, they suck on anything they can attach to. They chew, nudge, crowd, and trample each other with no qualms. It's a rough-and-tumble, ready-or-not free for all.

This is one reason that I've settled on hand feeding my kids rather than using some of the higher-tech and lower-work gadgets that are available. Some farms have really good luck with gismos like bucket feeders and lamb bars—milk containers of various shapes and sizes, studded with rubber nipples around the sides or bottom edges. They can either be set on the ground or hung from the fence. The goat raiser then just pours in the milk and lets the babies supervise themselves. But in my experience, there are always bullies who drink more than their fair share, and who shove the smaller or weaker kids out of range of the feeder so they can't get any milk at all. Hand feeding with bottles ensures that each kid gets enough, and it also lets me instantly detect if somebody isn't hungry or isn't feeling well.

For the first four days or so of a kid's life she's fed four times every day. After that I switch over to three times a day. That schedule lasts until kids are one month old, at which point they're switched to two feedings per day. At two months old we back off to just one feeding per day, and at three months old kids are completely weaned.

I introduce hay, grain, and water quickly, within about the first two weeks after kids have been born, setting them out in the pen so the kids can taste, touch, and experiment. They won't eat solid food until they're three or four weeks old, and even when they do start to nibble, they are dependent on milk for two or three more months afterward. But I want my kids growing, gaining weight, and establishing themselves as rapidly and as strongly as possible. The earlier they're introduced to solids, the earlier they'll begin to get curious about and begin eating the solids.

With kids on the place, each new day is an adventure. When things go right, it seems all is right with the world. But things can also go very rapidly wrong. I can never let my guard down in the spring of the year, and I've learned to be prepared for anything.

The most dramatic event I have experienced so far was the time I had to pull two kids. They arrived early one morning just as I was staggering out of bed. Or rather, they tried to arrive. By the time I hustled out to the barn and assessed the situation, they had gotten themselves stuck tight. Both apparently wanted to be born at the same time, and when I showed up, they were jammed together shoulder to shoulder. One had its head out already, the other's front leg was stretched out alongside. They couldn't go forward, and with the contractions of the uterus pushing them hard, they couldn't go back. They weren't budging.

The mama, a huge Toggenberg doe named Wister, strained with everything she had and screamed. My knees were beginning to shake. I knew what had to be done. I had read about it. I had imagined doing it. And I knew I could do it, but. . .

Wister hollered and heaved, desperately turning her head and wild eyes to me, pleading to know why she was in so much pain and why her shepherd wasn't helping her. I gulped, dropped to my knees behind her, and went to work.

The one with the foreleg extended was the one I methodically began to push back into the birth canal. The other, with its head thrust forward and both front legs folded way back underneath its chest, would have to come first.

Between Wister's contractions I cautiously eased the second kid back, back, reaching up to my elbow, until the first kid was finally free of the crush. Then the job was to straighten that first kid's forelegs. Kids should be born headfirst in a diving position, front legs straight out and the head cradled on top of them. This little one was coming all wrong. Straighten first one leg, then the other. Then catch hold of both front feet, slimy and solid, wait for Wister to push, give a gentle tug to help her, and we had one kid born, slippery and wet in the straw.

I was scared, shaking, and filthy. And I had one more kid to get out. I went in again, reaching up to the elbow, babbling incoherent promises to Wister that everything would be all right and that we would get this mess sorted out.

My fingers closed around that errant foreleg, then reaching farther, a little farther, to find the other front leg tucked way back under the chest. Carefully, carefully, pull that leg forward, straighten it out, and. . .

"Now push, sweetheart!" I told her. "Push! Push! You can do it, mama! We're almost there!"

And with one more groan and heave from Wister, the second baby lay in my lap. They were both alive. They were both beautiful. And they were both very hungry. I swaddled them up in the towels I'd brought, toted them off to the house, dried them, fed them, came back to check on mom, fed her, gave her vitamin B and a dose of antibiotics, told her what a wonderful girl she was, and finally trudged into the house, exhausted and victorious, to enjoy a very hot and much-needed shower.

Both kids alive and healthy and, as luck would have it, after all that work and drama, they were also both boys.

As I've explained, dairy breeders aren't interested in baby boys. Boys don't produce either kids or milk, and the services of one buck can take care of a whole herd of does. In other words, we don't need many of them. When my own does present me with the questionable blessing of a baby buck, I keep him for a week or so, just enough to get him started on the bottle and make sure he's healthy. Then he is sold, dirt cheap, to a family who raises him to market weight and then usually sends him to the sale barn. All my little boys go the same route. They're cute for the few days that they're with me, but I don't regret letting them go.

The doe kids stay two or three months longer. I get them well started, growing, dehorned, and vaccinated before beginning to advertise those I choose to sell. Some of them stay here on the farm and are never sold. It all depends on what I'm looking to keep, what kind of genetics they have, what kind of milkers their mothers were and so on. A lot goes into the decision of whether to sell or to keep a doe kid.

I always name the doe kids, and each year the naming theme is different. One year it was spices. Sage and Minty come from that spring. Another year it was fabrics. Paisley, Poplin, Silky, Velvet. More recently I named kids according to themes in literature. Fable, Legend, Mystery, Romance, Novel, Story. I have fun with names.

For about the first two weeks of their lives, the babies live in the cozy pen built into one end of my utility room. With absorbent bedding and straw underneath them and the space heater running fulltime, they stay snug and warm even when the spring cold fronts blast through and chill things down outdoors. When I'm sure the kids are thriving and strong, and after double checking that the forecast is warm enough, I take the next step and move them out to the mini barn.

The mini barn is a three-sided, low-roofed shed situated near the big barn where the adults live. It has a wooden floor strewn generously with bedding, and a swinging door at the front, open in the daytime and latched securely overnight. It lets out into a large corral, fenced by my backyard on one side and by the adults' pasture on the other. The babies get used to both the house dogs and the guardian dogs, they get acquainted with the big goats, and the goats and guardians also get familiar with them. All this while still keeping the kids separate and safe. The arrangement also makes them more accessible to me so I can more easily feed, doctor, and keep them clean. It's a good system.

Over the years, my girls have been pretty considerate when it comes to the time of day at which they have their kids. The majority of babies have arrived in daylight hours, the most popular time having been midafternoon to early evening. Occasionally a mama will decide to start her morning, and mine, off with a bang and drop her kids first thing. But she usually at least waits until I'm up, dressed, and in my right mind.

Keiko, however, isn't waiting.

By the time I yawn into my clothes, locate my boots, and start a bottle on the stove, she is in hard labor. The stars wheel frosty overhead as I hurry out to the barn. This is the deepest part of the night. It has that foreign, moonscape feeling of odd wakefulness, when everything except the night itself is fast asleep. It stands around me, immense and still.

The guardian dogs greet me at the gate, and I push my way in, clean towels wedged under one arm and my heart flip-flopping. It's half excitement, half fear, as I snap on the barn lights and ease into her pen.

She's in one corner, lying down, grunting and breathing hard. We're close. I hop into the milk room to unfold a towel on the floor, grab another couple of towels, and go back to Keiko to rub her shoulder and talk her through it.

Five minutes later I'm trotting back to the house, the latest addition to the farm bundled up in two towels and already beginning to nudge and nose for his breakfast. Yes, I did say "his breakfast." It's another little boy. *Sigh.* Way to go, mama. It's 2:14 a.m. as I slip into the house, slide the bottle off the stove, and settle down to begin coaxing another baby into the first hours of life.

CHAPTER 10

MILKING: TAKING THE STAND

As stressful and delightful as the arrival of kids can be, it eclipses the true obligation that spring ushers into my jam-packed schedule. Kids come in a rush, a tsunami of need and demand and worry and wonder. For one or two months they dominate the scene. In fact, for one or two months they dominate my entire life. I eat many meals standing up and catching more than six hours of sleep per night is a luxury. My entire world seems to revolve around filling bottles, warming bottles, cleaning bottles, and of course, feeding bottles to the starving hordes in the indoor pen and/or the mini barn. The kids are constant, here and now, a force of nature on the farm.

But what their presence overshadows is the staple of life and routine that actually keeps their little, demanding bodies and souls together. Twice a day, every day, rain or shine, freezing cold or frying heat, for better or worse, in sickness and in health, for ten months out of every year —March through December—I milk.

It's more than just a commitment. It is a way of life. Long after the kids are grown up and gone, morning and evening find me trudging out to the barn, a stainless steel pail clunking in each hand. The twice-daily obligation to milk the goats is no respecter of schedules. Regardless of whatever else may have to be done on any given morning or evening, milking supercedes it all. I may not get out to the barn on time every single time but get out there I will. Early in the pre-dawn chill before loading up and leaving for a dog show. Yawning my way from goat to goat after a conflict has kept me in town later than I had planned. So much to squeeze in to each morning rush, so much to cram in at the end of each overflowing day. But milking doesn't get scrimped. It happens.

Ideally it happens every twelve hours. This consistency keeps the goats at peak production. The amount yielded by each doe varies by individual, taking into account her age and genetics. A first freshener—dairy speak for a doe who has had kids for the first time and thus is being milked for the first time—will not produce nearly as much milk as a third freshener. Her lineage will also help determine a doe's milk yield. If she has heavy milkers in her ancestry, chances are pretty good that she will produce a lot of milk herself. Generally speaking, a mature doe from quality milking lines should give ten to fifteen pounds of milk every day during peak production. That translates to between one and one and a half gallons.

Milking becomes a way of life not only for me but for the goats as well. My goats love milking time. They get so impatient and pushy that I've implemented a tethering system to keep everyone somewhat under control.

Hanging along the fences in each pen are heavy-duty, nylon dog leashes. One for each goat. I fasten them long enough so that each waiting doe can turn around or lie down. But the leashes are short enough to keep everyone out of everyone else's business, and without enough slack to tangle in a goat's legs.

My first task at each milking session is to track down and tie up each goat. Every one of them has a designated place. The milkers who have been doing this for a couple of years know which tether is theirs, and will either station themselves at that spot along the fence, or else will lead me to that spot when I latch onto their collars. Each doe wears a large nylon dog collar, and naturally, each of my girls wears a bell so I can quickly find and identify her. I snap every doe to her assigned tether, and then it's time to begin filling grain dishes.

The impatience mounts. Excitement rises. The crowd of onlookers shift and shuffle, some tugging at their tethers, some hollering for me to hurry it up already. Bells jangle. Wire fences ping. Somebody knocks against one of the hay racks and the whole wall shivers.

They're ready to go long before I am, and when I finally get all the dishes filled, stacked and toted into the milk room, the barn is alive with pent-up energy. They simply cannot comprehend what in the world is taking this snail of a human such a ludicrous, ridiculous amount of time to get this show on the road.

At the beginning of the season, I milk in the order that the does freshen. No special preference is given to one or another. The one who drops her kids first and thus produces milk first is the one who gets milked first. But once everyone has freshened for the year, I'll take them up on the milking stand on a pen by pen basis. Eventually they learn the routine and the milking order, and they settle down as I go to work.

When she's untied, every single doe can be trusted to dash straight to the milk room, dive onto the milking stand and shove her head into the stanchion. She knows right where that grain is waiting for her. Munchies are the main motivator. The does are fed while I milk. That keeps them busy and standing still, and it also ensures that they maintain a healthy weight. Producing milk pulls a lot of weight off a lactating doe. Again, remember that she's yielding ten to fifteen pounds of milk every day. She needs to even things out by also eating several pounds of high-quality grain every day.

But besides the grain, there's the simple relief of being milked. A doe's udder gets pretty tight hauling around a gallon of milk at a time, and she quickly learns that having that milked stripped out just makes her feel better.

Training a doe to the milking stand commences long before she's old enough to have kids of her own. It begins with trimming feet.

Like horses, alpacas, and other hoofed farm animals, goats need their feet trimmed regularly. I do mine every four to six weeks, and I start them out young. The easiest way to trim a goat's hooves is to load her onto the milking stand. It keeps her calm and at an ideal height. The job needs to be done anyway, and doing it this way develops a good association in her memory. She learns that the milking stand is a place where she is fed and gets attention.

By the time they're a year or two old, have had their first kids and are ready to be milked, the girls know how to jump onto the stand.

The milking stand is a platform just wide enough and long enough to hold a large goat. It's most often constructed of wood, with a locking stanchion at one end to hold the goat's head steady. It sits about sixteen inches off the ground. That's just the right height for a person to pull up a stool, sit down, and milk comfortably. But it's a hefty step for a goat unaccustomed to getting up when requested. I teach all my does the command "step up" as they become acquainted with the stand. It has proven handy in other situations, too. There have been a number of times that I've needed to load a goat into the van or into a truck, and those familiar words "step up" have cued her to willingly step into an unfamiliar location.

By May or June, we've all settled in to the rhythm of the thing and it goes like clockwork. I plunk the first dish of grain into the tub at the front of the milking stand, and pivot out of the room to release the first dancing doe, Velvet. I unsnap her tether, she blasts out of her pen, canters down the aisle. She veers sharp left into the milk room, then the thunking of hooves on wood as she lopes onto the stand. I'm right behind her to pull the stanchion closed around her satiny neck and lock it in place as she begins to crunch her grain. Then scrape an upside down bucket into position beside her right flank, rattle the milk pail into place under her belly, and I get busy.

She crunches grain while I squirt milk. At first the jets foam into the pail with a metallic zing. Milk on metal. A keen, almost sparkling sound, loud in the high-roofed barn. As I keep filling the pail, the liquid noise becomes wetter, heavier. Before long the creamy streams don't zing at all. They swish and swirl. There are two inches of milk in the pail now, snowy white and frothy. I can hear the foam on the top crackle when I pause to switch from my right hand to my left.

From the far pen, Poplin lets out an impatient moan with a question mark at the end of it. She's next. Velvet is almost done. Poplin knows it, and she wants me to know it, too.

I snatch the empty grain dish out from under Velvet's snuffling nose, drop it under the milking stand, plop the next dish into the feed tub, unlatch the stanchion, and lead Velvet off the stand and back to her tether. Then three steps to the right, unsnap Poplin, let her go flying down the aisle, hard left into the milk room, hooves clattering onto the stand, me hot on her heels. And the cycle starts again.

Throughout all this hustle and bustle there has been another very appreciative audience. The cats have kept a pretty low profile throughout this story, but they've been here the whole time. Lounging in my lap, crouched on the desk, sprawled on the sofas, and skirmishing in the hallway. At the time of this writing there are eight of them. They purr and prowl their way through my life, as essential and special to me as the dogs, just not as flashy or portable.

The majority of them are black cats, most of them rescues. Some came to me almost feral, extremely skittish, and not at all used to being handled. It was a slow process to win them over and integrate them to the household. It took patience, persistence, and kindness.

Plus, a little creativity. There's Black Powder, for instance, a beautiful, athletic domestic shorthair adopted from the local animal shelter. Because of his upbringing in that sterile environment, Powder was not well socialized as a kitten. Socialization is just as critical to kittens as it is to puppies if you want a stable, well-adjusted pet. Powder didn't get it. He was raised behind glass. He interacted with many other kittens but with very few people.

When he came to me, he was wildly excited to be free of a cage. Curious, courteous, a smart and sensitive kitty. But never an outgoing personality, and definitely never a lap cat.

As he grew up, he became more and more aloof. By the time he was ten months old, I was finding it difficult to touch my own cat. And I'm sorry, but that's where I draw the line. If an animal lives with me, he has to be accessible. Independent and quirky is fine, but not standoffish, scared, or snooty.

In Powder's case, I think he didn't see the need for a bond with humans. He had been raised largely without them, after all. He had never been loved, handled, or played with. He had never experienced a home setting until he came here at about four months old. As long as they gave him food and shelter, people could come and go as they liked, and he was free to do the same.

Cats are often misunderstood and marginalized, especially by so-called "dog people." They are labeled as disinterested, self-serving, too independent, and maybe even nasty. But most of the time I think we humans fail to look deeper. We don't take the time or make the effort to attempt the understanding of a species that is quite unlike our own.

We humans are much more like dogs than we are like cats.

We are naturally social. We are very attached to our families, our friends, and our work. Most of us crave companionship and reward.

Cats are different. They are designed to be solitary creatures. They do not need a family group or a pack structure to thrive. They are patient hunters who find much more satisfaction in watching and waiting than we or our dogs ever will. They are natural control freaks who get out of whack if anything about their personal situation gets out of whack.

Put succinctly, they are complex. They take work and patience to understand. Cats are super smart and capable of great love and loyalty. They may not need me the same way my dogs do, and they may not relate to me the same way my dogs do. But to be loved and valued by an animal because the animal chooses to love and value me, not because it needs to do so, may be even more special than a relationship that is based squarely on need.

And then you meet a cat like Powder, who didn't see any reason to love or value the person he shared his home with. Sometimes dog principles really can apply to a cat. I decided to give it a try. The shortest way to Powder's heart, it turned out, was through his stomach.

Remember the work for food program? It works for cats just as well as it does for dogs. Powder has learned to do an impressive number of tricks to earn his kibble through the day. He comes when he's called, no matter where, no matter when. He speaks on command, waves, shakes hands, gives a high five, touches both front paws to my chest, spins in circles, jumps anywhere I indicate, and leaps onto my back when requested, and sometimes when not requested. We're currently working on playing pattycake.

Now Powder follows me everywhere—a long-legged, long-tailed, slender cat, sleek, black, and right where he belongs.

That includes tagging along with me out to the barn. Morning, evening, and any time in between, Powder is my regular barn buddy. He wouldn't miss a milking. He lurks in corners, or perches on the shelf, or more often than not, glides onto the milking stand like black satin to polish off any spatters of milk that might have landed there.

He does have competition. Bagheera and Lila, two other black cats, also often accompany me when it's time to milk. Bagheera, a young, boisterous Bombay, is something of a fair weather milker. He doesn't care for the cold, the rain, the snow, the mud, or anything else that isn't warm and comfortable.

But Lila has no such conpunctions. She knows no bounds. She minces through the mud of spring, braves the bluster of winter, and doesn't care about weather conditions in between. When she hears the clank of the milk pails heading for the barn, she rockets out the dog door in any weather to join me. She dashes into the milk room, waits for the goat to get up and for me to sit down, then glibly hops on the stand beside the filling milk pail. Powder hisses at her. She flips her tail in his face and darts to the other side of the pail. Minty, under whom the tiff is taking place, stomps at both of them and chomps her grain.

A dairy farm is a good place for a clowder of cats.

I love milking. Even though it takes some extra time, I hand milk all my goats rather than using any sort of milking machine or pump. I relish the chance to spend a little extra time with each doe, and to get to know her as an individual a little more completely. Each one has her own unique personality, characteristics, things she likes, and things she doesn't. Minty is sweet, tractable, and friendly, always obliging. Paisley is gentle and shy, intelligent and observant. Her sister, Poplin, is good-hearted and very vocal. Maybe not as vocal as Velvet, though, who always has an opinion or a comment, whatever the situation. She is solid and sociable, always happy to see me. And so it goes. Each one distinct, every one special.

And it isn't just the goats that are special. The practice of milking itself stretches back thousands of years. It's one of the first ways that humans and animals learned to cooperate with each other and share life together. When ancient peoples figured out that certain animals could be used for milk and not just for meat, a new kind of teamwork was born. It wasn't just about grabbing a bow and a spear and stalking prey through the savannahs anymore. Instead, a working, live-in relationship was developed, a mutual trust and respect into which two completely different species entered together.

And now all these millennia later, I'm doing the same thing, with virtually the same equipment, carrying on an eons-old tradition in the modern age. I think that's a special place to be.

Hunched there on my bucket, drinking in the smell of warm goats and fresh milk, listening to the frogs trilling down in the creek bottom and the meadowlarks fluting in the fields, I realize all over again how fortunate I am. The glory of the morning, the savor of life, the joy and privilege of relying on the lives of these animals entrusted to me—it all rises up in my soul. How many people get to experience this every single morning? And on a more personal note, how many blind people get to experience such freedom and fullness? There are some, but not many. I am one of a fortunate few, I think, as I turn the last doe loose and listen to the rich ringing of the bells in the high pasture grass.

For the first month or two, the lion's share of the milk goes to the kids. I strain it, pour it into the home pasteurizer on the kitchen counter, and heat it up to a scalding one hundred sixty-five degrees, then chill it down to measure into bottles later. But as kids grow up and are sold off, all that excess milk has to go somewhere. And that's when the fun begins.

I've learned to do a few things with milk. My first effort was the time-honored and very time-intensive process of making goat milk soap. Next, and much easier, there was thick Greek yogurt with unbelievable flavor, cream, and tang. Then came soft, mild Chévre cheese. Then paneer cheese and Mediterranean feta. I've learned to make kefir, Mexican horchata, cream cheese, and even hand lotion, all from the milk I harvest from my own goats.

Possibilities are just about endless when it comes to what a person can do with all that milk. Each spring I choose a few of the options that really catch my fancy and try something new. Learning to make some of the hard cheeses, like cheddar, and creating homemade ice cream and goat milk fudge are goals I hope to achieve next spring.

Milking my own goats has done me one more favor. To most people who can drive, shop, and generally do what they want to do when they want to do it, this will seem a small thing. But to me, it's one more step toward freedom—to realize that I will never run out of milk. I can always supply my own need. Sure, it would be simple enough to call up a friend or neighbor and pretty-please my way into a quick trip to the grocery store. There are folks who would do it for me, who have done it for me in the past. But that was before milking. Frankly, I don't like to beg. And now I don't have to. It's a small thing, yes, but the independence that milking has offered me looms large in my everyday life. If I ever get low on milk in the fridge, there are a few gallons of it walking around out in the pasture. And the goats are more than happy to volunteer their services.

Sometimes the greatest victories come in the smallest things.

CHAPTER 11

DUNDEE: DOG OF HEALING
GOLDENGREENE'S NOT DONE DREAMING

That winter was long and bitter. Heavy storms brought deep blankets of snow. Several rounds of ice moved through, turning the woods into fairy realms and the roads into treacherous glass. The snow dimmed into crust, and the sheets of ice on the gravel roads shattered into shards of dingy crystal. It dragged on and on, sunless day after vicious night. Nothing melted. More snow fell, drifted, crusted, and dirtied, hardening into cold and cankerous scabs over the dead fields.

Every once in a while, there would be a brief day of sunlight. Just enough to fan a flicker of hope that maybe winter's teeth would loosen their grip, if only just a little. Then, that evening, the wind would settle in the east, carding the woolly clouds into skeins and spools of gray, promising more ice.

December wore into January, a joyless Christmas and cheerless prospects for the New Year. Because as bitter and bad as the outdoor world might have been, the winter of my own heart was even more frigid and deadly that year.

I don't intend to delve into details, but the year of 2009 was one of the darkest in my life. Among other disasters, I lost four beloved dogs, all of them unexpectedly and all of them tragically. One of them in particular was my personal guide dog, an Australian shepherd named Mesa, who I had trained myself and who had also gone far with me in the obedience ring.

By the time I had laid her to rest, the third in the line of four losses, my eviscerated heart was finding it hard to get up again.

Added to these crushing blows were the failed attempts to bring in dogs in place of those who had departed. As dearly as I love my dogs, my philosophy has always been that the surest way to heal after losing one is to bring in a newcomer. It keeps me moving forward, keeps me fresh, and it helps me to honor the memory of the dog that is now beyond my reach by helping a dog who is not. However, that year I had tried three times with three different dogs, and none of them ended up working out. That sort of abysmal failure is also not typical of me. When I bring a new dog on board, I expect a few problems. There will be a couple bumps in the road before everybody is riding smoothly, and I'm okay with that. But these were big bumps, and my hope and determination had dwindled and grown small by then.

The last attempt was a wild, smooth-coated border collie who didn't even make it out of the vet's office before lunging ferociously at one of the clinic cats. Because the cat I had then was older, and because this dog had obviously never been around cats and couldn't be trusted with them, I was strongly advised to reconsider. I did, and the dog did not come home with me.

Besides the heart-stopping grief and numbing doubt overwhelming me, there was something else. It was my old enemy, fear, back in my face once again. Throughout that year, I had also had some nasty experiences with equally nasty dogs. I had been bitten badly enough to seek out medical attention. I didn't want to think that I had been scared worse, but I probably was. There had been another incident when one of my own dogs had been so stirred up by the neighbor's dogs that he had redirected his aggression toward me. A big dog with big aggression. If I can flash the victim card just for a minute, that is not a nice place to be when you're a blind, single woman, off on your own out in the country.

I hate to admit it even now, but I was afraid. I had, in fact, reached the point where I was becoming afraid of my own dogs. The two remaining dogs I had left, that is.

So when things fell through with that cat-aggressive border collie, I just about fell through myself. I have a hazy and humiliating memory of dialing my dad's number to let him know he didn't have to pick her up from the vet clinic where the incident had occurred. I remember breaking down in gut-wrenching sobs as I told the story.

"I don't know what to do," I gasped into the phone, clutching the receiver with one hand and pawing for a tissue with the other. "But I have to move on from this. I can't do this anymore. And maybe I've been doing things wrong after all." I sniffed, hiccupped, and took a deep, shuddering breath before forging ahead. I needed to tell someone. "Maybe I should just get another Aussie, you know? And maybe instead of an adult rescue—maybe I should just start over and get a puppy."

My dad muttered something unintelligible, confirmed that he did not have to collect the border collie, and got off the phone as quickly as possible. I didn't care. A timid shred of fortitude had seeded itself in my soul. It was a strangely unfamiliar feeling, that fortitude, and I clung to it. I do best with a game plan. And now, as tenuous as it might have been, I had one.

So, tiny shred of fortitude and a few larger shreds of optimism firmly in hand, I did something else that I'd never done before. I pulled up that morning's online edition of the Topeka newspaper and began sifting through the classified ads.

Always before when searching for a new dog, I had gone to the humane society, or through a rescue group, or a breeder.

Occasionally I had discovered a dog in need via word of mouth. At this point, I hadn't even encountered Craigslist yet. Combing the classifieds was new for me.

And there it was. A little blip t-boned between an ad for the local carwash and another ad for one of the first garage sales of the season.

"Australian shepherd puppies. Three months old. Dewormed and puppy shots. Call for more information."

I picked up the phone and called.

The next morning I was in the car, riding west toward a little town about an hour and a half away. There were two puppies left, the very nice lady who talked to me had said. Both boys, raised by her three daughters who sporadically bred litters of Aussies and border collies for their 4H projects. And more than likely, I would make the return trip today with one of those puppies. A small, plastic crate, cozied up with a towel at the bottom, jangled in the back of the car. I was nervous and excited and worried all at the same time. But I had a feeling about this puppy. This was right. This was my way forward, my way out of the darkness. It was time for spring. It was time for healing.

The March skies were high and blue, and the wind was in the south. The dull rimes of ice clinging to the north sides of buildings and barns were disappearing. The driveway, when we pulled off the road and headed toward the farmhouse where the puppies lived, was a morass of deep, chocolate mud. I caught the high whistle of a meadowlark as I stepped out of the car.

My driver and I introduced ourselves to the family, then trooped around to the back of the house to meet the really important individuals. The two youngest girls went dashing off to let out the puppies. Gate open, a flurry of fur and slush, and they came trundling right to me. Rolly-polly, button ears, big feet, and bob tails. I got down in the grass, paying no mind to how it squished or to the cold wet of melting mud seeping through my jeans. I hadn't held a puppy for a long time.

One was the traditional blue merryl color for which Aussies are best known. A black base color with mottled streaks and splashes of silver marbled through it. Blue merl is eye-catching and unique, and as ambivalent about color as I've always been, still the striking pattern appealed to me. The other puppy was jet black with tan highlights splashed on to his cheeks and legs.

They were both friendly, active, and adorable. They lapped at my nose and my hands, their fluffy puppy coats so soft and their baby-boy grins so contagious that I couldn't stop grinning myself.

We stood around for a good half hour, chatting, and chuckling at their antics. And I tried to decide. The blue merl slowly edged to the high end of my list. I loved the novelty of such a stunning and uniquely Aussie color. He was outgoing, active, smart. I could readily imagine that one growing up to be an obedience dog, a rally dog, or any other kind of competition dog I might train him to be.

The black-and-tan puppy waddled over, sat down right at my feet, tipped back his chin and gazed up. He had done that same thing several times over the last half hour. He was calmer than his brother, still chock full of puppy energy, but without the hyperactive spaz of the blue merl.

"Whenever there's a puppy fight, that one always ends up on the bottom," the oldest daughter told me.

Well, in my opinion that wasn't a bad thing. I have never been drawn to dominant males. And especially now, after the fears and failures of the last year, I did not need an alpha personality in the house. I needed a gentle, dependable, happy soul that could bring my own soul back to a state of gentleness and happiness.

I rubbed the black puppy's chest and thought about it. He keeled over onto his back, his paws paddling the air and his butt wiggling as he tried to keep wagging his nubby tail, even on the damp ground. His blue brother came by and began busily untying my left shoelace.

"The black one will be very attached to one person," the oldest daughter said. She was twelve or so, a quiet, confident kid, the kind who does well with horses, and with dogs. She knew these puppies, and I realized I would do well to listen to her. "The merl will like everybody," she said. "I mean, the black one will like people, too. But he'll really like especially one person and be very bonded to that person for the rest of his life."

It wasn't really a contest after that.

As I bundled the black-and-tan baby into his crate for the ride home, the mother of the three girls told me they had gotten a phone call the day before from somebody else who wanted to purchase a puppy.

"He was planning to get here a couple hours before you did today," she said, handing me the paperwork that went home with my new boy. "But he never showed up. I guess God wanted you to have first pick."

I guess He did. And it was a good pick, too, perhaps one of the best I've made over the years.

Dundee settled in just like it was meant to be. He knew his name immediately. He was an easy, mild-mannered puppy, eager to meet new people and new dogs but, as had been predicted by the oldest daughter in his first family, he gave his heart and soul to me. He didn't do it rashly or recklessly, but with calm trust and gentle devotion. The gentle, dependable, and happy soul that my own soul needed so desperately had, in fact, come to live with me.

The healing that Dundee brought to me really began the first hour I met him. But it was a slow process. In some ways, I have never quite recovered from the shattering blows dealt to me in that horrible year. There were some dark moments, especially in the first three or four months that Dundee lived with me, times when the fear and pent-up rage bottled up inside me threatened to blaze up and scorch us both.

One occasion occurred just a couple of weeks after he had come home. I had taken one of my other dogs to an area obedience trial. I can't recall now how we had fared in the competition but judging by my crabby disposition when I got back home, we probably hadn't fared well. I slouched into the house, shoving the door closed behind me with unnecessary force. Dundee and Storme, the two dogs who had been left at home, jostled and waggled behind the safe gate relegating them to the laundry room and back yard. Still grumpy, I propped the gate open and began dismantling it from the laundry room doorway.

Dundee, happy to see me after all those hours, shimmied up to me, wiggling his bottom and butting his silky head into my hands. He shoved himself against my legs, squealing and yodeling with that obnoxious Aussie whine. He was under my feet and he was hurting my ears. And all of a sudden, I was furious. Mesa, the amber-eyed, blue merl Aussie that I had lost only a few short months before, should have been with me at this dog show. She would have done well. She always did well. She was intelligent, intuitive, loyal, loving, and very competitive in the performance ring. Or at least she had been. Before she was so brutally and unfairly ripped away from me. Mesa had been a true Australian shepherd. Poised, athletic, and with tons of drive and work ethic. Not like this stupid, stumbling, bumbling baby.

"You little brat!" I snarled at him. "You don't even belong here! Who do you think you are? Oh wait, I forgot—you don't think at all. You're just a stupid, pathetic, blundering baby, and you'll never be even a quarter of the dog that Mesa ever was. Just get out of my way!"

I chased him and both older dogs out the dog door, slammed the flap down to keep it closed, and wrestled my grief into submission. My heart burned with the rawness and rancor of the past year, and my eyes burned with unshed tears. I knew I was not only being unreasonable, I was being cruel. I knew that just because life had been unfair to me, that did not entitle me to be unfair to Dundee. Of course Dundee would never replace Mesa. Nobody ever would. He wasn't Mesa and he wasn't supposed to be. He was sweet and eager and devoted Dundee. And even then I knew that he had more soul than his predecessor ever had. But in that moment I hated him. I hated the upside down injustice of life. And most of all, I hated myself.

Gradually I got a grip. I kept the dogs out for another half hour or so, then opened the dog door and let them come stampeding in. I sat on the floor with Dundee and let him love me and promised that I would try to love him better, too.

That was the worst moment. But there were other episodes when the shadow of the dark year still cast its pall over our interactions. One afternoon I had Dundee out in the yard, relaxing after a short training session. He flopped down beside me as I sat on the ground. He wanted a belly rub and was completely calm and docile. But out of the blue, the anxiety that had settled on me in that last year pinned me down. The random fear that he might snap at me reared its ugly head. It was ridiculous, absolutely irrational and silly, and I knew it. But the aggression and bites and mistakes of the year before still loomed on the horizon. They eclipsed the innocent sweetness of even this steady puppy, if only briefly. I had to sit back, take a deep breath, and mentally hit my reset button. I kept rubbing Dundee's tummy. And I stayed there an extra few minutes.

Sometimes when I was having a really bad day, Dundee's nearness would just grate on my nerves. I have never appreciated being sought out and fawned over. Perhaps odd for a person who enjoys dogs as much as I do. If I initiate the interaction I'm fine with a dog being lovey and demonstrative. And if the dog is respectful and polite, I don't have a problem with that dog soliciting attention. It's what dogs do. But on even my best days, I'm not partial to being forced into giving attention. Jumping, pawing, and climbing uninvited into my lap don't go over well.

On my nasty days, I don't even appreciate a dog following me around the house and pressing up against me.

Back in that dark and meaningless time, I had a lot of nasty days. And that was what Dundee did. He has always been a dog who is nearby but never underfoot. He's almost always with me but almost never in the way. In that first year of our life together, when the wounds of the year before were still festering and unhealed, his constant presence just plain annoyed me.

I know it doesn't make sense and looking back it seems obvious that he was responding to my need in the only way he knew how. Being the sensitive and intuitive dog that he is, he felt my pain and my lostness, and his natural Aussie response was to press in and comfort me with his physical presence.

But I was bruised, hurting, and resentful. I shied away from him. Dundee's insistence on being near me, gentle though it was, weighed on me. I felt trapped by his loyalty. His constant concern for me was easy to interpret as parasitic dependence upon me, and my scarred and weakened heart despised him as being weak himself. His anxiety when I was away made me want to stay away a little longer. It was becoming a "he may need me but I sure as heck don't need him" kind of mentality.

After all, I am an alpha female. I don't need anyone. I don't need anyone to follow me around, to monitor my movements, supervise my sit-down time, or generally think that he owns me. I do not, in effect, need to be needed.

And yet, of course, I did. I needed the routine of exercise, simple training, and out-and-about socialization that a puppy offered. I needed to learn all over again how to be patient, how to be kind, how to trust. I needed to learn how to love again, and I needed to learn how to be loved myself. I needed to let my weakness be turned into strength.

And little by little, as the months slipped by and became a year, and then became two years, it began to happen. Dundee transported his sweet constancy and loving-life sparkle into everything we did together. As a puppy, back in the darkest days when I was trying to get comfortable with a dog again, I had spent time with him playing fetch almost every day. Starting on a long line, I taught him to reliably return any kind of toy to me. Before long, he became one of the most eager and solid retrievers I've ever had. I taught him to sit, to lie down, to come when called no matter where we were, to stay in one position and place even when I was out of sight. He learned to spin in circles, to back up, to jump over high, bar, and broad jumps. He learned hand signals, and he learned how to behave in public. For a while, thinking that he might actually take Mesa's place and become a second guide dog for me, I took him everywhere with me. Wearing a service dog vest, he could go into supermarkets, restaurants, movie theaters, and meetings and always be relied upon to be quiet, calm, and do whatever I asked.

It happened so gradually that I did not realize for a long time how proud I really was of this young dog. I had brought him a long way. I had taught him a great deal. It would be many years before I understood what a long way he had brought me and how much he had really taught me.

Dundee was two years old when I put him in his first obedience trials. My preference is to wait until a dog is at least that age before showing him in obedience. Showing is hard mental work for a dog, even for one who thoroughly enjoys it, and that's especially true of a very young dog. So I let mine take their time before throwing them into the stress and pressure of the show ring. We work on stuff at home or at practice shows; the dog gets lots of social outings, and experiences as much of the real world as I can manage. But the show ring is off limits until that magical second birthday.

And then, if he is confident and socialized and mature enough—then I decide he's ready.

Dundee was ready. He earned his Novice Obedience title easily, qualifying three trials in a row. And that was just in one weekend. We came in Saturday morning with nothing—no ring experience, no titles, no real working relationship. We went home Sunday afternoon with a Companion Dog title behind Dundee's name and a newly forged bond that can be acquired only by working together in the ring.

We turned some heads, too. One lady from the training club came up to me and told me how glad she was to see me back in competition. "Everyone at the club knew what a rough year you'd had," she said, "and it's so good to see you back and showing again, especially with another Aussie," she added as Dundee wiggled and whimpered for recognition beside me. "I think he's a keeper."

By the close of that weekend, my heart was finally starting to open. I was beginning to trust this steady, dependable dog.

Of the dogs that currently live with me, Dundee was the first to arrive. He's been with me the longest and has brought me through the most. In a way, my life when he waggled into it was much like that first obedience trial. I joined up with him having almost nothing. Just deep depression, blossoming fears, and horrible memories. But as we went forward together, day by day and year by year, I regained strength and steadiness. At the beginning of the relationship I worried that my own dogs would prove untrustworthy and perhaps even hurt me somehow. Today I am the stable and confident leader of a group of ten dogs, all of whom I can trust and depend upon. None of us is perfect, but then, isn't that the point? We work together, strengthen each other, and maybe even become a little better thanks to any mistakes in the process.

It's obvious that this sweet boy has helped me tremendously in the psychological sense. But he is also on standby every day to tangibly help me in any way he can. As I said earlier, I had originally formed a tentative plan that Dundee might serve as a second guide dog for me. Despite the potential he showed for that type of training, I opted not to do it for several reasons. The main one was lack of need. Given the job I was working back then and the farm life style I've maintained since then, a guide dog just wasn't necessary. I had no busy hallways or crowded lunch rooms to navigate; I didn't need to catch the city bus or attend business meetings or crisscross a college campus. My environments both at work and at home were familiar and low-traffic.

So I satisfied both myself and Dundee with our long walks and our competition training.

However, along the way he developed a skill which has proved invaluable to me. Eager and dependable retriever that he is, Dundee has become the dog I turn to if I require help finding any kind of item that I've dropped. He will pick up anything, even tough stuff. Keys, sheets of paper, business cards, plastic bags. He will carefully scoop up fallen utensils, bouncing bottle caps, or mislaid leashes. He can retrieve full water bottles, quite a feat since they are heavy and unwieldy for a soft-mouthed dog to handle. There have been numerous times that he has found and returned gloves which I've inadvertently dropped along the road on our walks. He can even pick up and return the five-foot-long longe whip I sometimes carry on the road. Because of its length and unusually thin shape, the whip is another item that's not easy for most dogs to wrangle.

He isn't grabby or mouthy about it, either. He waits for instructions. If I drop something, he lets me hunt for it, then comes happily in to help when I call him. "Dundee, get it! Pick it up, buddy, get it!" And he does. Gentle and respectful as always, he will gingerly snag whatever the object is, then bring it close to my hand so I can find it. Or if it's a larger, more cumbersome item, he will brush it against my legs so I know he's got it and I can take it from him.

The remarkable thing about his retrieving is the perception he seems to have about exactly what I need him to get. If we're on the road and I drop a glove or a leash and am not quite sure where to tell him to look, he seems to just figure it out. Usually the search is within fifty feet of where the object was dropped, so it's not like he's covering miles trying to locate my stuff. But on a road which can have an empty soda can in the ditch, a fast-food wrapper farther down, a couple of hedge apples along the opposite side, and any number of scattered sticks and rocks, he still finds and returns the correct item.

The same applies in the house. Even though he could target a rug on the floor, a folded newspaper, a sock dropped in the laundry room, and a plethora of chew hooves, if something hits the floor and he knows I'm looking for it, that's the object he returns to me.

An example is when I was teaching him an obedience exercise called a go-out. This is an advanced exercise in the utility class which requires the dog to leave the handler's side and run across the entire ring, straight down the middle. There are a thousand ways to train go-outs, but they all focus on teaching the dog to mark and run to a specific target. At that time, I was using a hula hoop as Dundee's target. This isn't a technique I use anymore, but since he and I were both just starting in utility, the hula hoop was a good, solid target for us to begin with. It was easy for him to see, and because the dog is supposed to sit when he reaches the other side of the ring after leaving the handler, a hula hoop was just the right size that Dundee could sit in its circle.

The day before we had been training with the hoop. It was only the first or second time I'd had it out and introduced him to it. At the end of the training session I had walked away and left the hoop somewhere along the yard fence, probably distracted by throwing Dundee's toy as a well-earned reward.

Now a day later, I couldn't find the hoop. I searched and searched, back and forth along that fence, dragging my feet through the grass attempting to catch it with my toes, and trying to recall exactly where I'd placed it. No luck. Heaving a sigh, I finally turned to Dundee, who was hovering a few feet away and no doubt wondering what his strange human's problem was this time.

"Dundee!" I said, an undeniably whiny note creeping into my voice. "Where's your. . ." And then I faltered, not sure what word to use for a hula hoop that he had only seen a few times before this.

He came up beside me, glancing up at me with worry and questions in his eyes. He knew I was looking for something, and he was willing to help if I could just give him a clue. He shoved his soft head under my hand and panted.

Finally I asked the only question I could come up with that I thought he might understand. "Dundee, run!" I told him, using the command for a go-out. "Where's your run? Can you get it? Where's your run? Dundee, where's your run?"

He put his head down, hunting, searching, and I began shuffling along the fence again, hoping to catch the hoop with my feet. Then I heard him coming up behind me. He was hauling something in his mouth, rolling it along in front of him, attempting to figure how to carry a circular plastic hula hoop without stepping through it and tripping himself.

Another day we were trotting along the road, when I somehow managed the brilliant maneuver of dropping the bag of sausage I was using for treats. Jamming stuff back into the bait bag around my waist, I nicked the sausage baggie just right so that it flipped away to land somewhere on the gravel behind me. It took me a few seconds to comprehend that it was missing.

Then. . .*great*. Now how was I supposed to find my treats, or reward the dogs for coming to me throughout the remainder of the walk if I couldn't find the treats?

It was a longshot, but I tried it anyway.

"Dundee!" I called. "Dundee, get it! Get it!"

He bounded up beside me, understood which direction he was supposed to go, put his head down and began to search. He found it, too. Maybe finding a baggie half full of Vienna sausage wasn't a class act for a dog. But returning it to me was. Okay, he returned most of it. He did have to pause occasionally and sample the merchandise along the way. But he brought the baggie back to me, and a good portion of sausage was still in it.

The best story, though, I am still not sure how to explain.

It happened one afternoon when I needed to go up to the hay shed and retrieve a couple bales of brome. It wasn't a job I could conveniently do wearing my casual, slip-on shoes, so I went back to the closet for my hiking boots. And they weren't there.

In fact, I couldn't find them anywhere. I searched and searched, all through my bedroom, all through the entire house. I could not find them. Under the computer desk, under the kitchen table, beside the couch. Nothing. In the laundry room, the utility room, even the unlikely bathroom, and then, for lack of a better plan, back to the bedroom to begin the whole fruitless hunt all over again. No boots. Not anywhere.

I began getting suspicious. Surely none of the dogs had been bratty enough to haul both of my heavy boots out the dog door. It seemed doubtful. The dogs were all old enough and reliable enough not to pull that kind of prank. But I still wasn't finding those boots, and I was beginning to be annoyed. Getting that hay was not an option. It needed to be done, and I wasn't going to walk all the way to the hay shed, dragging the wagon behind me, in either my flimsy slip-ons or my rubber muck boots. I needed those hiking boots. So I began the search again.

I was ducking under the kitchen table for the third or fourth time when I heard a thud behind me. I turned just in time to catch Dundee heaving one hiking boot up in his mouth. He was headed my way. The boot was heavy and awkward, though, so he bobbled it. It hit the carpet with a thud.

Stunned, I scooped it up and stashed it back in the closet where it belonged. And then, of course, I asked Dundee where the other one was.

He brought it right to me. To this day, I'm not certain where he found those boots. And I'm still not certain exactly how he found them. Throughout the entire search, I had never said anything to any of the dogs. I had been quiet about it, only occasionally sighing and muttering. The dogs don't know the word "shoes" or "boots." It wasn't the time we usually go for our daily walk, and therefore, it wasn't the time I usually put on my boots. Throughout the entire search, Dundee had been relaxed and had seemed disinterested.

But somehow he had known. He had known precisely what I was searching for, he had known where the boots were, and he had known without being told that I needed him to bring them to me. It's one of the most amazing things I have ever seen a dog do.

And as Dundee has done in the little things every day, so he has done in the larger things throughout the years. He wants to be near me. He wants to help me. Whether that means finding stuff I've dropped, doing those go-outs in the obedience ring, watching out for me on walks, or even nudging me forward along the darker walk of life, he wants to help in whatever way he can. And in so many ways, he already has.

CHAPTER 12

DOG SHOWS: STRENGTHENING THE BOND

I have always been fascinated by what dogs can learn. The things they can figure out on their own are impressive enough. But what has really captivated me throughout most of my life is what we as humans can teach them to do. There are service dogs who can learn to open a door for someone in a wheelchair, flip on the light switch, pull off the person's shoes and socks, and then retrieve the TV remote control. There are search dogs who can riffle through the myriad of scents in sixty acres of wilderness and locate a missing child. There are trick dogs who can, on command, tug open the refrigerator door and carry a cold drink back to their owners lounging on the couch.

All kinds of skills and behaviors. All kinds of dogs. Some things we teach them are life-and-death serious, and some are just plain goofy. But the bottom line is—if we can figure out a way to teach a certain trick or trade—dogs can figure out a way to learn it.

They are amazing.

It wasn't until I was a teenager, self-conscious and painfully shy, that I took my first decisive step into the world of dog training.

Naturally I didn't do it alone. Right there beside me, or more accurately, way out in front of me, straining at the end of her leash and hauling me pretty much wherever she wanted to go, was Nikki.

Adopted from the humane society when I was eleven years old, Nikki would remain with me throughout my teenage years. She was half German shepherd and half Siberian husky. She was an adult when we got her, and she had very little knowledge of the outside world. She also had almost no manners. She was a medium-sized dog, but she toted a barrel chest and all the proud pulling heritage of her Siberian forbears.

To compound the problem, Nikki was also grossly overweight. When we met her, the poor dog waddled on to the scale at ninety-eight pounds, about double what she should have weighed.

She was dog aggressive. I recall one occasion when we put her on a tie-out chain, attached to a porch post, and the neighbors happened to walk their German shepherd past our front yard. Nikki shot to her feet, dug in, and went after him. The porch post snapped like kindling at the impact.

She was cat aggressive. Our cat survived most likely because Nikki was so often chained and the cat could scamper out of reach. But she tried to kill him more than once.

She was domineering and demanding; jumping up, licking, stealing food, and every once in a while, humping our legs. She had no concept of what it meant to come when she was called. In fact, she delighted in escaping. She would slip her collar, break her tie-out chain (or any unsuspecting porch post to which it might have been attached), charge through a screen door (the door still being latched, in case you didn't catch that), and later, when we moved to a house with a fenced yard, analyze the fence until she could puzzle out a way to slither free. She would then joyously run the neighborhood.

She bulled into life with a constant smile, a wagging tail and the heart of a lion. She was my solid rock through two cross-country moves and the resulting emotional roller coaster of new schools and no friends.

Because I was everything that Nikki was not. Timid, shy, oversensitive, and unsocial. I stayed in the background, quiet and unobtrusive, and I dreaded any task or interaction that might focus attention on me. I was studious and meticulous about school work, homework, music lessons, and memorization. I was terrified to meet new people and had no idea how to carry on a conversation.

Still, there was one thing Nikki and I did have in common. We were both strong-willed. When we set our hearts on something, we would end up getting it one way or another.

So it was that—when Nikki wedged her portly paunch through yet another gap under the back yard fence, kept right on running even as we shouted for her to come back, and attacked another neighbor dog—I put my foot down. I had just about had enough.

"This dog," I announced to my slightly bewildered mom and dad, "is going to obedience class."

That was how it began. At first it was just the basics. Walking on a loose leash, coming when called, staying in a specific place and position. But I saw the results. And I lived with the results. Gradually, Nikki became a dog who was calmer, more respectful, and more dependable. Within a couple of years, she was living with two other dogs, a few additional cats, and she was totally reliable off leash.

But there was more. She chose me to be her person. She enjoyed all the other members of the family and always had a kiss and a smile for everyone. But there was something special between the two of us. It was my first tantalizing taste of the depth of friendship, of partnership, that can develop between a dog and a person who work together.

I was hooked.

A handful of years later, I happened across an audio book that would literally change my life. It was a Susan Conant murder mystery. I can't recall much about the plot, the suspects, or the perpetrator. But I remember with total clarity that it revolved around dogs and the world of sports and activities in which they could participate. It was through that book that I learned about the different levels of competition obedience, and the obedience titles which a dog and handler team can earn.

I made up my mind to be one of those handlers.

Nikki was gone by then, but Chai, the cunning, grinning American Eskimo, had just joined the family. Eskies aren't exactly the premier breed for obedience competition. A typical Nordic dog, they have plenty of brain power—clever, quick, and easy to teach. They are also independent and easily distracted. That makes it a bit challenging to get serious with them in obedience, given the intense focus the sport demands. But you gotta start somewhere.

I put a Canine Good Citizen title on Chai, then a Companion Dog title, and then we got our feet wet in rally competition.

And it just snowballed from there. Quite a few dogs and quite a few titles later, the joy and the thrill of working with dogs, of teaching dogs, of encountering them in their own strengths and weaknesses and unique personalities, have never left me. In fact, as I have learned more and become a more proficient trainer and handler over the years, the joy has only increased.

There have been occasions when people have watched me work with my dogs in the ring, and then have cornered me afterward with the same basic question. *How,* they inquire, gazing with perplexed sincerity first at me and then at the dog beside me, *how do you do it?*

After the first time I figured out what they meant. They

weren't asking how to train a dog. Not how to teach a dog to heel off lead, or to respond to hand signals from thirty feet away, or retrieve a dumbbell both directions over a jump. What they're really asking is not a question of method or training technique. What they really want to know is: how can I do any of that stuff without being able to see?

I hate to disappoint you, but I don't really have a straightforward answer. If I want to be flippant about it, I fling out my favorite mantra, "Where there's a will, there's a way." And to a certain extent that's true. If you want something badly enough, you'll figure out a way to get it.

Take rally, for example.

Rally is visual. It's a series of consecutive exercises, mostly done while heeling, where the dog and handler walk through a designated course. The course is mapped out before the class, and the handler works through it by following printed and numbered signs. There are about fifteen signs on each rally course, and the handler has to take them in numerical order. Obviously, that's all a little tough to do when you can't read the map or the signs and have no idea how to stay on the course.

It can be interesting for me doing a rally class. We've come up with several strategies. Sometimes my dad, faithful to the end, will walk with me in the ring, calling out the signs to me. Sometimes one of the ring stewards is okay doing it. And every so often the judge will actually jump in and agree to read the signs so that no one else has to worry about it. As long as someone is willing to do the reading, I handle the dog and keep us both on course.

But there you go. Rally is a nice sport to get obedience dogs involved with because it's a little more relaxed and less formal than the more intense obedience ring. I can encourage the dog, repeat commands if needed, praise constantly, and even redo exercises if any of us makes a mistake. It gives the dog confidence and ring experience. It's especially helpful in proofing a dog for off lead heeling. For all those reasons I wanted to do rally. And I do it. But it did take some innovation.

It has also taken humility and courage. At the beginning, it wasn't easy for me to walk up to a professional judge, a total stranger with lots of clout and authority, introduce myself and say that I would need some help. Even today it isn't easy. But I've learned. I think of the dog beside me and how far we've come together, and how far we still have to go. And at every single show, whether it's a rally trial or an obedience trial, I walk up to the judge, offer a friendly smile and a firm handshake and say, "Hi, I'm entered in your next class, and I'm blind, so we'll have to be a little bit creative."

On the surface it's rally, with its printed signs and numerical order, that appears to be the most challenging sport we participate in. But as I've said, rally is actually the easy one. There's wiggle room in rally, both for the dog and for me. It's the competitive focus and formal precision of the obedience ring that can be daunting. I've had to be creative in obedience, too, and much more determined and implacable than I've had to be in rally trials.

First there's the bell collar. AKC regulations strictly prohibit anything dangling from a dog's collar. When a dog is in the ring, it needs to wear either a chain collar or a flat, buckle collar. No tags or bells attached. The reason for this is mostly safety-based. Accidents do happen. It is possible for a dangling tag to get snagged on a jump or something else, with nasty consequences. Jingling tags and clanging bells can also be distracting to other working dogs. Plus, with all the retrieves and jumps that an obedience dog is required to do, dangles just plain get in the way.

The problem for me is that, without tags or bells, my dogs virtually disappear. I know each of my ten dogs by sound. Behavior and habits play into it, of course, but no two dogs have the same jingle. I know them by their tags, by their feet, even by the way they lap water. When I'm in the ring with one of them, it's doubly important that I know where the dog is and what the dog is doing. When I ask for a jump I need to know the dog has jumped. When I give a "stay" command I need to know that the dog is not moving. And the issue was: without dangles on the dog, how was I going to know any of those things?

The solution I concocted was to take a regular buckle collar and sew small and very lively jingle bells around it. They don't hang or dangle. They're studded along the length of the collar, just two or three bells to prevent them from being too loud. They don't snag on anything, but they ring freely enough when the dog moves that I almost always know what's going on.

With the bell collar, I could take my dogs into the ring and have a pretty good idea whether or not they were with me. But there were still the challenges of navigating the ring and each of its complex exercises.

It's in the utility ring that I've had to be the most creative. Utility is the most advanced level in obedience. Its hallmark is that the dog has options in each exercise. Multiple hand signals, not just one. Two jumps, and not just one. The directed retrieve involves three gloves, only one of which the dog is commanded to fetch. And there's scent discrimination, which requires the dog to find and return only one article out of a pile of ten. It should be easy to see why the class has been dubbed "futility" by exasperated and discouraged competitors.

A sightless handler negotiating this world of hand signals and extra equipment is, to put it tactfully, a challenge.

The great thing about dog people, though, is that most of them aren't put off by a good challenge. Obedience people in particular are usually smart, motivated, and determined. Yes, we can also be competitive, nit-picky, and perfectionistic. But underneath that veneer is the drive to succeed, and it usually translates into wanting others to succeed as well. Obedience people know how to praise, how to cheerlead, and how to encourage. We know how to think outside the box.

The signal exercise in the utility class presents an especially unique challenge. No verbals are allowed in this exercise, either from the handler to the dog or, more importantly in my case, from the judge to the handler. All commands are given only via hand signal. Of course, I have no clue when the judge is signaling me to signal my dog, and to ask the judge for a verbal command would compromise the integrity of the entire exercise. So the solution I invented was to have a ring steward stand directly behind me and tap me on the shoulder whenever the judge signals. Judge signals a down, steward taps me on the shoulder, I signal the dog to lie down. Same for the sit, the recall, and the finish. And exercise finished, and hopefully the dog has cooperated and we qualified.

We make the same modification on the go-out exercise. The ring steward once again hovers behind me and drops a tap on my shoulder at the moment I'm supposed to tell my dog to stop and sit. And on the figure-eight exercise, where the dog and I do a heeling pattern around two people standing eight feet apart, each of the people is allowed to talk so that I know where each person is. As soon as the dog and I step forward to start the pattern, the soft murmur of "post, post, post" begins, each human figure-eight post reminding me where they are as we circle each of them in turn.

So much for the ring exercises. But no chapter about training and showing my dogs would be complete if I left out one of the key characters. Always on call, always game, always ready for orders, and almost always patient about it. Dependable driver, even at six in the morning. Willing dog walker, even when it means fishing one of those fateful baggies out of a pants pocket and doing you-know-what with it. In a word: my dad.

He is not a dog person. He's not really even an animal person, although if he had to choose it would be cats. But he goes along with it. Technically, I suppose it's better to say that I go along with him. He gets us to the shows, gets me to the right ring, helps me check in, keeps tabs on which classes are competing and how many dogs still have to show before mine. He lugs crates from van to building and then back from building to van. He hunts down and eyeballs areas for each dog and I to warm up. His weekends are more flexible than my mom's, and he doesn't mind driving my mammoth tank of a cargo van. And so away we go.

"Do you have any dog stuff this weekend?" delivered in a morose and taciturn tone of voice, laced with a heavy dose of despair. If he remembers, he asks me this most Thursdays. Or sometimes Fridays, Saturday being a fairly regular day to commute to a show.

He puts up with a lot. Early hours, miles of boring Midwestern roads, my stress and demands, and usually hauling four or five dogs, none of which he's crazy about. I'm not going to speculate as to his motives. Maybe deep down he secretly does enjoy the chance to break out of his own routine and do something different. Possibly he does like watching his little girl accomplish a few things with those mutts of hers. I personally suspect that it's a bit more basic than that. . ."She sent in those entry fees, after all, and that's a lot of money, and who else is gonna get her to the silly show, anyway?" Duty calls, and Daddy is there.

But whichever approach he's taking, the dogs and I all appreciate it. Without his help, we would all quite simply be stuck at home. So, Dad, whether you truly do enjoy the trips or whether you're just doing it because you have to—from me and the pack—thanks.

And now back to the original question. How do I do it? As to the nuts and bolts of how I as a blind handler can compete in the ring, I've just shared the major secrets. Be determined, creative, and whip up the right mixture of confidence and humility before stepping through the gate and onto the matting.

But there is a little more to it than that. How do I do it all the time? At home, in the front yard, in the living room, and at different training locations? To know that a dog is sitting when I ask, to be sure that he actually does lie down when given the hand signal to do so, to teach him to take a jump or pick up a glove from a good distance away. And doing all that without sight, before even getting anywhere near the performance ring. I think, at the heart of it, this is what those curious questioners really want to know: how do I do any training at all?

I'll sum up the answer in two words: repetition and relationship. First of all, I don't rush when I train a dog. And I'm never afraid to go back and retrain something to clarify it. So we start small, with short distances and low jumps. This arrangement is as much for me as it is for the dog. If he's right next to me or only a few feet in front, I can tell if he jumps, breaks a stay, or picks up a dumbbell. And if he doesn't, I'm right there to step in and fix it. We work hand-in-hand, as you might say, until the dog is understanding the task. Then I ask for a little more, move a little farther from the jump, or toss the dumbbell with a little more distance.

Repetition. Not drilling a dog, demanding the same action over and over until he's even more sick of it than I am. But requiring and rewarding the same skill day by day, until he gets it and I know he's reliable. I don't stand ten feet away on the signal exercise until I'm sure the dog is reliable at five feet away. And even then, I'll increase the distance incrementally, to seven feet, then to eight, then to ten. If I've been careful and consistent and haven't fast-tracked the training, eventually I'm standing thirty to forty feet away with the dog's attention riveted on me, lying down, sitting, racing across the ring to me, and then jumping back into heel position at each of my hand signals.

Repetition. The dog knows what I'm asking and knows that I expect it. Because I do check. Every time. I am fairly convinced that most of my animals, and certainly all of the dogs, know in a basic sense that I can't see. They may not know it logically, in stone-cold fact, but they comprehend that I'm not like other humans. I don't make eye contact. I don't always know where they are, even if they're two feet away from me. I have to touch them after giving a command and before praising them for doing it right. I think they know. But they also know that I'm not weak. I expect them to do as I ask, and if they blow me off I will dart in to correct it. I would never stoop as low as the harsh domination and abusive corrections of old-school obedience. There is never a time or a place for that kind of nonsense. Instead I am fair and firm. When I ask a dog to do something I mean it, and I can and will make it happen. But we can still have fun in the process.

Perhaps even more important than repetition is the bedrock relationship I have with each of my working dogs. We know each other. We have an understanding. We're in this thing together, and we find joy in each other's company. It's something special to work this closely with a dog—with multiple dogs—to learn each other's minds and hearts. It's more than a student-teacher or a master-servant rapport. We are allies and partners. We are good friends. In fact, we love each other.

And it's a good thing, too, because after all that warm-and-fuzzy stuff, the truth is that my dogs have to tolerate a lot from me. I don't even know the half of it, and if I did, no doubt I would stand amazed at their patience, perception, and good humor. Try as I might, jumps are still set up at crooked angles. There are times when I inadvertently point to the wrong glove or gesture to the wrong jump, or can't find the article that I expect the dog to find. Yeah, how does that work again? There are times when a dog makes a mistake and is rewarded anyway, since I can't always tell if they sit on a go-out or dodge around a jump, or if one of them steps in between the boards of the broad jump rather than sailing over it high and clean. So occasionally a dog is rewarded for the wrong behavior as the right behavior, which naturally leads to confusion the next time he does it wrong and gets corrected for it.

My sweet, stalwart babies. They put up with so much, yet they always come to the training sessions with flailing tails, doggy smiles, and eager enthusiasm.

Somewhere along the line I made a subconscious decision. The fact is that I'm unusual in the dog sport world in another respect. Most people who train and compete with their dogs only have one, or at the most, two. Every once in a while, you'll meet a daring soul who works with three or four dogs. They don't have six or seven that they train. My self-diagnosis of obsessive canine disorder came as no surprise to me. But it has come at a cost. And I'm not just talking about my dog food bill.

The fact of the matter is that, if I followed convention and only had one or two dogs to train and show, those one or two dogs would be much more advanced than the six or seven I'm working with now. We would have gone all the way. Rally Champion, Obedience Trial Champion, and probably lots of other advanced titles in lots of other sports as well. Fewer dogs mean more focus. Not necessarily more attention, but definitely more in-depth and intentional training. My dogs would do more and be titled sooner in whatever they did do. They would be incredible, as close to perfection as a dog could get.

And it would be so fantastically boring.

So somewhere along the way I made the subconscious decision to have multiple dogs and simply enjoy the experience. If I had fewer I would go farther. But I would miss out on so much. True, if I only had one or two they would be super trained and super titled. But there's more to life with dogs than competition. I want to learn from them as much as I want them to learn from me. There are so many unique and amazing breeds I would still like to own and to do life with. I want to delight in each of them, in all of them, and in many of them at the same time. So as much as I dream about and strive toward those rally

Champion and Obedience Trial Champion honors, my first choice and first priority is to just enjoy the experience of living with multiple dogs.

There is one canine sport in which it doesn't matter whether the handler is sighted or not. That would be tracking. Just as it sounds, tracking is a sport in which the dog is trained to follow a trail of human scent. The track can be laid by anyone, and in competition it's never a person that the dog knows. The idea is that the dog will follow any trail of scent indicated by the handler. Emphasis is also placed on the kind of surface or terrain over which the track is laid. Advanced dogs can track through the easy stuff (dewy grass and scattered brush) and the tough stuff (gritty gravel, dry concrete, and even supermarket aisles).

Vision is not necessary for a handler to pay out a tracking line and tag along dutifully after the dog. It's all about that dog leading the way with his incredible nose.

I enjoy tracking. Brio and Tassie are both in training for it, although we haven't gotten far enough to actually compete and earn titles yet. One great thing about this sport is that it allows a dog to just be a dog. Obedience and rally condition our dogs to think like we do. But tracking allows us to plunge into their thought processes and their world.

To follow my dog's nose, I don't need eyes. I just snap the thirty-foot tracking line to her harness, give her some slack and let her do the rest. My job is just to stump along behind. It's Brio or Tassie's job to filter through the plethora of scents wafted to her in an open field, the residue of smells clinging to moist stems and clumps of grass. I don't know where the trail leads, and neither do any of the sighted handlers who trial their dogs in tracking events. Only the trial judge and the snuffling dog know.

Tracking is a different world. It's quiet, almost contemplative. It's another one of those ancient modes of communication between dog and human. It's a slower, deeper brand of teamwork. Reading the wind and the ground, measuring the moisture in the air, accounting for the time of day—early morning, midafternoon, twilight evening—and understanding that each time of day has its own, specific smell. The ropy line playing through my fingers, and me letting it out and taking it in as the dog speeds up, adjusts, slows down. I can hear her sniffing. She inhales eagerly, snuffling, her whole awareness saturated in a dimension of odor that I can never fully understand. There's a wuffling snort as she snaps up a treat, dropped strategically between the feet of the track layer to keep the dog fresh and on task. Birds sing. A wind gets up and shuffles through the shin-high grass. It's blowing from my right to my left, across track, fanning the scent and spreading it out. My dog will have to work a little harder to stay on the exact trail. Sure enough, within thirty seconds she pauses, hesitates, and I stand still to let her work it out. No words, no encouragement or remonstrance. Just keep the slack out of the line and wait for her. She'll figure it out.

And she does. The wind quiets, and I feel a change in the line. Certainty, movement, and then forward. I give her some line, take a few slow steps, a few faster steps, and break in to a jog-trot to keep up. She must really know where she's going. And just for fun, I close my eyes, shutting out even the blurry light and dark of my regular horizons. My trust is in that dog out in front of me and in her stunning ability to take me where we're supposed to go.

To me, the best thing about tracking is not the confidence boost it provides for me, but rather the confidence boost it provides for my dogs. Brio and Tassie are both dogs who tend to be timid and insecure. Obedience gives them mental stimulation and emotional stability, and those are things they definitely need. But tracking gives them courage. It lets them get out ahead and pull. They can put their heads down and tell me what to do for a change. It lets them call the shots, set the course, and the pace and lead the way. Super good for them. A pleasure for all of us.

There's far more to training than simply bending a dog to my will and forcing the issue. If I have a dog who doesn't thrive on obedience, then we don't compete in obedience. I try to tailor our activities to the talents and abilities of the individual dog. If it's something they enjoy doing, then I try to make it happen.

And that's where the ducks come in.

They are Indian Runner ducks, and I have been told that they look like bowling pins with legs. A better description might be to say they look like penguins, only in the wrong color. They stand almost perpendicular to the ground, their heads high and their little wings tucked up tight against their bodies. I keep a handful of them around most of the time.

Unlikely as it seems, ducks are categorized as livestock at AKC herding trials. At most trials, dogs can work any of three species of livestock—sheep, goats, or ducks. Indian Runners are the preferred breed of duck that is used, because, unlike most other poultry, they don't frantically flutter their wings as they scamper away from a working dog. They keep those wings closed and simply run.

They're my preferred type of stock on which to work my dogs, even though I have goats. Sheep and goats are big and blundering when a dog has them on the run. They will scoot and scatter and knock you down if you aren't prepared to move fast or jump out of the way. And they don't make much noise until they're basically right on top of you. Not great for a person like me.

The ducks are much smaller, slower, and frankly, safer. They crowd together in a knot as they move, scurrying as one unit across the pen or the pasture. They won't knock you over. And just as good, they make lots of sound so I can tell where they are. Not only do they quack, but those big, webbed feet drumming across the ground make plenty of noise.

Tassie and Gem have each shown definite drive to work ducks. Gem with her swift, assertive intensity, Tassie with a lighter touch: careful, focused, and precise. Two or three times a week, I take each of them up to the round pen and let them organize the ducks. Blocking, circling, stealthy stalking, sudden bursts to block again. But up to now, that's as far as it's gone. No trials or titles. Just some new dreams, new challenges. Just something else to keep my busy mind occupied and, better still, to keep the busy minds and bodies of my two working stock dogs as occupied and active as possible.

I haven't quite figured it out yet—how to take the next step and get ready to compete in herding trials. At this point, the dogs and I are just having fun. But my guess is it will come. The lure of a new canine sport, with all its thrills and challenges, will be too much for me to resist. And so will the chance to love and bond with my dogs a little more. One of these days we'll just jump in and plunge ahead. And for this blind handler, with my smart, patient, and loyal dogs beside me, there will be no looking back, and no end in sight.

PART 4

SUMMER

By mid-May, warm weather has really arrived. Not hot yet, but warm, tepid, and a bit lazy. Everything is green. Gardens are going in all over the place. The crop fields are rough with growth, and the farmers are cutting alfalfa in the hay fields. Everyone tied to the land watches the weather, scintillating between praying for rain when we've gone a week without, and begging for a dry spell if it's time to bale hay.

The frogs are still trilling, a richer, more textured chorus now with croaks, peeps, and twangs thrown in. All the migratory birds have returned from pilgrimage and now commence the hectic duties of building nests and raising babies.

Lush and lavish life overflows the fields, ponds, and hills.

The days lengthen and the sun strengthens. Twilight lingers until well past nine in the evening, and dusk lingers far beyond that. Mornings are still fresh, sun-kissed, and dew-drenched, but the spring sparkle and softness have faded. These mornings are harder and shorter, the glaring sun drawing them swiftly upward and forward into long, smothering, sizzling days.

June unfolds the humidity, shakes it out, and settles it like an eiderdown across her lap. Across the steamy pastures and the sweltering cornfields. I push open my front door and pause on the patio, and the stifling wetness of the air engulfs me. It's like a woolen blanket, just hauled out of the wash and barely wrung dry. It's hard to breathe. Plodding up the driveway, I plow through waves of humidity. They rise from the ground, from the depths of the deep grass, wet waves breaking over my legs and slapping into my face.

Sweat. I drip with sweat, even just sitting at the milking stand. The big, industrial barn fan roars at my shoulder, gallantly forcing out a breeze, and I still drip. Three or four T-shirts flung into the laundry every day. Sweat. Greasy and sticky with it.

Sun. Harsh and oppressive, bearing down on the land. The growing things love it. Everything else gravitates to the shade.

The wind dies in June. The trees, full and vibrant green, stand motionless. The wind chimes rarely stir. The air lies limp and thick, drowsy in the heat.

It feels unnatural to me. The very word "Kansas" translates to "people of the south wind." And now with the wind gone and silent, it seems to me that the entire known world struggles without air, fighting to draw breath. I open my own mouth and suck in a steamy lungfull of humidity. Gasp, and try it again.

Through the first part of July the thunderstorms still come. Their mood has changed since the violent jubilation of spring. They are slower and more ponderous in the summer. They march soddenly across the plains, slow and deliberate, trudging under the great burden of the rain they carry. They dump rain in prodigious amounts—in torrents and solid walls of water. No longer the lone-ranger super cells of wild spring, these are storm complexes. They cluster and congeal into massive rainmakers. They creep eastward at ten to fifteen miles per hour, drenching and deluging. Five, six, even seven inches of rain can fall in one storm.

The gutters overflow, pouring water onto the patio so that it pools almost ankle-deep. Even above the tumult of the rain and the continuous roll of thunder, I can still hear the guttural rushing of the creek. It's running high and fast, drunk on abundance, reeling with rain. There is no wind or hail. The storm has one purpose and one purpose only: to dump its staggering, stunning, soaking cargo of rain.

July and August, though, turn dry. The earth and fields bake brown. The sky heightens and hardens into shimmering brass. Dust rises from the gravel roads like smoke. The air dries. Its perfume deepens from the sweetness of clover and honeysuckle to the fragrance of baking bread, frankincense, and rich iced tea. The grasses crisp and scorch. The weeds still thrive, thick in the ditches and along the fence rows. The sunflowers lift their tawny heads, smiling up into the burning and glorious face of heaven.

The corn is tall now, over my head. A reluctant breeze rises, ruffles, sinks down again in the heat, and the long, sharp leaves grate and rustle, sigh and subside. It's hot. When the wind hushes, the rows still incrementally vibrate, whirring and crackling with insects.

Yes, the bugs are back. Cicadas and locusts scrape and chafe in the corn, in the high grasses and leafy trees. Their racket is the bane of my existence this time of year. I involuntarily wince at the first shrill sawing of a cicada. They start out one by one, just testing out their equipment, and it already hurts my ears. I subconsciously tune my radar to catch their first hideous songs, probably just to brace myself for the inevitable. They usually begin in mid-June, and by July the individual performers have melded into a horrendous and deafening chorus.

Then come the locusts, even worse than the cicadas. They specialize in late-night concerts. Actually, they start in the morning as soon as the blazing sun has dried the grass. But by ten or eleven p.m. they are in full cry. Long, rasping, sandpaper calls, thousands of them at a time. I can hardly think, the sound is so overwhelming. It's like fingernails on a chalkboard.

The flies buzz and swarm, settling on the goats like dark and evil snow. Stinging and biting, humming and hovering, relentless irritation. They find the Pyrenees as well and torment them, strafing and biting the dogs' noses until the skin turns raw and opens into sores. Every morning I smear repelling ointment on each of their noses. The dogs hate it, as do the flies, so I stick to my guns and make it part of the routine.

The Pyrenees suffer in the heat. Their luxurious coats are heavy and suffocating. In summer they blow their coats, and the fur comes out in puffs and clods of cotton, but even so they're hot. These magnificent guardians for whom I have no fear whatsoever in the bitter cold are now at the top of my worry list. They dig holes into the hard-packed earth, under thickets out in the pasture, or in the floor of the barn. Drifter has a hole he's been working on for a couple of years. He's excavated it in one corner of the middle pen, right against the floor of the milk room. I keep wondering when he's going to go all the way and dig underneath the raised floor completely, but so far he's content to lie panting in front of the fan in a hole about fourteen inches deep. I keep the industrial-strength fan blowing through the barn in the heat of summer.

I also press the hose into service. Anything above ninety-five degrees and I'm snaking its coils out to the pasture and hunting down the dogs. They despise getting hosed down, so I have to be stealthy about it. Only after I corner, catch, and soak them do they appreciate the wet coolness and the reprieve from the heat.

The heat of summer is just as hard on the animals as is the cold of winter. And like the cold, it requires extra work and longer hours from me. I lug buckets of water up to the corrals. I refill the twenty-gallon water tubs at the barn. Week after week, I scrub all the water tubs to keep at bay the green slime that constantly attempts to grow.

The fans work hard.

The air conditioner works harder. The house has its summer smell now, a combination of pine shavings, road dust, cut grass, damp dogs, and Glade. The house has its summer feel, too. Cool, quiet, a refuge from the heat, the humidity, the hardship. The ceiling fan whispers unceasingly. Kola crashes flat out on the hardwood floors, soaking in the coolness. The lawnmower drones outside. My sweat has almost dried.

The wind begins to rouse itself in August. Sometimes it blows like a blast furnace, gusting from the southwest, its bellowing breath stoking the fire of its heat. More often, though, it yawns and huffs, as if shaking off the reverie of the past months. It stirs, stretches, scuffles in the golden grasses. It's not quite the same wind that it was back in May. Laboring up the hillside with a full wheelbarrow, I stop short, turn to the northwest, raise my head and feel it. Breathe it in and smell it. The sun burning into my back, sweat soaking my T-shirt, the cicadas rasping in the trees like miniature power tools. But that wind has an edge to it. The sun blazes down, and I drag dripping sweat out of my eyes. But I feel it. I can sense it. The wind has snatched up the news and breathed it to a place of awareness deeper than my ears.

Summer is fading. Autumn is coming close.

And then the wind falls and more sweat trickles into my eyes, and I remember that it's only August. Summer still ruling supreme, and hot, sticky work still to be done. But I have heard the wind, and I tuck the secret away, back in one of the cubbyholes of my consciousness.

Summer is a time of fullness. Each day full of work, full of heat, full of life. And for now, I am content to walk ahead and to let its fullness fill me.

CHAPTER 13

GROWING UP: FROM BABIES TO BIG KIDS

Baby goats grow fast. Weighing in at five to ten pounds when they're born, by the time they turn three months old, they should tip the scales at thirty to forty pounds. By the time they mature to eight or nine months, they should be eighty to ninety pounds—good-sized and big enough to breed that fall.

But in the meantime, let's just enjoy the kids being kids.

They certainly enjoy it. To baby goats, the whole entire world is one giant, fascinating, and wonderful playground, put there especially for their personal use. Growing up goat consists of eating, running, hopping sideways just for fun, eating some more, jumping on and off of anything within reach, messing with things, eating some more, and finally, at the end of an action-packed and exhausting day, curling up into a big pile of heads, legs, and ears. They play hard, sleep hard, and you could even say that they eat hard.

By the time they reach two months old I've weaned them down to just one bottle per day. They anticipate it as only a young animal can anticipate anything. The yells and demands begin at about 6:30 a.m., and as soon as they see me step outdoors, they redouble their efforts.

When the breakfast buffet does arrive, there is unrestrained mayhem at the gate. The kids surge forward en masse, heads and chests lowered to press their way through. I insist on taking only two at a time. I do, after all, have only two hands, which makes juggling more than two bottles at once a slight problem. The kids naturally don't follow this logic and assume I should be able to feed all ten of them at once. So we grunt and tussle at the gate, swaying, pushing, and each of us resorting to dirty and underhanded tricks as necessity arises. I won't deny that, during these fracases, I've yanked a few ears, slapped a few butts, stepped on more than a few toes, and uttered a handful of words I'm not proud of. But in my defense, how many times can a girl be pushed, scratched, have her head jumped on, and get head-butted in the crotch before she feels the need to retaliate?

Two kids finally extricated, the gate jerked closed and latched, accidentally trapping the head of one kid, who begins to scream so that I wheel back to open the gate and give an almighty shove to the miscreants once again straining to get out. Now grab two warm bottles out of the bucket hanging on the fence, drop them down to nose level, and pull in a deep, calming breath while the juvenile delinquents drink their milk.

Actually, they inhale their milk. How they manage to slug it down without drowning themselves is a mystery to me. But less than a minute later, they're desperately sucking on empty bottles and it's time to repeat the whole rough-and-tumble procedure all over again with two new starving children.

However, throughout all this hullabaloo I have not been alone. I have had help. Gem has been with me.

The thing is, just because they've inhaled their milk in record time, doesn't mean the little pigs dressed in goats' clothing are satisfied. Nope, they're still hungry, and being out of the corral and in the front yard provides a fabulous opportunity to sample the weeds and grasses that flourish along the fences. Once the bottles are empty, the two kids I've been feeding are done with me. And there are the weeds, right in front of them, and nobody said they couldn't—and even if somebody did say they couldn't—that wouldn't really matter. Except if the one saying so is Gem.

She slinks and pants in circles around them while they chug their milk, and as soon as I thunk the empties back in the hanging bucket, she gets to work. No baby goat is gonna eat weeds on her watch. She crouches, darts and stares, offering an occasional slam or nip if it's needed. But it very seldom is. She really has them quite well-trained. They scoot to the gate in a hurry, no questions asked, wait for me to open it, and go jostling back into the corral where the dog is not allowed. It's a simple help, but without Gem to watch and guide them, I would be running all over creation trying to find and retrieve the little rascals.

At three months old the kids are weaned to strictly solid food. Now the business of putting on height and weight really takes off. They have brome hay free-choice, grain twice a day, and alfalfa hay when I can get it. They eat and frolic and eat some more. They get bigger, fatter and, if possible, sassier.

There are few things more entertaining than watching eight or ten baby goats play. I provide play equipment for them each spring, and they absolutely use it and love it. Anything they can jump onto and push each other off of is fair game. This year their playground consisted of a wooden platform on concrete blocks, a big, heavy railroad tie, and a fifty-five-gallon plastic barrel turned on one side. I'm always on the lookout for goat play equipment. The best I've brought home so far is an old picnic table. The kids would hardly leave it alone and eventually broke it with all their jumping and bouncing.

By autumn, the kids to be sold have usually been sold, and the kids to be kept are large enough to be moved into the big barn and pasture with the adults. There's always an adjustment period when this happens as the older does grudgingly accept the juniors into the herd. The dominance hierarchy is re-enforced and sometimes restructured at this point, but the juniors always end up on the bottom. I pen them up separately overnight when everyone is shut in the barn, but daytimes out in the pasture they're free to mingle and establish whatever silly caste system they need to. No one gets hurt, but there is certainly a lot of chasing, posturing, and head-butting that goes on.

Long before breeding season comes around, I've already played the matchmaker and figured out what doe gets paired with which buck. And I'm already hoping, planning, wondering how next year's kids will turn out and grow up. These junior does have grown up so fast themselves. And as I stand among them, their warm, solid sides pressing against my legs and two of them chewing on my T-shirt, I'm proud of these girls. I imagine putting each of them up on the milking stand, how each will learn her name, how each distinct personality will emerge even more decisively than it has already. And I'm ready to start the cycle over again and find out how these kids have really grown up.

CHAPTER 14

MEG: SHOW ME THE WAY
GOLDENGREENE'S EVERYDAY MAGIC

I finally got my border collie. Meg arrived as a four-month-old bundle of black-and-white energy. She came just a few months after Dundee joined the household, and more than two years before Gem showed up. My first true border collie, and a respectable poster child for the breed.

I met her thanks to the summer horseback riding lessons I was taking with a lady who had just moved to the area. She had thirteen dogs, a number I could only goggle at back then. They were all border collies, all flashy black-and-white, and when they rushed the fence to announce anyone who had just broached the property, they presented a front that their owner laughingly dubbed "the Border Patrol."

Three of the thirteen members of the Border Patrol were puppies. I was tempted. I was there to ride horses, but my heart, still bruised and riddled from the horrors of the Dark Year, was magnetically drawn to the dogs. I thought about them. When my mind should have been focused on posting to the trot, it wandered to thoughts of working a border collie. We could do obedience. We could do herding.

Was I ready to canter? No, not really—I was thinking more ready to try tiring out a border collie puppy. Heels down, sit deep in the saddle, shorten up those reins. . .

I wanted one. I wanted one really bad. And maybe we could even try something really unique, like search and rescue work. Wow, it would be neat having a mission like that with my own special dog. And a border collie would be an ideal breed for the work.

I wanted one really bad. Or did I mention that already?

I named her Meg. I had named her Meg ten years before, back in the days when I only had my dream border collie. It was the right name. Feminine but strong, Celtic in origin, and the one syllable traditional to naming working sheepdogs. There was nothing dazzling about the way I picked her out. She was friendly, active, and interactive, not pushy and not aloof. I just picked her. Scooped her up, toted her to the car, and brought her home.

Even in those first few days I could see Meg's potential for obedience work. It wasn't just that I wanted her to do obedience and therefore saw what I hoped to see. It was a case where she wanted to do obedience. Needed to do it. Needed to work, to learn, to excel. As border collie as they come, Meg has always desperately craved a job to do and things to learn. She thrived on work. She waited for training time every day, still waits for it, ever attentive to the front door and to my comings and goings. Even the slightest jingle of the bell collar will get her up and pacing. If it becomes apparent that the bell collar is actually entering the house to be put on a certain dog, Meg's pacing intensifies. She pants, whines, and begins quivering with anticipation. Learning is her life. Work is her world.

By the time she was two years old we were beginning to seriously prepare for more advanced obedience classes. Meg earned her Novice Companion Dog title easily, but it was the Open and Utility classes toward which I really wanted to train.

Up until this dog, all my previous obedience hopefuls hadn't quite made it. Mesa, the Australian shepherd before Dundee, had come the closest. She was my first dog to earn the Companion Dog Excellent title, but even that had been accomplished through the coaching of a training mentor with whom Mesa and I had taken classes.

Now my focus was squarely on Meg. She and Dundee were the same age, and of course, I expected success with Dundee as well. But Meg was sharper, quicker, and more mature than he was. And so I set my sights on her and began pushing for that CDX title.

To catapult a dog from the Novice class to the Open class takes a lot of rocket fuel. A good comparison is to say that it's equivalent to a human student making the abrupt transition from third grade to high school and nothing in between. Open obedience exercises are accomplished completely off-lead. The leash is taken away as soon as the team enters the ring, and the dog is required to do a heeling pattern and then a figure-eight pattern without it. There is also a recall exercise where the dog is asked to come to the handler from across the ring, then to stop midway and lie down at the handler's command before completing the full distance recall. There are two retrieves in the Open ring, two jumps, and two stay exercises.

It's tough stuff. Compared to the safety and simplicity of the novice class, with its mostly on-leash exercises and basic recall, Open demands tremendous attention, commitment, and drive from a dog.

Meg had it all. It was, as usual, her handler who was a bit lacking.

This being my first advanced dog to train without a coach, I made my share of mistakes. And, naturally, so did my enthusiastic but mismanaged dog. It seemed like every single exercise in that Open Ring brought us down at one trial or another. We would work on retrieves and jumps, get to the next trial, and she would goof up on the drop on recall. Then we would take a step back, polish up the drop, and at the next show she would bobble the retrieve over high. I got frustrated. I got annoyed. But I never got discouraged. I didn't see much promise or potential in myself, aside from my innate stubborn determination. My focus was, instead, on the dog. Her eager intensity, her mercurial intelligence, and her boundless joy to do the work were all the promise I needed. I knew we would do it. I knew she could do it. I was only the helmsman, tweaking the rudder just enough to guide her, and riding the wave behind.

Even with such raw potential on the end of my leash, I must admit that the thought of going back to a training mentor never again appealed to me. It did flit across my mind, but I only paid it enough attention to bat the pesky idea away. Somehow, I just didn't want anyone else working with this dog. The usual arrangement in a mentoring situation is that an owner takes their dog to the mentor's training location. It's often for an hour at a time, perhaps once a week, maybe once a month depending on the cost and distance involved. The training mentor actually trains the owner much more than the owner's dog, offering feedback, advice, and suggestions as the dog works through certain exercises. I, as the owner, would be the one with my hands on the dog, doling out treats, praise, and occasional corrections. Just under the supervision and direction of someone else. It would still be my thing—my work, my dog.

And yet, somehow, it wouldn't. Not in the way I wanted.

Meg was my first border collie, a dog I had dreamed up and picked out all by myself. I had started her myself, bent over backward to socialize her, taken her into the obedience and rally rings thus far without coaching. I didn't want to sully that connection. I wanted this to be about my own dog and my own relationship with her.

Maybe it was just a tricked out case of good old-fashioned pride, but I wanted to do this on my own, with nobody else's name or technique or reputation attached. And so we stuck with it. I asked questions, talked to folks, took a few suggestions. But this was something I was going to do myself.

The first CDX leg we earned came almost as a surprise. Meg was right with me on heeling, quick on the drop on recall, and picked up both retrieves. The jumps were good, the stays were solid. And they called our number as one of the teams that had qualified. All of a sudden, this endeavor was real. We had earned a score toward a CDX title. One down, two more to go.

After that it didn't take long. A few weeks later and Meg and I were in the ribbons again, me grinning like a fool, Meg smart and serious beside me. As she handed the ribbon to me, the judge glanced back at my dad and said, "I'm not sure this girl can smile any bigger, but I bet she will when she earns that title next time."

As it turned out I didn't just smile. I cried. I took our ribbons, took the handshaking and congratulations of the crowd, and then I took my dog to a quiet corner of the show building, sat down in a metal chair and opened my arms. "Hup!" I told her, and Meg was in my lap, wiggling her body against my chest and licking my face and ears. CDX. What an achievement. What a great dog. Yes, there are higher obedience honors—way higher—and way harder to earn. And while Meg and I are still working toward those accomplishments, this particular CDX title will always stick with me as one of the most stellar achievements earned by any of my dogs. It was a testament to my own grit, tenacity, and hope. It was proof that I could dream big and that I could back the dream up with work and pioneer spirit and make it reality. But all of that is just the byproduct. It sounds good in print, and it's a great moral to the story. But sitting there on that cold chair with that warm, living, loving, working dog in my arms, it was about so much less and so much more.

I simply had a wonderful dog.

Of all my dogs, Meg is the one who in many ways has

brought me the farthest in obedience training and competition. She is the first dog I have ever trained for Utility, and so, she is the dog on which I've made all my mistakes. I have learned so much from her and through her. My continued refusal to work with a mentor has slowed our progress, and no doubt has in some ways stunted our training. Much like the quandary over whether to own many dogs and go only so far with each, or whether to own just one dog and go as far as possible, my decision to train alone has meant compromise. Utility is not for the faint of heart. If a handler wants to succeed, it's almost a given that she has to either train with a coach, or else be a highly experienced trainer already.

And finally, my lack of sight has put another kink in the whole process, since it limits what I can glean from watching other trainers and competitors with their dogs.

Some days my thoughts take a dark turn, and I start to consider how good Meg could have been in someone else's hands. High-scoring, high-in-trial, Obedience Trial Champion, and probably agility champion titles as well. She could have been an incredible show dog—titles, ribbons, awards, maybe even shown across the country instead of just piddling around at little local trials. But she got stuck with me, and it's obvious that I've held her back. Her career isn't over, but she's a middle-aged dog now, and sometimes I can hear the clock ticking. And I look at her: her drive, her enthusiasm, her total lack of limitations, and I look at myself: my fumbling mistakes, my misguided techniques, and my very definite limitations. And I curse myself for my slowness and my failures with such a gifted dog.

And then I jerk my own mind back to heel with a vicious correction that I would never use on an actual dog. I tell myself that I had to start somewhere. I remind myself how much I've learned because of Meg. I look at a dog like Tassie, young, brimming with potential and already largely trained through Utility. She would never have gotten so far so fast without the lessons I've learned from Meg. Meg is the giant on whose shoulders Tassie and many other amazing competition dogs in the future will stand. Her greatness is what will make their own.

That's who she is in the ring. But there's another thing about Meg that makes her a great poster child for her breed. In a word, she's weird. I think most border collie people, if they're honest, will tell you that the breed is just like that. They're weird. They do strange and quirky things that make no rational sense to anything except a border collie brain.

I remember one time I had a neighbor couple over, spending an hour or so in the house. The husband was installing window perches for the cats, the wife was just hanging out and lending an extra hand if it was required. As he stood at the window overlooking the backyard, the guy made a comment about "that dog climbing the oak tree." I did a double take.

Then, cautiously and not quite sure I wanted to know, I ventured, "Which dog?"

"Oh, that black-and-white one," he said, and his wife concurred enthusiastically. "What is it, a border collie? Sure looked like it was trying to climb that big oak tree you've got right beside your patio."

His wife nodded encouragingly. "Yeah, I saw it, too," she said. "That dog just came racing across the yard and leaped four or five feet up onto the tree trunk. Never saw anything like it."

I had to admit that I never had, either. Upon further questioning, it became clear that *no,* the dog had not been chasing anything into the tree and *no,* there apparently hadn't been anything up in the tree already. No cats, no squirrels, no Andean condors. It was just Meg, being a weird border collie.

She is, like many members of the breed, also extremely sound sensitive. Any kind of thunder or gunshot sends her into nervous pacing and cowering, and you can forget the Fourth of July.

On our walks Meg seems to specifically listen for noises

that will startle her. A car door slamming, a truck engine firing, even a horse snorting in a pasture along the road, and Meg is bolting forward, eyes wild and ears pinned down in fright. Gem is always on hand to corral her so that she doesn't run far. I often wonder if Meg really would run, or if it's all just a part of the border collie mind games. Maybe she pretends, letting herself be spooked in order to bait Gem into coming after her. I wouldn't put it past either one of them.

Be that as it may, there are other sounds that trigger bizarre reactions. For a while, Meg went through a faze where the scraping of my kitchen chair did the trick. I would get everything ready and laid out on the table for breakfast, and she would be calm, quiet, and disinterested. But let me finally be ready to sit, and the scuff of the chair drawn back across the laminate flooring would send Meg trotting out the dog door. It happened morning after morning, and it only happened in the morning. Not at lunch, not at supper. Only at breakfast, consistently day after day.

I never could fathom why. Eventually I just gave it one of my eloquent eye-rolls and closed the dog door.

Then there are the noises associated with the ritual of bottle feeding. Water pouring into the kitchen sink spikes Meg on to high alert. The snick of the stove burner being switched off is another trigger. And by the time she hears the rattle of the warm bottles being loaded into the transport bucket, it's time to tear out the dog door and run the fence line.

Running the fence line is its own separate topic. It's another border collie thing. Meg doesn't do it obsessively; for one thing I would never put up with that, and for another thing, she's usually energy-drained enough that she doesn't need to go that far. But she will never quit doing it completely.

Meg is an adrenaline junky. She does not have an off button. I honestly believe she's one of those dogs who would literally collapse before stopping. She is incredibly competitive—the first one out the dog door, the first one out the front gate, the first one down the road, and of course, the fastest in all three of those events. She's not nippy or nasty or aggressive about it. She is pure, dynamic energy. Lightning and no thunder. But compelled to be the first regardless.

One of the ways she gets her adrenaline rush throughout an average day is by determining every situation in which it might be even remotely acceptable for her to go streaking out the dog door. Once she's concluded a dog door dash is warranted, all systems are go and it's a race to the far end of the back yard and a manic run back and forth along that section of fence.

It doesn't take much. Me going out to the barn is always a good reason. Once I'm at the barn, she stations herself along the yard fence, watching. Most of the time when I come out of the barn again, or when I open and move through a gate along the way, I hear Meg's tags chinking. She moves along her own fence because I'm moving along mine. Or simply because I'm moving at all. She is keen, aware, tuned into every sound and every signal.

Barn visits and bottle feeding are good excuses to get up and trot out, but to Meg, they aren't the really important stuff. Her forays into the yard are conducted at half-speed on these occasions. Quick trot, forward action, bright eyes. But not the high-flying, hard-hitting wallop of her real mission—these excursions out to the corrals and barn pale in comparison to training time. Meg not only loves her own training, she is an avid fan of watching the other dogs get their turns. As soon as she hears the jingle of the fateful bell collar, as soon as she comprehends that it's been buckled onto somebody else instead of around her own neck, she bounds into position directly in the entryway leading from the kitchen. The kitchen is where I get each dog ready to train, shucking off the regular collar, clinking it onto the countertop, then securing the tinkling bell collar in place and buckling it snugly, chattering and pep-talking all the while. Meg quivers and stares, hovering in the entry between the kitchen and the laundry room, one ear cocked to the strategic dog door. She waits there, tense as a bowstring, shaking in desperate anticipation. Then let me turn from the counter toward the front door and the race is on. She squeals, her feet scrabbling frantically on the hardwood. She falls down at least twice, slams her head against the stove, then gets her feet under her just in time to avoid trampling by three other dogs, just in time to be the first, the very first one, crashing through the dog door, cutting the sharp right turn onto the back patio, and driven by brute speed and frenzy, sprinting furiously for the back fence. By the time I and the lucky training dog arrive in the front yard, Meg is dashing back and forth, back and forth, panting and whining along the stretch of fence separating back yard from front.

I have tried crating her, calming her, closing the dog door, reprimanding her. Nothing works. She's a border collie. This is what they do. They work. They run. They compete. End of discussion.

A good day for Meg is as follows. Seven or eight miles on the road in the morning, running off-lead like a maniac. After lunch, a rousing game of fetch, in which she chases down and retrieves a wildly bouncing toy forty or fifty times. Then a session of obedience training. With this breed, it's just as important to exercise the mind as it is the body. And finally, a one to two-hour fence-running frenzy as the other dogs get their work sessions in for the day, while Meg obsesses and cheers for each one of them.

Even after all that, I'm not convinced that Meg is truly tired. She is always vigilant, never quite relaxed, always ready. For anything. There are times, listening to her patter and pant along the yard fence, or hearing the distinctive jingle of her tags simply because I've turned off the burner under the kettle on the stove, that I wish Meg were just normal. I wish she could just kick back and chill out and forget about the sounds and the stimuli and the competition. And then there are other times, as she sweeps up the driveway in utter abandon, or joyously completes any task that I give her in the ring, that I'm so glad she is who she is. A true border collie, a passionate worker, she really is one of my dream dogs.

My fear is that those reading this chapter might label Meg as unstable or neurotic. And that would be such an injustice to her. She's not neurotic, she's a border collie. And maybe we should just leave it at that. She is a loving, friendly, sensitive dog who adores people, and who adores her work even more. In many ways, Meg is the dog who keeps me the most honest and the most grounded. She is the one who pushes me, the one who reminds me to strive and not to settle. She needs more. She wants more. Why settle for seven miles when we could go eight, when in fact we should go eight? Why not give that Kong toy one more throw—make it fifty-five, not just fifty-four. Take that jump just one more time, better, higher, faster. I can't settle for less, or even for mediocrity, with Meg in the lead. After all, she never will. She spurs me on to be a better owner, a better trainer, and perhaps even a better human being.

CHAPTER 15

BRIO: COMING TO LIFE
GOLDENGREEN'S READY OR NOT!

The first time I met Brio she was hysterical. After about five minutes, I almost was, too.

It was a gas station, a cloudy afternoon in August. She was a wiggling, whining, freaked-out armful of scared and very loud insecurity. She was wide-eyed, wound up and half-panicked, flailing and squirming against my chest, washing my face with desperate licks.

She was my new dog.

As we bundled her into the crate for the ride home, her constant whining became a wail. And as we eased out into traffic and the volume went up, I asked myself the question that is always uppermost in my mind when I'm crazy enough to get yet another dog. *Why exactly am I doing this again?*

Brio came all the way from South Dakota. She started life with a 4H family who raised Sable dairy goats and miniature Australian shepherds. They lived on a ranch in the middle of nowhere. The nearest town was De Smet, the settlement near which Laura Ingalls Wilder spent her teenage and early married years. Spacious, untamed country, in many ways the land was unchanged from the rough-and-ready days of the pioneers. Brio tumbled into it with abandon. Running riot with her littermates, she reveled in the freedom of a rural farm dog. No boundaries, no training, and nothing even close to socialization.

She was actually more of a toy Aussie than she was a mini. Standing about thirteen and a half inches at the shoulder, she just barely brushed the minimum height requirement of thirteen to be considered a mini. Anything below thirteen inches is classified as being a toy Aussie.

The debate between the Australian shepherd crowd and the mini Australian shepherd crowd has simmered for decades. By 2015, the rift became wide enough that the mini Aussies were designated as a separate breed. Since that year, they have officially been called miniature American shepherds.

My rationale, especially since welcoming Brio into the herd, has always been that the smaller size provides a very nice alternative for people who love the Australian shepherd as a breed but want something more portable. A well-bred mini allows a person to enjoy all the intelligence, energy, and trainability inherent to the breed, condensed in a package of about fifteen to thirty pounds. It's a nice option to have, especially for people living in housing where there is a weight limit specified for pets, or for those who just prefer a small breed but still like the herding dog style.

As we pulled out into traffic and the noise from the back of the car increased, I just couldn't seem to find an acceptable answer to that nagging question. Seriously, why WAS I doing this again? I did not need another dog. Especially one that screamed like a demented maniac.

And she did scream. She wailed and shrieked and yapped at such high frequency that I wondered how soon either the windshield might crack or my eardrums might rupture. I winced and turned around and stuck my fingers through the wire door of the crate.

"You're okay, honey," I said, and honestly, I wasn't sure whether I was trying to calm her or myself. Either way, my reassurance was smothered beneath a crescendo of manic whimpering and warbling. She licked my fingers frantically, then began a salvo of rapid-fire yaps so loud that my ears rang and tears sprang to my eyes.

My dad, the unfortunate driver, shouted something unintelligible from right beside me.

"What?" I yelled back, and there was another frenzy of shrieks from the back of the car which, if possible, were even louder than the ones before. He tried again, but after another couple of shouts we both just gave it up. I scrunched my eyes closed and turned up the radio.

It went on like that for days. Every time we did anything, Brio would yap and scream. If we went outdoors, she yapped. If we came indoors, she yapped. If we went for a walk, she yapped. If we came home from a walk, if I put her in her crate, when I left for outings, when I came back home again, the response was ear-piercing, window-shattering yapping. Think of the loudest, highest-pitched, most drill-bit sound you can imagine, and then crank it up by about forty decibels. That was living with Brio for the first week or so.

Have I mentioned how I feel about loud, ear-splitting noises? They do not make me happy. But I knew that Brio was just coping the best way she knew how. She was anxious and insecure, suddenly yanked out of her familiar existence and flung into a completely new setting. New place, new people, new rules, new routine, and lots of new dogs.

She tried to be brave, racing to keep up with the other dogs and dashing after me with piercing chirps and squeals. She tried to understand and to adjust, wiggling and whining and pressing up against me whenever she could.

And for my part, I tried to be patient and to remember to love her through this transition. I tried to understand and adjust, too. And I also tried, from the very first hour and with very minimal success, to teach her the word "quiet."

But in spite of all the noise, something happened between us within those first couple of days. I recall one moment in particular as I sat at the computer, Brio plastered in my lap and silent for a few blessed minutes. As I held her snugly in my arms, I felt a connection with this little dog. It was deeper than the connection I usually develop with an animal so early in a relationship. I felt honest affection and a concrete bond with her. There was a rapport between us that I couldn't explain.

In a word, it was chemistry.

As much as I love all animals, and specifically my own animals, chemistry isn't something I have felt often. My initial love for an animal is not emotional. It is a deliberate decision. Emotions often come with it, of course, but they do not define it. My love for an animal is a commitment. I determine that I will give this special being whatever it needs to thrive—food, shelter, veterinary care, exercise, fulfillment. And along with those basics, I also give my heart. Emotions and chemistry don't matter. They arrive sooner or later, usually sooner, but they don't have to be part of the initial bargain.

And yet with Brio, they were. I felt that emotional connection with her almost immediately. It was an unbreakable bond—she was my dog, I was her person. It was meant to be that way, and it would always be that way. Put succinctly, I just liked her.

Apparently, the feeling was mutual. Brio became a total mama's girl. She was friendly enough with other people when she had to be, but she was never really excited or curious about meeting them. At home, she has never been what is dubbed a "Velcro dog," meaning a dog who has to be with its person at all times. She chose a few comfortable spots, usually lounging on either of the couches in the living room, and she would set up shop there for most of the day. But she was always conscious and concerned about where I was. Years later, she continues to be a dog who chooses her own space but who still checks in on me. Not constantly hounding or hugging me, but keeping tabs on me. Every so often, she will hop off the couch or pad out from under the table to find me and say hello.

However, when we went out in public it was a different story. As long as I held the leash, she was okay, or as okay as Brio could be out in public in those early days. Let me hand off the leash to someone else, though, even someone like my mom or dad whom she knew well, and Brio suddenly transformed into a frenzied, panicking mess. I could be only three feet away from her and she would become frantic, leaping and spinning and making those incredibly high-pitched Brio noises.

That hyper-insecurity became the number one problem for me with Brio. And for the first three to four years of her life, it kept us from doing much of anything together. We walked the roads, we played fetch in the yard, we tinkered around every once in a while with some basic training stuff. But when it came down to the nuts and bolts of socialization, training in new environments, and any sort of show experience, it just wasn't happening. It couldn't happen. It's hard to give a dog social opportunities when her first reaction upon bolting out of the car is to start bouncing, twirling, and screaming.

Brio would get so worked up with anxious excitement in any new situation that general hysteria was the inevitable result. It started before I even let her out of the car. As soon as we slowed down to park, the whining would begin. As we unbuckled seat belts and opened doors, she was up, fidgeting, her tags jingling as she threw her head around and wove back and forth. By the time I had opened her door and snapped the lead to her collar, she was in full cry, announcing herself with long, drawn-out screams or gut-punching yaps. Both if we were really lucky.

Once out of the car, she would set herself in constant

motion, zipping and zig-zagging to the limits of her leash. She would shimmy and spin in tight circles or rocket herself three to four feet in the air. And naturally, the soundtrack continued with ear-splitting shrieks and her signature drill-bit yapping. If I managed to stop the wild motion and keep her still, her tactic then became to sit right in front of me, staring into my face and barking, barking, barking.

Going out in public with a dog like that is hard. The irony of it was that going out in public was precisely what Brio needed. What appeared at first glance to be excitement and enthusiasm were actually anxiety and insecurity. Whether it was a learned behavior or just her natural personality, this frenzy of motion and commotion became Brio's strategy for coping with new and stressful situations.

Taking her into a dog show setting was out of the question. Even taking her to less formal and very pet-friendly establishments was difficult and definitely not enjoyable.

Over the years, I tried everything. High-value treats for calm behavior, high-value treats to distract her and produce calm behavior, simply ignoring the behavior until she got tired of it and stopped on her own. There were sharp corrections, there were time-outs, there were no-bark collars and spritz bottles. I brought her to play group sessions where I would leave her for half an hour to an hour. The idea was that without the security of having me close by she would be more likely to interact with other people and dogs. Instead, she panicked and barked the entire time.

Eventually, I ran out of ideas. And frankly, as much as I hate to admit it, I basically ran out of patience.

And so the upshot of it was that Brio stayed home. From our very first week together, I had seen that she was a very insecure dog with zero experience of the outside world. She was young and unsure with a ton and a half of pent-up energy. Knowing that, and given how impossible it was to heavily socialize her, my game plan for that first year was just to let her run it off and grow up. Give her lots of hard exercise and a good, structured routine. She'd settle down, mature, and gain some confidence. Just give it time.

That first year rushed by and Brio was still happily out in left field. A second year passed and still she was largely untouched and unchanged. By the time a third year had elapsed my attention just wasn't on Brio anymore. Meg and I had recently earned our CDX title, and I was working hard to get the same title on Dundee as well. I had a Labrador puppy that I was raising for an assistance dog training program. I was really beginning to get into dairy goats, and the demands of milking, bottle feeding, and general herd maintenance were crowding my daily routine. I had started a new part-time job, too, and that stole even more hours from each week.

And so, while Brio was never neglected physically, her psychological and emotional needs languished. She ran like a wild child on our long walks, commented from the sidelines as a parade of other dogs relished their own training time, and for the rest of the day and night, she vegetated on the couch. Was she unhappy during those years? Probably not directly. She was well fed and well exercised, she had a soft couch and companionship, both canine and human. She was secure enough in her routine.

But that's all it was, a routine. There was nothing new, no mental stimulation or challenge. One of my bedrock principles has always been that a dog's body isn't the only thing that needs care and conditioning. That's true for any dog of any breed. But particularly for an intelligent and driven breed like a mini American shepherd, mental exercise is essential to true fulfillment and happiness.

And Brio wasn't getting it.

Besides the reasons I've already listed, there was one other obstacle that had slowed me down when it came to getting serious about her training. Besides Gem, Brio was the toughest dog I had ever worked with. She had a complex personality, full of corkscrews and contradictions. Of my current ten dogs, Brio is almost certainly the smartest. But that brain power is combined with a babyish immaturity extremely tough to overcome. She would revert to very puppyish behavior at times—wiggling, squirming, and refusing to make eye contact. If yapping and squeaking didn't work, she would flop over on her back and paddle her paws in the air.

She was anxious and unsure but there was another side to Brio that was controlling, bossy, and bratty. The most obvious example of that was to watch how she interacted with the other dogs on our walks—barking, baiting, and biting whenever she could. It wasn't aggressive behavior; it was all calculated control—herding instinct gone haywire.

Her first reflex, of course, was to use her voice before using her mind. In Brio's book, yapping, chirping, and screeching were usually preferable to thinking. It was how she coped, how she solved her problems. She was also manipulative. She knew what she wanted and about ninety-eight percent of the time she also knew what I wanted. But the desire or motivation to give it to me just wasn't there. She had drive but no work ethic.

That is an extraordinarily difficult dog to unlock. Immature but controlling, smart as all get-out but with no motivation, possessed of all the clever creativity inherent to a herding breed and with no place to put it.

As a mentally-neglected almost-four-year-old, Brio was a hot mess.

There really wasn't any specific event that clued me in to her condition. Life went on as usual for both of us. But as that year progressed and we neared her fourth birthday, her situation just began to rankle with me. Why wasn't I doing anything with this dog? She was just living her life as a wind-up toy, going through the motions with no real mind or heart. Or was that describing myself instead of my dog? Why was I okay with settling for less, again less for both of us? Because, really, this was not the kind of relationship that I wanted with any of my furkids.

So I got busy. The first drastic change I made was to put Brio on the old work-for-food program. You don't work, you don't eat. For every bite of kibble that came her way, Brio would have to achieve some sort of task. Nothing like this had ever been required of Brio before, and it got her attention. Forget dumping her food in a bowl and shoving it under her nose twice a day. All of a sudden she was learning to jump and retrieve and to keep her focus on me. She was learning to think and to process. And in a healthy sense, she was learning confidence and control, and to take charge of a job when asked to do it. She was learning that life had purpose besides just lying on the couch or going for walks. And she was learning that purpose was a good thing. It was good because, obviously, it gave her access to food every day. But it wasn't just about her stomach. Brio's mind was beginning to awaken.

The other thing I did at about the same time was to enroll her in a scent work class. Scent work is a fairly recent phenomenon in the world of canine sports. Its main emphasis is on teaching a dog to recognize specific odors, and then to find items scented with those odors in different settings. There are multiple levels that become more complex as the dog advances. It's a lot of work and a lot of fun. That being said, it isn't a sport that I've chosen to pursue as far as to compete and title my dogs. But teaching a dog to use her nose is an incredible confidence builder for that dog, and confidence was one thing Brio sorely needed.

The class I put her in was very rudimentary, but she thrived. She became the star student, and there was a new spark in her attitude. I wasn't going to let it burn out. I shielded that spark, breathed on it with hope, and fed it with shreds of challenge and encouragement.

Brio began to look forward to training time. The lackadasical, apathetic immaturity was replaced by bright and eager desire. The dog who would once have flopped and floundered on her back when asked to complete a simple task was now making eye contact, maintaining attention, and really trying to understand.

Not that it took much. As I've said, she was a quick study. The right motivation and approach were what she needed.

There was still the challenge of taking her places. The hyperactive hysteria did not go away just because we had put our big-girl pants on. But now Brio wasn't the only one who had some motivation. I had caught the spark, too, and once I see the potential in something and set my heart on it, I don't turn back easily. I saw the potential in this little dog, saw her coming to life right in front of me. And that was something worth fighting for.

So we attended the scent work class, and we went other places to practice obedience, and we began to drop in at store-front establishments. And Brio squeaked and yodeled and chirped at top volume. I'm not going to say it was easy, and it certainly didn't subside overnight. But I had a vision to strive for now, and I could tolerate a few shattered windows and ruptured eardrums along the way.

Armed with lots of patience and even more Vienna sausage, I would arrive at our class or training location just a little early and gradually get Brio out of the car and into the building. The best strategy I adopted was to show her a handful of treats, pressing them right on her nose so she was totally fixated if only for a moment, and then just wait for her to figure it out. Work for food. You calm down, even for a second, and I give you this handful of sausage. You jump and squeal and yap and spin and you get nothing. I would simply turn away and concentrate on something else. I would sometimes even scoot back in to the car and close the door, Brio still attached to the leash in my hand but suddenly alone and without an audience. As soon as the clamor and motion stopped, I would open the door and lavish her with treats.

It took time. There were embarrassing moments, and there were moments when I wanted to strangle her. But before long that mini Aussie mind began to percolate. It helped that she was hungry. It also helped that she knew what to expect once we arrived in the building.

As she calmed and quieted, we would walk forward, me still showing her the treats, and Brio more and more focused on them. There were still tantrums each time we made the trek from vehicle to building. We would have to stop, I would turn my back and shorten up the leash, and Brio would have to realize once again that acting up only got her ignored. As soon as she settled and focused, there were treats, praise, and more forward movement toward the desired destination.

About halfway through the scent work class, we entered our first rally trial. Just an easy novice class, but it was a big step for this little girl who, just a couple months before, hadn't even wanted to get off the couch when the training collar came out. Compare that to the eager little worker warming up at ringside, attention fixed on her handler, her mind active and alert. She is all business as they step into the ring, as they navigate the course. She is quiet, listening for the words and commands she knows, unintimidated by the cones and signs and the other people in the ring. She gets a little squeaky when they go back for ribbons, but when her handler is called forward and presented with first place, she sits right in heel position and watches to see what comes next. She is unfazed by the applause, or by the congratulations from complete strangers as they leave the ring. But when they go back to the crates and mom gets down on the floor with her, then she understands that she's done something really good, and there are fistfuls of sausage, and she can roll on her back on the cool floor and then flip onto all fours again and start vaulting up in the air and making some noise about it.

From Rally Novice we progressed to Novice Obedience, and then into Advanced classes in both sports. Brio is now working toward her CDX title and is competing at the excellent level in rally. She has scored as high as a 195 out of 200 in Open Obedience. And even though we haven't pursued scent work, she is one of the dogs with whom I do tracking. That continues to strengthen her resolve and confidence.

No matter how rewarding it might be to see how far Brio has come in the ring, as always, the real reward is the strengthened bond between us. Relationship has now been added to chemistry. The deep connection we shared from the outset all those years ago has now been fortified with learning, life experience, and true teamwork. Not just in the ring, but in everyday household living.

Brio has come off the couch. Well *okay*, she still likes her sofa time. But whereas before she was practically attached, now she has the freedom and confidence to come and go. She's more engaged with me and with her surroundings, and I've gotten to enjoy her as she enjoys her life.

She still delights in our long walks, and she's assigned herself several unique and endearing tasks to help me on the road. For one thing, she will almost invariably let me know a car is coming. She usually hears it before I do and will sidle closer to me, flicking glances first up at me, then back toward the oncoming vehicle. When she sees that I've realized the danger, she will zoom to my side and begin a panting and sneezing session. There may even be a few squeals thrown in, just to be sure that I get the entire message.

This special communication from Brio comes in handy particularly on breezy days when it's harder for me to hear vehicles coming. Or sometimes a day is just noisy—lots of leaves crunching and rustling on the ground in the fall, or when the buzz-saw cicadas are going at it full throttle and drowning out a quiet car in the summer. On those days, Brio's alert is often what cues me that a car is coming long before I would hear it otherwise.

She also cues me when we've reached a corner or an intersection in the road. Her signals then are similar to what they are in her car routine—racing back to me as we get near the corner or the crossroads—shimmying and hopping, and bouncing beside me until she figures out which way we're supposed to go. It's another trick that comes in useful, this one especially helpful when the roads are snow-packed and it's harder for me to identify precisely where we are.

One other special, quirky thing about Brio is that she has a hedge apple habit. For those who don't live in the Midwest, hedge apples are big, bumpy, green balls produced by the Osage orange tree. The trees themselves are thick, thorny things native to the prairie and resilient enough to withstand any drought, drench, or bitter cold. Farmers and ranchers appreciate their iron-tough, rot-resistant wood for making fence posts. And every autumn, they drop their payload of scaly, lumpy, pungent "apples."

Brio loves them. Not to eat or to play with, but to fetch and carry. For reasons unknown, on almost every walk in the fall, she will select a hedge apple, usually one bigger than her own head, and carry it for an hour or more. The bigger and harder the apple the better she likes it. She will trot along behind me, that day's trophy clamped in her jaws, and we'll travel like that for miles. If a car comes along and I call all dogs back to home base, Brio will plunk the hedge apple down, dash to her place at my left side, then shoot back to reclaim the apple as soon as I give the word. Many times, that hedge apple will make it all the way back to our front gate, where Brio will spit it out and streak into the house. And there it molders until the next walk when she trots back to reassume the treasure.

Brio will always be a dog who just needs a little extra. Each time we unload at a show or head for the entrance of the farm supply store, I still have to take just a minute and let her calm down and settle herself. And once she's squeaked and chirped a few times and done a few mambo maneuvers, she's ready to go. It can still be a little awkward when we sachet into a show building and Brio is whining and snorting with anticipation. But I've learned to smile at anyone we pass and say, "Boy, I wish I got that excited when I had to go to work."

Gets them every time, and most of all, it's true. The joy and the purpose this little dog has discovered in life are wonderful. May the same also be said of me.

CHAPTER 16

LILA: THE CAT WHO NEEDED A FARM

The meow was imperious. It wasn't loud, and it wasn't really unique. But there was a quality to it, a certain note that cut through everything else and brought me to a sudden standstill.

We were walking through Petsmart, just a quick, routine stop. I was mentally thumbing through the items we still needed to find, shuffling along beside the cart, and only half-conscious of my surroundings. Most Petsmart stores have a cat adoption center, where kitties from local shelters who are having trouble finding homes are presented to the public. The idea is that people who might never set foot in an animal shelter, who might not even be searching for an adoptable cat, might still come in contact with these kitties at the store and decide to bring one home.

I knew about the cat adoption center and had absolutely no interest. Six cats already called my house their home, and I was not even considering adding another one. We had a good thing going. Why mess with it? Five of them were rescues; two were senior citizens; one was a special needs kitty; and two others were black cats. Pure black cats have a special place in my heart because of how hard it often is for them to get adopted. So I had two of them. I was doing my part. Not to mention the other members of the clouder who were each needy individuals in their own right.

This Petsmart cat was black, too. I knew that because I asked my mom. I had to. After that commanding, imperious meow, after hearing the undercurrent of pleading, I had to find out more.

I dug in my heels, stopped the cart and asked, "Who is that?"

As many times as I've meandered through animal shelters and adoption events, as many times as I've met puppies and kittens, dogs and cats, horses and goats, as many times as I've trolled the pet pages of Craigslist and Petfinder, yet I have never in all those years had an experience like this one. With Brio it was chemistry. With Lila it was a call. It was as if she'd been waiting for me, for me and only me to walk past the entrance to the cat room at that particular moment at that particular store. And after all those days of waiting, here I was, walking right past her, and she knew I was the one. It was a summons, an urgent and assertive appeal.

My head pivoted toward the sound as if strings were attached. "Who *is* that?" I asked again, and we left our cart and ventured into the little alcove where the cat cages were stacked.

She was coal black, sleek and glossy. She was right at the front of her cage, and as I came to her she reached for me through the bars, purring and mewing softly.

"What a sweety," I said, pushing my own face against the bars of the cage and rubbing the kitty under the chin. My mom agreed. She was indeed sweet, a friendly little charmer.

Reading the cage card, we learned that she was a year old and had lived at a local shelter since being found as a young kitten. What that translated to was that she had been living in a cage for the past twelve to fifteen months of her life. My heart squeezed. My orange kitty, Julius, had lived in a cage for three years before he came home with me. Horrendous for a cat, but at least he had been a low-key adult during that time. This kitty was a young and active teenager who had lived behind bars even as a hyper, curious kitten. She had never known anything else.

Yet she was so gentle, friendly, and easy to handle. I felt a familiar ache, questions and possibilities beginning to mushroom in my mind. What if I were to. . . I pulled my fingers out of the cage, shook my head and turned away.

"Why hasn't anyone adopted this little girl?" I asked. Not really expecting an answer, because there really wasn't one. Surely the fact that she was solid black didn't help the situation. Whether it's the way the human eye is attracted to color or whether it's just old-fashioned superstition, studies have shown that people tend to shy away from adopting pure black cats. The tabbies and tuxedos, the grays and golds and calicos find homes much more readily. The black cats stay put. Or maybe it was just the location of the rural shelter where she had grown up. Yet she had been here at this Topeka store for a couple of months already and still no one had wanted her.

"Life just isn't fair, baby girl," I told her. "I'm really sorry, honey. But you'll find the right one," I added as we backed away and she watched us go from her cage. The eager purring and chatting had stopped. The friendly rubbing and patting paws were still. Only her eyes tracked us as we left the room. No more meowing.

We kept shopping, found the other items on my list. We slogged through the checkout line, plopped into the car, merged into traffic. We went on with our day. But the cat stuck in my mind. I couldn't forget. That pleading, imperious meow. A whole year in a cage. Hours of boredom. Hours of waiting. Waiting.

But life goes on. There were lots of kitties in cages all over the country. They would find the right homes. She would find the right home. So I went on with my schedule, my chores, training, walks, work.

I did mention the black cat to one of my clients, though. She was a real pet person and always wanted to hear about my critters and their latest exploits. She came in that week and I told her the story of my interrupted shopping expedition.

"You need to take that baby home," she informed me. "Honey, I think she was waiting just for you. Just think of that: a whole year all alone, and finally there you are, and she's been waiting for you that whole, long time. That poor baby. You may not know it yet," she concluded smugly, "but that girl has it figured out. She belongs with you."

The next weekend Mom and I were back at Petsmart, laying in supplies for the coming week. We were both thinking about it, but I was the one who finally broached the subject.

"Hey," I said as if it had just popped into my head, "let's go see if that black kitty is still here. I hope she isn't," I added as we made a sharp turn and headed for the cat room. "Surely somebody's adopted her by now."

But nobody had. There she was, still in a cage, so friendly and so happy to have visitors.

We didn't stay long. I, at least, couldn't. My heart was starting to get too involved. I couldn't take another cat. And someone would find her. Someone would adopt her. That's what I told her, and it was what I kept telling myself during the next two or three weeks.

My pet-friendly client was back to see me at work during that time, and she rushed straight into her report. "My hubby and I went to see that black cat at Petsmart a few days ago," she said. "And oh, honey, she is a doll! Absolutely black, and you could tell just by looking, such a sweetheart. But you know how you said she was so friendly with you and your mom? Well, she wouldn't even come to the two of us. She just lay in the back of her cage on her blanket, and it was just like she was telling us, yeah, you're nice people, but you're not the right ones. I'm waiting for my Reyna to come and get me."

I smiled reflexively, but my heart was doing that painful squeezing thing again. That kitty had been friendly to everyone when Mom and I first met her. The fact that she was beginning to hang back concerned me. Most likely it meant that she was getting depressed and beginning to give up hope. There are only so many people who can pass by an animal's cage before the animal simply stops expecting them to notice her and stops trying to get attention.

I told my mom about it later. Resolve was weakening for both of us. Neither one of us knew quite what to do. I had six cats, my parents had three. It was hard to justify adding another to either household. On the other hand, it was becoming harder and harder to justify not doing so.

That weekend my mom was back at Petsmart, buying a few items. She peeked into the cat room, and there was our orphan, gazing back at her. There was no excitement or friendly greeting this time. The cat glanced up at her and made one, tiny sound, then turned dully away.

"It broke my heart," Mom told me later. "And I just thought, that's it, I'm gonna get her out of here. So if you want her, that's what I think we should do."

With the last of my flimsy defenses shattered, I agreed. I was willing to adopt her and bring her home. However, since I wasn't with my mom to fill out the requisite paperwork, the result was an interesting hiccup in Lila's life story.

She didn't come to my house for about a year. Instead, she went to live with my mom and dad.

My mom said it was because she felt obligated. After recording her own name and address on the adoption application, and since I wasn't there, she just did what she felt was the right thing and took the cat to her own house. It was one of those questions of conscience, and she just didn't feel honest recording the adopter's name and address as one thing, then taking the animal to live with a totally different adopter at a totally different address.

I felt like I'd been punched in the gut. The decision to add yet another cat to my household had been made suddenly, and now just as suddenly I was informed that same cat was not joining my household at all. Perhaps it was petty of me, but I felt betrayed. It is true that a very small part of me breathed a tiny sigh of relief. Without a new cat coming in, the stability and status quo of my home would be maintained. No upset, no adjustment, business as usual. But the bulk of my emotions was stunned and angry. I felt as if a promised and needy child, and a child who had chosen me, had been ripped out of my arms. I was also totally blindsided by the fact that my mom would do such a thing.

For days I wrestled with my grief and outrage. Mom and I never talked about it. I didn't want to fight about it, and furthermore, I knew my parents would give her a wonderful home. That was the bottom line. Meanwhile, my own home was at peace. So I worked through it in private, taking solace in the critters already under my care, and in the realization that they were enough.

There was one detail, however, on which I put my foot down. That was on the cat's name. My mom, unaware of the psychological turmoil she had inadvertently caused, immediately began calling the new arrival "Lila," the name I had selected for her even before I had decided to adopt her.

I bristled at that.

"You can have the cat," I told her, "but you can't have the name."

Not very charitable I admit. But nonetheless, the name Lila was special to me, and it was a name I wanted to save for one of my own black cats in the future. It was a name I already liked, breaking my long tradition of not christening animals with human monickers. It was also a Hebrew word that meant "night." I could think of few names better for a female cat black as night itself, and I was going to be obnoxious about it. Lila was my name, and I wasn't willing to share.

So they called her Ebony instead and set about making her feel welcome. As friendly and curious as she was, it didn't take long. After a couple of days spent in the big guest bathroom to acclimate her to the sounds and smells of the house, she came prancing out into the wider world.

It began with the house. Ebony explored, experimented, and approved. She met the three other resident cats, fluffing a few tails and earning a few unflattering growls and hisses. She shrugged it off and moved on to bigger things.

The outdoors was bigger. Much, much bigger. She went out tentatively at first, cautious but curious as ever. She had never been outdoors before, except perhaps as a tiny kitten just before being surrendered to the animal shelter. Since then, she had spent more than a year indoors, and she couldn't get enough of this new and wonderful outdoor world.

My parents lived on a very quiet cul de sac and so felt comfortable letting her out. At least they did at first. But as the weeks wore on, their kitty began to disappear. What had initially started as excursions of an hour became absences of two or three hours. Then four or five. By the time Ebony had lived with them for several months, she was vanishing for stretches of seven or eight hours at a time.

She had arrived in late summer, and we all assumed that as autumn faded and the cold drew down on us, she would be back, content in the warm indoors. Let her run and explore, was the general consensus. It was another case where this animal, a young and restless teenager, had been cooped up for so long that we all felt she needed the chance to burn off energy and learn about the world.

That would have been okay if she had confined her world to

the cul de sac and the creek bank. But Ebony simply didn't stay home. She disappeared. No garden variety sun bath or saunter for her. She would completely leave the property, and for all we knew, she would leave the neighborhood.

As winter settled in, all hopes that Ebony would do the same were abandoned. By December she was staying out for as long as twenty-four hours at a time. My parents shook their heads. We posited all kinds of theories. Had she adopted another family somewhere? She wore a bell collar, so although she had no ID tag, it was obvious that she was owned and well cared for. Was she snitching food from an outdoor feeding station of some kind, either from somebody's back porch or perhaps even from a location set up for feral cats? Or was it a situation where she didn't feel comfortable coming home for some reason? Was the inside world forcing her out, rather than the outside world drawing her in?

Nobody knew. After those day-long disappearances, she would come in like she owned the place, jaunty and confident and always hungry. She would eat hard and sleep hard, then be up and dashing for the door within a few hours.

We talked about keeping her in by main force, transforming her into an indoor-only cat and hoping that somehow, she would be satisfied. But as nice as the sentiment might have been, the practicality was anything but. She fretted and paced, crying desperately as she scampered from the front door to the back door to the garage door. She refused to be held or distracted, either by toys or by food. She was on edge and distressed, always alert to the remotest possibility that a door might be opened. If one was even slightly cracked, no matter where she was in the house she would go sprinting to it, and nine times out of ten she would get through it. Then it was another eighteen or twenty hours before Mom and Dad would see her again.

Throughout these months, I had maintained a mostly hands-off approach to my ex-cat. At first it was to let my parents bond with her and to keep myself from following suit. She was not my cat. To be fair, when Mom eventually realized how disappointed I had been when she adopted Ebony, she did offer to let me have her after all. But by then, Ebony had been with them for several months, and I didn't feel right about yanking her out of a stable home where everyone had already gotten comfortable with everyone else. So I smiled and edged away, saying no, I wouldn't take their kitty from them. Then as the months slipped past and we all saw less and less of her, the discussion just didn't seem relevant anymore.

On the rare occasions that Ebony was at home when I visited, I would greet her, run my hand along her sleek back, then try to squeeze out the door while my mom shouted behind me, "Don't let her out!"

But I had an uneasy feeling. Things couldn't go on this way. Someday, she just wasn't going to come home.

Then one Sunday afternoon, I arrived to find Ebony curled up and unmoving on a chair. Assuming she'd just had another one of her late nights, I stepped softly over to say hello. She seemed deeply asleep, almost unresponsive to my voice and touch, and I ran a hand down her back in my customary greeting. About midway, I felt a hard, hot lump under my palm. An absess. I was the first to find it, and my parents had no clue what had happened. A trip to the vet didn't tell us much, either, except that the injury had probably been caused by a large dog. Nothing broken. No permanent damage done. But the ugly thought crossed each of our minds that it was only a matter of time.

Within two or three days, Ebony was back to her regular routine. Still no one knew where she went or what she did. My mom and I once tried to follow her after one of her sprints out the garage door. She flashed to the end of the driveway, cut a ninety to the right, and set off along the cul de sac. She moved at a trot, brisk and businesslike, as if she knew exactly where she was going and was intent on getting there. We kept pace with her in the car, but she crossed three yards, then four, oblivious to our attention and calls, totally focused on her own mission. Eventually, we lost track of her. She didn't come home until the next day.

Spring smiled on the plains and blossomed into summer. Ebony had been with my parents for ten months, and each month they saw less of her. The head-shaking and bewildered speculation had deteriorated to eye-rolling and ambivalence. The frantic shouts of "Quick, shut the door, don't let her out!" had faded to resigned sighs of "She wants to go out again, just open the door."

I stayed out of it. The feeble few suggestions I had offered eight months before just didn't seem valid. In a sense, my parents' four-cat home had downsized itself to three.

Nobody was happy about it. It was just one of those things.

And then there was an intervention. As a gift to themselves, Mom and Dad took an unexpected plunge and purchased an Alaskan cruise to celebrate their fortieth wedding anniversary. They would be gone for ten days in July. Plans were laid, arrangements were made, and everything was settled except for one nagging question. What were they going to do with Ebony?

Shutting her up indoors for that amount of time seemed unthinkable. If they could even catch her beforehand, that is. And even if they could, it was almost guaranteed that she would dash out again when the pet sitter came to feed everyone. Then things would get really complicated. Boarding her at the vet seemed even less likely. It was bad enough to consider locking her in a house for ten days. Locking her in a cage, especially after her history of being locked in cages, seemed downright cruel.

With one week to go, I gingerly hinted that I could possibly keep her while they were away, and it was as if storm clouds had been sheared from the sun. Stark relief was the order of the day. I said I thought she would do fine at my place. I'd start her in the computer room, gated off from the rest of the house so she could get used to the dogs and the other cats, and we'd go from there. I'd send them emails every day to let them know how she was doing. She wouldn't get out of the room, and on the off chance that she somehow did, I would just close the dog door, nab her, and pop her back in the room where she belonged.

"And then what?" Mom asked me. "What about when we come home?"

I knew what she meant. Was I going to keep her?

"Why don't we just see how she does," I said. "We'll have ten days. We should have a good idea by then how she's feeling about things."

I think we all knew she wasn't going back.

My dad carried her into the computer room. Set down the crate, opened the door, and let her come slinking out. Low body, big eyes, but no bolting or panicking. She was installed with a cat tree, a high bookshelf, and several other places to perch and lounge above floor level, plus two litterboxes and a water bowl. Across the entrance to the room was a wire panel, three feet high, so that she could get acquainted with the family without being overwhelmed. She had never been around dogs before.

Dad banged out the front door, grumbling about the hassle of preparing to leave for ten entire days. I turned back to my new baby who, naturally, was now to be called by the name I had originally chosen for her. She wasn't Ebony anymore.

"Okay, Miss Lila," I said, leaning over the wire gate and noting that she was already ensconced on one platform of the cat tree. "Welcome aboard. I think you're gonna do just fine here."

And so she did. It took her a couple of days to realize that she could vault over the barricade and brave the rest of the house. More accurately, it took her that long to feel comfortable enough to try it. But after sizing up the other animals and acclimating to the rhythms of the house, she sprang lightly over and began to explore.

The main fear at this point, of course, was that she would make a break for it, get outside, and never be heard from again. I thought that unlikely, since this was a completely new place for her. She didn't know where the doors were and didn't know how to use a dog door. She was in a completely new situation—new animals, new routine, new human. Still, I wasn't taking any chances. So when she hopped out and began a self-guided tour of the house, I slid the flap down on the dog door, locked Lila in my bedroom, and instituted Plan B.

It took some work, but within an hour I had hauled in a six-by-six-foot chain-link panel and secured it in the doorway to the computer room. The panel came from an old dog run that hadn't been used for years, and it was equipped with a gate. With the addition of some hardware cloth around the top, the whole ensemble fit snugly into the arched doorway, and the room was once again catproof.

All these precautions took care of the physical reality of Lila's joining the family. They kept her safe and contained, they let her orient herself to a home environment very different than any she had ever known. But they didn't address the deeper issue. They were the prevention, not the cure. Why hadn't she stayed home originally? That was the problem I really needed to solve.

My best theory was that Lila had wandered from home because she didn't know it was her home. As a kitty who had been raised in the animal shelter, she had no concept of attaching herself to her own personal territory. During her year at the shelter, she had not even remained in the same cage, but had been shifted around as need and space demanded. Then she had been moved again, this time to the adoption center at Petsmart, where she had once again been juggled between cages as necessary.

Cats are animals that first attach themselves to place. Of course, they bond with people, too. But they naturally bond with a place more completely than they do with a person. Dogs are the opposite. They attach themselves to both people and property, but when the chips are down, dogs are usually more connected to the person than they are to the place.

Lila had never learned to bond with either. Her upbringing at the shelter had not only prevented her from learning to bond with a place, but it also meant that she had never gotten the chance to bond with a particular person or family.

When she landed at my parents' house, my guess is that it was all too much too fast. The sudden freedom of being uncaged, of having an entire house to roam, and then, within only a few days, of being allowed outdoors was well-meant. But it was freedom with no foundation. Lila went racing into it without a sense of her own space or her own territory. She didn't even know she could have those things. The whole world was a dazzling place after the cages and confinement she was used to. All people were nice and kind and sometimes gave her food. But as a cat that had been constantly uprooted and shuffled from cage to cage and from shelter worker to shelter worker, there was no reason for her to attach herself to any one house or human. There was no working knowledge that attaching herself to either was even a possibility.

My strategy was to keep her confined not only to help her adjust, but also to help her begin learning to bond with me and with her new territory. By the time she had been jailed in the computer room for two weeks, I decided it was safe to begin letting her into the rest of the house for short periods. So, once again shutting the dog door, I took a breath and squeaked open the chain-link gate to give her some freedom.

Just for half an hour or so at first. She would come jingling through the gate, tail high and eyes bright, and would make the rounds. Onto the back of the couch, onto one window shelf, then down again to survey the kitchen floor, the kitchen counter—*whoops,* that wasn't allowed—so back to another perch on another sofa. And so on, until she had examined the dog room, my bedroom, and the laundry room with its tantalizing dog door.

After these explorations, it was time to call her back to home base, sprinkle some kitty treats on the floor to keep her busy, and gently secure the gate behind her.

She got comfortable. Her confidence grew. She was unworried by the dogs or by the other cats. She was becoming part of the pack.

Then one day I opened the front door to introduce her to the utility room. This enclosed front porch is one of my favorite things about my animal-friendly house. Not only is it the place where the baby goats spend the first weeks of their lives, but it also has space to store grain, chicken feed, and dog food. That means it has convenient storage tubs, complete with pads and blankets for cats to lounge on. It also has windows and two litterboxes. I toted Lila through the door and set her on one of the tubs to inspect the area. The glass panel on the screen door was raised to let in air, but the door itself was firmly latched.

Lila soaked it all in. The outdoor air, rich with all sorts of new smells and peppered with birdsong, and the sunshine streaming across the room. An hour later, I found her lulling on one of the storage tubs and definitely content with the state of the world.

For all intents and purposes, she was still an indoor cat. But I knew it was only a matter of time before she discovered that fateful dog door and the liberty it offered. That would be the test. My tummy fluttered when I thought about it. My mom was fairly convinced that Lila would vanish within days if not hours. I was less convinced, but I was still nervous. I had decided never to let her out the front door, no matter how she might beg or fuss. If she wanted outdoor time that badly, she would have to do it herself. The only exit I would make available was the dog door, and she could get through it without any help from me. She would have to take the initiative to get into the back yard, and if she still wanted to wander beyond that, it was up to her to negotiate the fence.

On the flip side, she would also have to take responsibility to come back in if she wanted food. She wasn't at Mom and Dad's house anymore. No more of this game in which she got as much food as she wanted whenever she wanted just for showing up. Here, if she came back indoors on her own, she would get a warm welcome and even a few treats. But meals were at scheduled times, and the schedule wasn't going to change just because she wasn't there. If she wanted to eat she would be here at the scheduled times, or at least come when she was called.

It might sound harsh. To some cat people, it might even sound too much like dog training. But I believed Lila needed both the routine and the responsibility. She needed to understand that she didn't make the rules or set the schedule. Besides that, most animals thrive on a routine. If events in their day are predictable, it gives them a sense of security and stability. And that sense of security was another thing Lila absolutely needed.

Finally, she needed to learn to trust and to be engaged with me even when she was free in the outside world. She could come and go, hunt, hide, or just hang out. But at the center of it all, I was her person. That did not change. The routine did not change.

Freedom and responsibility had to meet in the middle.

When I caught her pawing at the flap of the dog door one afternoon, I knew the rubber was about to meet the road. The flap yielded as she scrabbled at it, opening a fraction, letting an inch of air and light spill through. Within an hour, Lila was out.

I was tense. More tense than I wanted to admit. I monitored her movements as best I could, praying that she would stay close and would come back, or would at least allow me to catch her if she seemed confused or reluctant to come herself. She ended up hanging around near the garage and front patio, and after a couple hours had gone by, she acted content to come back indoors. I scooped her up, deposited her in the computer room in her familiar safe space, and doled out a generous helping of kitty treats.

So it was a good beginning. By September the chain-link gate had been dismantled and dragged back outdoors. No more checks and balances. Lila could come and go as she pleased.

She easily learned not only how to exit via the dog door but, more importantly, how to come back in the same way. She was also comfortable coming in through the front door, although for a good year I kept my vow not to ever let her out that door even if she asked. And she never did ask. She just figured it out.

With Lila, I have always insisted on a curfew. In the mornings she got her breakfast like everyone else, but she was left out of the evening feeding frenzy. Once again, I would employ my strategy of giving her several yummy kitty treats to take the edge off. But if she wanted a full meal, she had to show up before lights out. I would squire her into her old haunt, the computer room, slide her dish of kibble onto the bookshelf, switch off the light, and close the folding doors which had replaced the chain-link gate.

There were a few nights that she missed, and after calling her several times, I just closed up shop and tucked in for the night. She would always be there by morning, usually curled up on a couch with one or two dogs, happy to be home and definitely hungry. *Bad decision*, I would tell her, and the food would not come out again until that evening. She never missed two curfews in a row.

Lila was a talented and obsessive hunter. I still believe that's one reason she stayed out for such extended periods of time when living with my parents. She loved the outdoors and was enamored of the challenge of stalking and capturing prey. It isn't the part of cat ownership that I enjoy, but it's who they are. Cats are skilled and lethal hunters, and Lila proved to be more skilled than many. Mice, locusts, cicadas, birds, baby bunnies, small snakes, and at least one squirrel all ended up in the vice of her jaws and claws at one time or another. As she became accustomed to the property and the smorgasboard it offered, Lila began to stay away from home longer. Never all day, but perhaps all afternoon and half the evening. It was enough to make me worry. Maybe I hadn't solved this puzzle yet. I was sure she was close by and not wandering, because there would be times when she would be gone for three or four hours, but then suddenly show up when I called or while I was out training dogs. She always seemed to be home whenever I got home myself, either from a walk or from my part-time job. I guessed that she was just out hunting or lying under cover waiting for an opportunity to ambush something. Even so, I wasn't going to take chances. It worried me, and so I once again dusted off my thinking cap and attempted to solve my kitty conundrum.

Bells are so handy. Lila earned the right to wear one of her own, besides the little jingle bell already attached to her collar. It was a medium-sized sheep bell, the same type Tassie wears on our walks. It was light-weight, but it was still large enough to make stalking, grabbing, and climbing cumbersome. And it was loud. To make it as safe as possible, I slid her collar directly through the metal loop at the bell's top. That eliminated the need for keyrings or coach clips, both of which could easily catch on trees and fences.

She stayed home, more visible and more accessible, and these days she wears the bell less and less often.

Lila is a free spirit. She still treasures her time outdoors, even in the cold. Physically speaking, she knows no boundaries and will blithely vanquish any fence or obstacle standing in her way. She has learned, even with her bell on, to leap into the rafters of the barn, where she strolls around and terrorizes the sparrows that flutter there. But she is at peace. Often on an average day, usually when it's chilly or wet, I will find her snuggled down on her favorite sheepskin in my bedroom, or cuddled up in one of the cat trees. She does know when it's time to come home.

So far, I've talked mostly about Lila's physical activity. But there is a real depth to this cat, a depth to which I haven't yet come to the bottom. She is one of the smartest cats I have, and she is keenly sensitive not just to her tangible surroundings, but also to the needs of the people and animals around her. Her intuition is uncanny. Only a few days before Glacier was euthanized, and as his strength really started to fail, Lila made it a point to stay near him. A number of times I witnessed her come to him as he lay weak and lethargic in the shade. She would curl up right beside his massive head, and she would stay with him. These days she tends to do the same with Caspian, my ancient gray tabby who is nearing the end of his own life.

Recently, she also showed the same insight with people. Mom was at my house, taking a breather after a rough day. Just that morning, she and my dad had made the decision to have one of their own cats put to sleep. We were in my bedroom, talking it over. The dog door clicked, and I heard Lila jingling into the house. She trotted straight down the hallway, paused at the baby gate, trilled, then sprang over the gate and into the bedroom. Then without hesitation, she jumped up beside my mom and chirped. Now that Lila lives with me, she seldom initiates direct contact with anyone else. But there she was, at a time when Mom specifically needed kitty comfort.

Lila is a cat who knows. She is one of those animals who sees and hears and understands more than most of them do, and since most animals understand far more than we imagine, that's saying a lot.

In a word, Lila is just special. I'm glad she chose me. I'm glad she's finally come home.

CHAPTER 17

TASSIE: OF HOPE AND DREAMS
GOLDENGREENE TARTAN SWEET

I know I shouldn't have been on Craigslist again. But I honestly did have a legitimate reason.

The black Labrador puppy that I had raised for the past two and a half years was gone. She belonged to the regional training organization for assistance dogs, and the time had come for me to return her to the program. I had known it was coming, of course. Anyone who volunteers to become a puppy raiser knows it's coming. But that doesn't really soften the blow when it does come.

It stung, and I was still wobbling from it a month or two later. Turning to Craigslist was my therapy. Again, I am not condoning this website as a perfectly reputable place to acquire animals. You need to be careful, look with both eyes open, and ask lots of questions if you're truly interested in a certain dog.

But I wasn't looking seriously. Somehow, just scrolling through all the ads for cute and unique dogs and cats diverted my attention from the ache of losing my own cute dog. It dulled the pain.

I wasn't really looking, though. . .

Even so, the ad titled "short-haired and long-haired collies" did give me pause. First, my inner dog show snob contributed some snide remarks. There was, after all, no such thing as a "short-haired collie." The collie is technically divided into two separate breeds. The breed usually referred to when using the term collie is the rough collie. This is the stereotypical Lassie. Not always the Lassie coloring, but the same classic head and ears, and the same glorious rich coat. Then there is the other breed called the smooth collie. Looks just like it sounds—a collie's head, body, and behavior, but with way less coat. This time, think Lassie with a haircut.

So the term "short-haired collie" was completely incorrect. I rolled my eyes. What a yahoo.

There were apparently two litters for sale, one about eight weeks old, the other already several months old.

I thought about it. Collies of both coat types have always appealed to me. They are sweet and active dogs, intelligent and eager and loyal to a fault. Of course, the Lassie movies and TV shows have been exaggerated, but the collie is still an incredibly insightful and perceptive breed. They thrive on exercise, work, and human connection. A perfect dog for me.

I kept scrolling. Then I gave myself a shake and pushed back from the computer. *Waste of time*, I told myself as I marched out to tug on my boots. I had chores to do and my own dogs who needed exercise, work, and human connection. I needed to quit dinking around and take care of my own babies and my own business.

I did begin to look at Craigslist less. Time really does heal wounds, and as I busied myself with the farm and its projects, and with my own dogs and their activities, gradually my heart hurt less.

A couple weeks later, though, I skimmed the site again, and there was that same ad for "short-haired and long-haired collies."

Well, I thought, *I really do like this breed.* You almost never see collies in this area, especially not the smooth variety. I would just drop a quick email and ask how many were left. Nothing major. No commitment. Just a quick question.

And that's how Tassie came to live with me.

The lady who owned the parents had two puppies left. One was a little rough-coat about ten weeks old; the other was a smooth-coat about three and a half months. I couldn't decide which I wanted. I love dogs with lots of fur, and the younger puppy would also be easier to introduce to my established pack of adults. Still, the uniqueness of the smoothie intrigued me, and the fact that she was a little older meant we could start walking and training together right away.

I waffled, said I needed to think about it. Decided on the younger rough puppy. Then got back to her and said no, I would go with the older smooth-coat. As it turned out, I had made the right choice.

She hadn't even arrived yet and I was already calling her Tassie. It was another one of those names I'd had bouncing around in my data banks for decades. I had discovered it in a short story that I'd read long ago and had latched onto it as a name I would use someday for the right dog. A tassie is a kind of pastry from the British Isles, and collies, of course, hale from Scotland. The word also sounds suspiciously like Lassie without being too gauche. I have always liked it, and it was perfect for this little girl.

She came home on a muggy July morning. My best friend, Barbie, had offered to transport her to me, with the help of two intrepid teenage girls who sat in the back seat and comforted the disconsolate puppy.

She needed comforting. Within the first fifteen minutes or so, Tassie was carsick. The totally new sensation of riding in a vehicle, combined with the anxiety of doing so with complete strangers, was enough to upset her stomach. The swath of dryer lint she had scarfed down before embarking didn't do her any favors, either.

By the time she got to me, Tassie was sick, scared, and more than slightly damp.

They hefted her out of the car, and she cowered. I crouched down to greet her, and she cringed as far away from me as the short leash would permit. Not that she was leash-trained. She skidded and skipped and put her head down like a mule as we eased her toward the front patio. *Well,* I thought philosophically, *she will figure the leash out soon enough.* That was easy. I had taken on worse. She was just spooked and not very well socialized. And she had come to the right place to take care of all that.

The plan was to introduce her to the other dogs right there in the yard. I latched the front gate, the girls dropped the leash, and I went indoors to retrieve the first member of the welcoming committee.

Kola. She was gentle, calm, and steady. Not much ruffled her, and under me, she was the unofficial leader of the group.

And she was also very big.

Tassie took one look at her and lunged. Flashing teeth, hideous snarling and yowling, and she rushed straight at Kola. My big girl bounded backward, as stunned as the rest of us.

I was not pleased. It's one thing for an adult dog, or even a more mature teenage puppy, to act up when meeting a new and very large dog. Even that wouldn't have made me happy, but it would have been understandable. But this little stinker was only three months old. And she was on Kola's turf. She wasn't defending her own territory. She was far too young to be acting like such a snot. In canine society, she was way out of line and was being very rude.

Kola recovered herself and stepped forward to try another sniff. She received the same reaction. Tassie screamed, snapping and menacing. Kola reeled back, shook herself, and came to stand beside me.

"That's enough," I said. "Get hold of her leash and just try to calm her down."

One of the girls snagged the leash and tried to soothe her. Tassie did quiet, but she was still tense and suspicious.

"Okay," I said, "if that's how she's gonna be, we'll just let her meet everyone at once and see how she feels about that. Drop her leash and get ready. I'm letting them all out."

Everyone except Pixel. If this little fart was going to be so unpredictable, I didn't want my smallest and oldest dog in the line of fire. But she was going to meet everyone else like it or not. And she was going to drop the attitude.

They surged out the door in a torrent. As usual, the border collies led the charge, followed hard by the two shrieking Aussies. Their assumption that we were headed out for a walk took a sharp detour when they saw the new arrival. They locked onto her and within seconds she was surrounded. Kola went with them, galumphing in for another inspection.

I kept all the humans in the yard away. The dogs would have to sort this one out for themselves.

Engulfed by five other dogs, all bigger, older, and more dominant than she was, Tassie's bravado melted. She crouched submissively and let them sniff. Head and tail down, body close to the ground, and her teeth in her mouth where they belonged. She was not comfortable, but she was calm, and she was finally starting to act like a normal puppy.

Once the pack had checked her out they lost interest. Meg and Gem vasculated between a meet-and-greet with all the new people and furious rushes toward the closed front gate. Brio yapped and harassed everyone, and Dundee and Kola hovered near Barbie and me.

Tassie, forced to choose the lesser of two evils, came slinking closer to us as well. She cowered behind whichever person was nearest when any of the other dogs cantered past. Meanwhile, I ordered everyone to walk around the yard so that

Tassie would be forced to mingle. I didn't want her to hide. In fact, at this juncture I didn't particularly want her at all. The temptation to toss her back in Barbie's SUV was so strong that I found myself shying away from both the vehicle and the dog.

Reminding myself to quit being a moron, I bent down and gave the little girl a rub under the chin. "You'll figure it out!" I said as she velcroed herself to my left leg. "It's all pretty scary right now, huh, sweety?"

After we had milled around the front yard for ten minutes, I judged it was time to brave the house. There had been no more blow-ups from Tassie and she had actually started to trot around with the other dogs. Her mouth and tail were relaxing, and she was taking stock of her surroundings instead of just trying to hide from them.

Still, as we tromped into the house I felt less than enthusiastic. Barbie came up beside me and I glanced back at her. "So far I don't like her," I said. "I hope she gets her act together, because frankly, I'm not impressed with a puppy acting this nasty. But let's see how she does with Pixel and the cats."

Here we were in for another surprise. When introduced to Pixel, Tassie showed no animosity whatever. In fact, she wagged her tail and went forward to greet him. And when Black Powder, then a kitten, pranced into the mix and whisked his tail under her nose, Tassie became ecstatic. She swished her own tail wildly and got down on his level to wash his face.

Flattened by such delight, Powder sprang to the back of the couch and shook himself. We all laughed. I breathed a sigh of relief. My worry that Tassie's aggression would transfer to my smaller animals was completely unfounded. That was one hurdle we wouldn't have to fuss over.

As the next two or three days went by, I began to understand her, and to piece together some of her past.

My best guess was that she had been bullied by larger dogs in her previous home. Her snarky reactions were always directed toward dogs bigger than herself. They also seemed to occur most often when she felt cornered or trapped. There were several occasions during that introductory period when she was accidentally blocked into corners by my other dogs, and it never ended well. In one instance she was shoved back in an angle of the hallway as two or three other dogs turned around to follow me. Another time she was trapped under the kitchen table. Each time she flew at the other dogs in a flurry of fangs and ferocity. But now that I knew what to watch and listen for, I could hear the note of panic in her voice. Her nastiness all stemmed from fear.

So when she lashed out, I would grab hold of her and tell her firmly, "No. That's enough. You don't act that way in this house." Then I would bring her out of the corner where she'd gotten so scared and keep her there for a minute. We would both breathe, both recover. And I would let her go and continue with whatever work I'd been doing.

The crate was another flash point for Tassie. Once she understood that it was a safe space and that no other dogs could go in with her, she began to shark out on any of them who came close to the crate when she was inside. Again, it was the same problem. She felt cornered. She knew she couldn't get away from another dog when in her crate, yet she also perceived the crate as her own personal territory. So she began to become what dog behavior people call "crate aggressive," snarling and snapping at any dog who ventured within a foot or two of her sanctuary.

However, by this time I was onto her. My initial skepticism and annoyance had mellowed to compassion and my typical determination to make things better. Tassie could snark and bluster, but I knew her secret. I knew she was just scared. And I wasn't going to let her stay that way.

I began dropping treats into her crate whenever another dog came close. It became a practice exercise whenever it was time to crate dogs. I would crate Tassie first, hand her a small treat, then reach for the stash of treats in my pocket. As each of the other dogs was called to be crated, I would make sure whoever it was passed Tassie's crate as they went to their own. She watched suspiciously as the other dog approached, and as she began to tense, I would drop chunks of sausage into her lair.

"Good girl, Tassie," I would tell her softly. "Good for you." And another treat would come her way.

Repeat with the next dog to be crated, then with the next. And before a week had gone by, all Tassie's crate aggression toward other dogs had been replaced by expectant focus on me.

As the months passed, Tassie grew in confidence and comfort. I socialized her as heavily as possible. We went to practice shows, real shows, herding trials, and the dog park. We went to pet stores and farm stores and even spent a day at the area Renaissance festival. She grew in mental maturity and learned how to learn.

She grew in every way except physically. By the time she was one year old, my would-be smooth-coated collie, a breed that should stand about twenty-four inches at the shoulder and tip the scales at seventy pounds, stood a mere seventeen inches at the shoulder and weighed about thirty pounds. Everything about her, from her head to her coat to her coloring and temperament, was smooth collie. But somewhere along the line there had been a glitch. Whether she had some Sheltie or other small breed mixed in, or whether she had just been a runt and Mom just wasn't healthy we would never know. She had no official registration papers and I hadn't met the parents. So the upshot of it was that I had to apply for a registration number for Tassie as a mixed breed.

No biggy. In all the essentials she was a collie, and it was rather nice having a compact, medium-size dog instead of a strapping seventy-pounder.

Far more important to me than the breed question was the

question of when to start showing Tassie. She was only a year old, so according to my regular time table, she wouldn't enter the ring for another year at a minimum.

She was so mature, though, so judicious and attentive, that I began contemplating breaking my own rule. It would just be a simple Rally Novice class, after all, the way I start all my newbies in the ring.

So we gave it a try. She nailed it. Three qualifying scores in a row, and she earned the RN title and swept on to Novice Obedience.

The first effort was lackluster. Okay but not great. A solid score in the 180's—nothing to brag about, but a qualify nonetheless. One down, two to go.

And from our next attempt would come one of the greatest moments of my life with dogs.

It was the first show of the year. She was looking good, feeling good, happy and eager, but as typical Tassie, she remained self-controlled and focused. We did our thing in the ring and came out with a qualify. It was a nice run. I hadn't felt anything remarkable about it, and none of the spectators made any special comment. But I knew we had done well, and I was happy with her. We trooped back to our crates and chairs and hung out, just loving on each other until the class was called back to the ring for ribbons.

It was a big class. Including Tassie, fourteen dogs had qualified, somewhat unusual for novice. It was a competitive class, too. When I heard the judge call the first-place team forward with a score of 199 out of 200, my dim hope of netting a ribbon faded. Wow, a 199. Almost unheard of in a novice class. My best score ever was a 196, and that had been earned with Mesa, a much more experienced dog in a more advanced class.

Second place was called forward with a score of 198.5. *Wow*, I thought again, *this class is cut-throat*. Just half a point between first and second place.

I reached down to the little dog beside me and rubbed her silky head. Any handler will tell you it isn't the ribbons that matter. It's those qualifying scores that get you titles, and titles are what everyone is working for. I was just happy that day to be one of those qualifying people.

"And in third place today," said the judge, "with a score of 198, are dog and handler. . ." And then she called my number.

I gasped. Literally gasped, like some sort of scene in a movie. I looked down at my dog, my mouth still gaping, and tears burned in my eyes. They didn't stop. I stumbled forward to collect that chintzy, yellow strip of fabric, that third-place ribbon which was so, so much more than just third-place.

By the time we finally left the ring I was sobbing. I heard voice after voice, blurred, distant and unrecognizable—"Congratulations. . .congratulations. . .congratulations, Reyna." I felt the supple leather lead in my left hand and my dad's fuzzy sweater in the other hand, and I felt the presence of the quiet, alert, little dog at my left knee, and I smiled and tried to say "thank you" and "I'm so proud of her," and I knew that everyone understood and that nobody truly understood. *198.*

And the tears just kept coming. I sat on the floor with her, and hugged her, and slashed my sleeves across my face again and again. *198.* She had done that well for me. I had brought her that far. We stood on this pinnacle together. I can still barely believe it.

We were still flying high when we hit the next trial. A score of 195 and a first-place ribbon, and that was Tassie's novice obedience title. Now began the real work of fine-tuning her skill set in preparation for the more advanced titles and classes.

Much of the groundwork had already been laid. And as we practiced and perfected and polished, I continued to learn about this unlikely little farm dog.

She is a born watchdog. Naturally more reserved and suspicious than any of my other dogs, I've learned to pay attention to Tassie's barking. Barking is something she seldom does, but when she does, there's a reason. Once while doing chores up in the ducks' pen, I neglected to latch the gate behind me. It was pulled closed but not latched. Enough to keep the ducks in, but not enough to keep the inquisitive and ever-ready Snowstorm out. As I hosed down the ducks' wading pool and checked their grain supply, I heard Tassie growl from her vantage point in the back yard. She followed up with a sharp woof. Not thinking much about it, I finished up the duck chores, latched the gate behind me, and was ready to bulldoze onward when I heard another growl from Tassie and the clanking of Snowstorm's collar bell. It sounded like it was coming from inside the ducks' pen. Only then did I realize my mistake and Snowstorm's sneak.

It wasn't that Snowstorm would have hurt the ducks. She was more interested in their food and their droppings than anything else. It was more that Tassie was alerting to a breach in the farm's code of conduct. Snowstorm wasn't allowed in the ducks' pen. Only ducks were allowed in there. No goats, no guardian dogs.

I witnessed that vigilance again a few months later while my dad repaired one of the corral gates. It only took a minute or so of inattention on his part, and next thing we knew Snowstorm was loping up the driveway and Mocha, the donkey, had wandered into the pasture. Once again, it was Tassie, riveted from the back yard, who sounded the first alarm.

She looks out for me on walks, too. There is one house in particular where the resident border collie makes the trek tricky. He has even nipped me on one occasion. That was before Tassie was on the job. There is no growling or aggression on her part when we pass his place. Yet Tassie, keeping to a steady trot, stations herself between the perimeter of his yard and me. She keeps pace with me and keeps watch on him, and when he rushes forward to intercept us, she will match him stride for stride. She hedges him in, not allowing him near me, still without growling or showing teeth. It's more of a game to her than anything.

This quiet vigilance is what has given her the right to sleep in my bedroom every night. Just before lights out, I open the sacred baby gate and let her come trotting through. She heads for the fluffy sheepskin rug beside the bed, softly lifts the cookie from my hand, and curls up for the overnight. Even in those dark hours of rest, my own vigilance sleeps only lightly. I hear a baby goat if it cries in the nursery pen. I hear Meg flopping over, restless, in her crate. I hear the pack of coyotes start yammering across the pond and the Pyrenees when they bark a response. I am aware of the air conditioner kicking on and the rising of a north wind, and distant thunder never fails to rouse me.

But as good a watchdog as I might be, Tassie is better. I can trust her ears to be sharper than mine. I can rely on her eyes to be stronger than mine. And I am learning to value her perception and understanding.

Conscientious is a good word for Tassie. Attentive, intuitive, a stickler for the rules. She is a dog who wants to get it right, and she is a dog who usually does.

Just how right, I learned only recently.

It was an early Sunday morning. I shuffled into the computer room, sleepy-eyed and cranky, to check email. There is no such thing as sleeping in on a dairy farm. So as I opened up my inbox and began thinking through all the things to be accomplished that day, I still wasn't fully awake.

Not until I opened the message from the American Kennel Club at the top of the email list. Expecting just another advertisement, I yawned and began reading:

AKC 2018 Obedience Classic — entry eligible

Congratulations, your dog (Goldengreene Tartan Sweet) has met the eligibility requirements to enter the 2018 AKC Obedience Classic in Orlando, Florida!

There was more—dates and details—and I had to read the information three times before it really began to register. But I finally got it. Tassie had done it again. She had rocked my world. She had propelled me to a level of honor I had never before achieved with any of my obedience dogs.

The AKC Obedience Classic is one of those stratosphere events for dogs and their hard-working handlers. It is by invitation only, and it is based on the scores a dog has earned in the ring for that year. Tassie's kick-booty scores had been stellar enough for even the American Kennel Club to sit up and take notice.

I said yet another "wow!" and gave Tassie yet another hug. What an honor. What a dog. For the rest of the day, I was walking about six inches off the floor.

The irony, of course, is that we can't go to Orlando. I have a farm to run. I have goats to milk and pens to clean and hay to feed. The other nine dogs need to be walked and worked and cared for and loved. The cats need to be cuddled. The rabbits need to be groomed. The eggs need to be gathered. Somebody has to stand guard over the farm and monitor the wind and the weather. Somebody has to take care of everything. And nobody does it quite like I do.

So for this time, Tassie and I will stay home on the farm. There will be other times, other dreams that will come true. For now I'm happy here. I'll meet each new day early and hold onto it late. I'll welcome the wind and find strength in the storms. I'll shine in the sun and revel in the rain. I'll find the joy in each new season. And in spite of it all, because of it all, I'll watch over my land, and take care of everything and everyone that is in my hands.

The author walking on her farm while Gem herds the goats.

The author moving quickly and confidently in the baby goat corral.

The author and her baby goats on their play equipment.

The author bottle feeding baby goats while Gem supervises.

The dairy goats are milked twice a day by hand. Powder the cat knows the milking stand is a great place to hang out.

Hungry goats look for warm bottles while the pyrenees stand guard.

It is obvious the goats love the author!

Off lead heel work with Meg.

Signal exercise with Meg.

A successful jump!

A successful broad jump by Brio .

Well-deserved praise for Brio.

Gem

Brio

Meg

Dundee can't contain his pride in finding the author's missing boots!

Quite a pose by Tassie.

Pixel enjoying his priviledged place on the bed.

Lila at home.

Kola taking a cozy nap.

95 pounds of Kola.

Cinder, a hard worker, also knows how to relax.

The author and Tassie heading down their farm lane on a perfect Kansas day.

ACKNOWLEDGMENTS

A huge and heart-felt thank you to all the following—I couldn't have done this without you!

First of all, to the Lord of heaven and earth, who has given me life, and who has specifically allowed me to live this life.

To my mom and dad, who have supported me, believed in me, and generally put up with me.

To Ann Palmer, my incredible photographer. Because of your skill and generosity, this book has truly come to life.

To my friend, Dorothy, who was the first person to give me the kick in the pants I needed to begin this project. She once asked me, half encouraging, half exasperated, "Why don't you just write your book?" I couldn't find a good reason not to. So, Dorothy, here it is.

To my publisher and editor, Thea Rademacher, who took a chance on this book and had more true vision than I did at times.

To Carolyn Thomason, who freely gave of her time to set up my computer so that I could do the tangible writing.

To Kelli Bausch of Camo Cross Dog Training, who graciously allowed us to take photos in her building.

ABOUT THE AUTHOR

Blind since the age of fifteen months, Reyna Bradford homesteads her own hobby farm in northeast Kansas. She has always loved animals, and currently shares her home with nine dogs, multiple cats, and Angora rabbits. She raises registered Nubian dairy goats and has learned to do all kinds of things with the milk, including making cheese, soap, and yogurt.

Reyna is passionate about training and showing her dogs in companion and performance events with the American Kennel Club. She is a proud Kansan who loves to share the beauty of her home state with her readers.

Besides her farm and her furkids, she also loves film scores, thunderstorms, and dark chocolate.

Follow Reyna on
Instagram: Reynaoftheflinthills
Facebook: In My Hands – author Reyna Bradford
www.flinthillspublishing.com

Made in the USA
Columbia, SC
08 March 2020